The Liberties

A HISTORY

Mary Makebelieve lived with her mother in a small room at the very top of a big, dingy house in a Dublin back street. She knew every crack in the ceiling, every spot of mildew on the ancient wallpaper was familiar, at night-time the cockroaches came rattling, the grime of many years had encrusted the glass of the window, the chimney pots of next door continually hurled jays of soot against her window, and water had to be carried from the very bottom of the five-storey house up hundreds and hundreds of stairs to her room ... she disliked having to use too much water ...

(James Stephens, *The Charwoman's Daughter*, 1912)

With the passage of time the tenements were depleted and demolished, the families banished to the outskirts of the city to housing estates... but their relations, friends and neighbours weren't there. The shops, schools, churches, dealers, pawnshops, hustle, bustle, atmosphere, bumping into people they knew all their lives. The security of the community was gone ...

(Former resident of The Liberties)

The Liberties

A HISTORY

MAURICE CURTIS

The
History
Press
Ireland

First published 2013

The History Press Ireland
50 City Quay
Dublin 2
Ireland
www.thehistorypress.ie

British Library Cataloguing in Publication Data.
A catalogue record for this book is available from the British Library.

ISBN 978 1 84588 771 1

Typesetting and origination by The History Press

CONTENTS

Acknowledgements 6

Introduction 11

1. The Gaelic, Viking and Norman Origins of Dublin 15
2. Henry II: Liberties or Franchises? 19
3. The Middle Ages: Barbers, Blackpitts and the Black Death 23
4. From the Tudors to the Georgians 26
5. The Huguenots: Weavers and Dutch Billies 30
6. The United Irishmen: The Wearing of the Green 35
7. From Daniel O'Connell to the Irish Tricolour 43
8. Forged in the Smithy: Poverty and Tenements 49
9. The 1916 Rising and The Liberties 65
10. The Wood Quay Campaign and the Knight 70
11. Boots, Brews, Biscuits and the Golden Triangle 75
12. Stairways to Heaven: Landscape of Spires 90
13. A Tour of The Liberties: By the Sign of the Leather Bottle 120
14. Celebrating The Liberties 223

Notes 241
Bibliography 253

ACKNOWLEDGEMENTS

Many organisations made this work possible including the Office of Public Works, the Dublin Civic Trust and in particular its study, 'Thomas Street – Proposed Architectural Conservation Area' and other studies on The Liberties. The Dublin City Council's Heritage Office (Dr Howard Clarke/Dublinia, Charles Duggan and Seamus Donohoe) has undertaken significant studies of the area and these were of help. The Irish Architectural Archive, An Taisce (National Trust for Ireland) and in particular John Ducie for detailed information on the significance of Tailors' Hall; the Architecture Foundation, the Irish Georgian Society, the National Library of Ireland, the National Gallery, the Gorry Art Gallery, the National Archives, the National Museum, Dublin City Council, and the Dublin City Public Libraries (Hugh Comerford in the Gilbert Library/ Archives) were all of assistance. Dublin.ie forums were indispensable for chats on The Liberties. Thanks to Archiseek (and in particular Paul Clerkin) for its many contributions on Thomas Street and Wood Quay. Excavations.ie is excellent for archaeological information. Thanks also to the Heritage Council, Friends of Medieval Dublin, and Irish Architecture for its many examinations and reflections on the area. The Royal Society of Antiquaries of Ireland was a great source for articles and old images. Dr Christopher Morash and the Smock Alley Theatre provided help on the history of the theatre. Thanks to Emmeline Henderson for her landmark Thomas Street study and likewise to Graham Hickey for his outstanding work on Meath and Francis Streets. Their studies are a must for a greater understanding of this historic and unique area of Dublin.

Particular thanks to John Gallagher of the Coombe, who combines being a local community leader, social worker, historian, campaigner and much more. He is based in Carman's Hall and is the founder of The Liberties Heritage Association (LHA) (with Bernard Warfield who has an encyclopaedic knowledge of The Liberties, and is ably assisted by John Brogan, Wayne Deane and the team in the LHA project), and director of St Nicholas of Myra Parish Centre. The Liberties Association and St Nicholas of Myra Heritage Projects, based in Carman's Hall Community Centre (and Gerry Graham and his busy staff), are inspiring. Additional biographical details on John Gallagher were compiled from interviews he had with Michael O'Flanagan in 2008, and author and historian Kevin C. Kearns in 1994 – particular thanks to all involved. The Liberties Living Heritage Project is proof of his energy and the vibrancy of this fascinating historic neighbourhood of Dublin.

Thanks also to Liberties poet, Christine Broe, for her inspiring poem on John Gallagher and her biographical compilation. Her poem does indeed encapsulate profound respect for all the work John has done for the people of The Liberties over a lifetime.

Much praise to the SICCDA (South Inner City Community Development Association), organisers of the annual Liberties Festival. Founded in 1982, this is a committee of local residents from The Liberties who are committed, on a voluntary basis, to tackling the social, educational, health, economic and environmental problems facing the local community. In particular their annual Festival, still going strong after more than forty years, is an inspiration. The sterling work of Liam Fenlon (Snr), Chairman of the SICCDA and The Liberties Festival for many years, and ably helped by an outstanding committee, will never be forgotten. Liam, speaking on the twenty-fifty anniversary of the festival, noted that it is not simply a concentration on the past, but signifies an act of concern for the future of The Liberties. As Maurice Stewart, former Dean of St Patrick's Cathedral, put it – it has always been a festival of The Liberties, for The Liberties, by The Liberties.

Tessa Fleming was helpful on the Royal visit to The Liberties in 1911. For local writer Liam O'Meara's books *The Bayno* and *Zozimus*, many thanks. Other local writers were inspiring, including Deirdre McMahon, Isobel Smyth, Mairín Johnston and Liz Gillis. That great Liberties poet, Gerard Smyth, has captured the essence of the life of the people and places that is The Liberties in his many poems, and is well worth reading. Another poet, Padraig J. Daly, with a fresh perspective and in a different era, portrays the customs and story of The Liberties. Artist and writer Chris Reid deserves fulsome praise for his imaginative and inspiring plaques on the Iveagh Trust buildings. Of course Eamon MacThomáis and his Liberty memories, both in print and on film, are the stuff of legend. Kenneth Milne of Christ Church Cathedral undertook an indispensable landmark study on the four Liberties which was most useful. Muriel McCarthy of Marsh's Library opened the cage doors in her splendid library and has also written on The Liberties.

To the Deans of St Patrick's Cathedral and Christ Church Cathedral, the deans/ rectors/priests and staff of St Audoen's church (both C of I and RC), John's Lane, St Catherine's, Thomas Street (CORE) and St Catherine's, Meath Street, St Nicholas of Myra, and the various other churches – a special thanks. Charles Reed and Sinead Hernon of St Patrick's Cathedral were of particular help. I found the studies of Kenneth Milne and Stuart Kinsella on Christ Church Cathedral to be of great assistance. Tony Dolan of the OPW has an encyclopaedic knowledge on St Audoen's (C of I). The Holy Faith Sisters of the Coombe, the Presentation Sisters of Warrenmount (in particular, Sister Pauline) and the Mercy Sisters on Cork Street were also helpful. The Augustinians of John's Lane church and Brother Giles O'Halloran in particular, were of immeasurable help.

Thanks to Eddie Rice for buttoning me on Robert Emmet and the Liberty Rangers. Mícheál D. Roe of the famous Roe's Distillery and St Patrick's Tower, Thomas Street, was helpful with the family history. Eugene Coyne of the Digital Hub was a fountain of information on the distillery and St James's Cemetery. Some of the staff of *The Irish Times* have written on The Liberties from time to time and I am particularly grateful for this: Gerry Smyth for pointers on The Liberties in literature and Áine Kerr for her article on architect George Boyle who set up the Fumbally Exchange when the Celtic Tiger disappeared. Thanks also to former Blackpitts resident and *Irish Times* journalist Karl Whitney, for his articles and blogs on the River Poddle, Newmarket Square, and Charles Dickens in Dublin. Alison Walsh of the *Sunday Independent/Evening Herald* helped set the compass. To the *Irish Independent* for information on the renowned Irish music player John Potts of the Coombe, grateful thanks also. And thanks to Miriam Lord, formerly with the *Irish Independent*, for her coverage of President Mikhael Gorbachev's visit to The Liberties in 2002.

That renowned teacher, music historian, flute player and much else, Mick O'Connor, originally from The Liberties, was of immense help with regard to the musical heritage of The Liberties and in particular the huge influence of the Dublin Pipers' Club on Irish traditional music. James Ferris advised me on O'Donovan Road in The Tenters and Sharon Fitpatrick was a source of much useful information on the old Fever Hospital on Cork Street (*Brú Caoimhín*).

Thanks to Isobel Smyth for her 'A Southside Childhood' memories. Likewise to *Irish Archaeology* for notes on the archaeological roots of Dublin in The Liberties. I found the Heritage Council helpful for notes on archaeological excavations in the Back Lane/Lamb Alley area. Ken Finlay's *Chapters of Dublin History* resource and out-of-print books about locations in Dublin, many of which no longer exist or have changed beyond recognition, was very helpful. Douglas Bennett's excellent resource on local history, the *Encyclopaedia of Dublin*, is indispensable. Turlough O'Riordan of the *Dictionary of Irish Biography* was helpful with Pue's Occurrences. To Millie Lawler for her thesis, 'St Nicholas of Myra and its Two Architects, An Historical and Architectural Survey', a big thank you. Emmet Scanlon of Tom De Paor Architects was helpful with the 'Double House' on John Dillon Street.

Thanks also to Eleanor Fitzsimons of the *Evening Herald/The Dubliner* for information on Darkey Kelly and The Dolocher. Cathy Hayes of the *Irish Central*

Irish American magazine also provided information on Darkey Kelly. Eamon McLoughlin and Phil O'Grady of 93FM undertook revealing research on the legend of Darkey Kelly, which added to the story. Thanks to RTÉ Library and Archives for information on Wood Quay. Professor Howard Clarke and Professor Mary Daly of UCD have produced landmark research on different facets of Dublin social history. My research brought back fond memories of the late and great Professor FX Martin of UCD and the Friends of Medieval Dublin. He greatly encouraged his students of medieval history (myself included) to get up and march to preserve our history and heritage even if that involved missing lectures. Sincere thanks to Ronan Colgan and Beth Amphlett for their patience and encouragement, as well as professionalism. June O'Reilly of the Business Depot of course can still walk on water!

William O. Frazer and his study on the Newmarket and Weavers' Sqaures (and to Dr Ruth Johnson, Dr Paddy Ryan, Katrina Bouchier, Jill Siddall, Peter Walsh, Dr Clodagh Tait, Chris Corlett, Antoine Giacometti, Kevin Lohan, Franc Myles and Claire Walsh for their contribution to that work) were of immense help. In this respect, the Dublin City Council has made tremendous strides in raising awareness of the architectural, archaeological and environmental heritage of The Liberties. I found a number of their publications to be of particular assistance in this regard. Peter Pearson provided interesting interpretations of the paintings of Alexander Williams. Noel Haughton of the St Vincent De Paul Back Lane Shelter and the Dublin Bird Market is a great story teller and was of invaluable help. Sam Smith of Plant Life of Cork Street gave me useful leads on the area.

Thanks to Damtheweather and Bernard Warfield of Dublin.ie Forums for the history of the Mushatts and much else on local history. Tony O'Rourke of Oh Rourke's on Bridgefoot Street, besides being very welcoming, is a mine of information on the old traditions and customs of The Liberties, some of which are very much alive. Thanks also to Kevin C. Kearns for his book *Dublin Tenement Life: An Oral History*, and for the interviews he undertook with Liberties residents. Author and long-time Tenters resident, Anto Howard, gave an enjoyable description 'Ode to the Smell That Lingers' from his memorable book *Slow Dublin*. Thanks to author Joseph O'Connor for his memories of his father's influence on him from his home in Francis Street. The Ark Children's Centre in Temple Bar was also of help. Jonathan Hynes, manager of the Harding Hotel at Copper Alley, provided access to Dublin's oldest alleyway. Rory Delaney of the Dublin Unitarian church was helpful with street names in The Liberties. Son of The Liberties, Jimmy Dent of Viking Splashworld, was a fountain of information on The Liberties. Young Calum McPartland of Fallons Capstan Bar helped on legendary boxer Dan Donnelly's association with the old pub. Declan Larkin of Larkin's Butchers on Meath Street was of immeasurable help also. Likewise, Foley's Chemists and Noel Fleming of Londis Supermarket on Meath Street were of particular help. Jack Roche of the Roche's Green Grocers on Meath Street was an inspiration for his reminiscences on meeting President Mikhael Gorbachev in The Liberties in 2002. The residents of The Liberties are often the best for a clear appreciation of the character of the area. In this respect my grateful thanks to Mona Farrell and her son Rory Farrell of James's Street for their hospitality, memories, reflections and fascinating insights into the essence of The Liberties. Similarly, Liberties stalwarts Christy Lawlor and Paddy Nealey, for their help and humour. Finally, thanks to all the people of The Liberties who helped make this work such an enjoyable undertaking.

INTRODUCTION

James Malton in his work, *A Picturesque and Descriptive View of the City of Dublin*, gives a glimpse of Dublin at the close of the eighteenth century. Malton was 'struck with admiration at the beauty of the Capital of Ireland and was anxious to make a display of it to the world'. His comment and many of his illustrations included the oldest neighbourhood of Dublin – The Liberties. And the 'beauty' of this part of Dublin has not been lost, and in fact has been enhanced since Malton's visit to Dublin, and is there for all to see.[1]

John Gallagher, long-time Liberties resident, activist, campaigner and stalwart advised me that any history of The Liberties would run to ten volumes. And he is quite correct. This book therefore is a mere introduction to an ancient area and neighbourhood in the city of Dublin.

The area known as The Liberties is the south-west part of Dublin's inner city, approximately west of Dublin Castle, Werburgh Street and Bride Street and stretching to James's Street and Cork Street, including Pimlico, the Coombe, Newmarket and The Tenters; south of the River Liffey from Wood Quay, Merchant's Quay and Ussher's Quay, extending to the Coombe Hospital, New Street and Kevin Street – predominately in the Dublin 8 postal district.

The story of The Liberties begins shortly after the murder in 1170 of Thomas à Becket, the Archbishop of Canterbury. King Henry II came to Ireland and visited the ancient church of St Catherine at what is now the western end of Thomas Street. The king declared that an abbey be founded in memory of Thomas à Becket. The founders of the monastery, the Augustinian monks, were given complete freedom of city laws, i.e. they did not have to pay rates or taxes. This first 'Liberty' spread out to take in the lands of Donore. This area became known as the Liberty of Thomas Court and Donore (later the Earl of Meath's Liberty), and had its own palace, prison, courts and hospital.

In return for supporting the ruler, the Liberty of St Sepulchre (under the Archbishop of Dublin) also received privileges such as freedom from various taxes. These were the two most important Liberties in Dublin. Today the term 'The Liberties' comes from these two ancient areas and jurisdictions.[2] Over time, however, The Liberties included different parts and places of the south inner city, and have meant different things to different people.

The Liberties was always regarded as being an intrinsic part of the real old Dublin. It is one of the oldest and most interesting areas of the city, and played a vital role in Irish medieval and revolutionary history. It occupies a unique place in Irish political, social, economic, religious, cultural and literary history. Some of the most pivotal events of Irish history took place in and were inspired in or by The Liberties.

It is of particular significance that the last official function of former President of Ireland, Mary McAleese, was to The Liberties. In the course of her tour, she visited Back Lane and the St Vincent de Paul night shelter. The locals, adults and children alike, gave her a huge welcome. This was not her first visit to The Liberties as she had previously visited the historic Liberty Crèche on Meath Street for its centenary celebrations. And she was not the first head of state or leader to visit the area. British royalty had visited The Liberties in the early years of the twentieth century and in early 2011 Queen Elizabeth II visited the area when she toured Guinness's Brewery. Former Taoiseach Bertie Ahern was a frequent visitor particularly during election times and Pope John Paul II made it his business to visit the area in September 1979. In addition, Ireland's first Taoiseach (or President of the Executive Council as he was called in the 1920s), William T. Cosgrave, was born in The Liberties (174 James's Street in 1880) and was educated at Francis Street Christian Brothers School.

Unique Spirit of The Liberties

There is no doubt that The Liberties holds a special place in the heart of Dublin people and in fact of people from all over Ireland. But why the fascination? Why the aura, magic and mystery that seems to surround the area? According to some of the residents themselves the reason is that the people of The Liberties are the 'real Dubs': this location is the area of Dublin where the city started and evolved more than a thousand years ago. Secondly, they say that over time, the area developed a great community spirit which gives a unique stamp and character to the people and place. The Liberties was also where some of the most pivotal events in Irish history occurred, ranging from the coming of Henry II, the Reformation, the United Irishmen and 1798, the 1916 Rising and the Wood Quay marches of the late 1970s.

Some of the finest and most historically significant churches in Dublin are to be found here, along with some of the city's most important industries and businesses. Weaving, tanning, brewing and distilling started and developed in The Liberties and some of these industries are still located here; Guinness's Brewery, in the heart of The Liberties, is one of Ireland's foremost tourist attractions.

W.T. Cosgrave, 1922. He was the first Taoiseach of the Irish Free State 1922–1932 and was born at 174 James's Street, Dublin. (Courtesy of UCC Multitext Cultural Project)

As far back as the 1950s conservationists were particularly aware of the historical significance of The Liberties. Attempts were then made to preserve Chamber Street with its terrace of Huguenot 'Dutch Billy' houses. In the 1960s, the Irish Georgian Society took the Tailors' Hall under its wing and subsequently An Taisce (National Trust for Ireland) took it over as its headquarters. Most significantly the campaign by the Friends of Medieval Dublin for Wood Quay, which included Coombe resident and activist, John Gallagher, did a huge amount to focus national and international attention on the major historical, cultural and archaeological significance of the area. As recently as April 2012 the Dublin Civic Trust launched a plan that aims to reverse the 'blight, dereliction and vacancy of Thomas Street, one of Dublin's most historic streets, through the restoration of its historic buildings, the promotion of indigenous businesses and the development of visitor attractions'.[3]

The indomitable spirit and sense of place that characterises The Liberties can be seen in many contrasting things: the South Inner City Community Development Association (SICCDA); The Liberties Festival committee (and Larry Dillon its first Chairman who spearheaded change); Mrs Ryan of Meath Street Public House; the inspiring Liberties singer Imelda May; footballer Kevin Moran;

The Liberties and Wood Quay campaigners and local activists John Gallagher and Fr F.X. Martin (the local Augustinian priest); and the many active and committed residents' groups, heritage associations, parish groups and businesses. Think of Declan Larkin's butcher's shop going strong for more than sixty years, or Hanlon's of Cork Street still longer, or Tony Byrne's enterprising spirit, or Jimmy Dent's Viking forays, or Gerard Smyth's memorable Liberties poems, or Sean Foley's Mushatt cures! These encapsulate The Liberties today.

1

THE GAELIC, VIKING AND NORMAN ORIGINS OF DUBLIN

As The Liberties are an intrinsic part of the history of Dublin, let us first look at the history of the wider city.

Settlement in the area can be traced back to the Early Christian period. One of the most significant settlements was the church of St Patrick, sited beside the River Poddle and very close to the present-day St Patrick's Cathedral.

Baile Átha Cliath is the ancient Irish name for Dublin and it means literally 'the town of the ford of the hurdles'. The Vikings built the town they called Dubhlinn, named after the Black Pool, which was formed by the meeting of the rivers Poddle and Liffey. Viking Dublin stretched roughly between Wood Quay, Winetavern Street, Christ Church and Fishamble Street.

A network of ancient routes (*slighe*) linked the early settlements with other locations in the country and familiar streets such as Augustine Street, Francis Street, Thomas Street and New Street in The Liberties are all descendants of these Gaelic routes. The city walls were constructed around the hill of Christ Church. This established it as the heart of the medieval city on high ground above the river, and drew the populace into the impressive cathedral. Further routes were developed, building on the *slighe* to develop an early urban network of streets. John Speed's map of Dublin, 1610, showed the city centred on Dublin Castle, with Thomas Street and Patrick Street being significant routes to the west and south.[1]

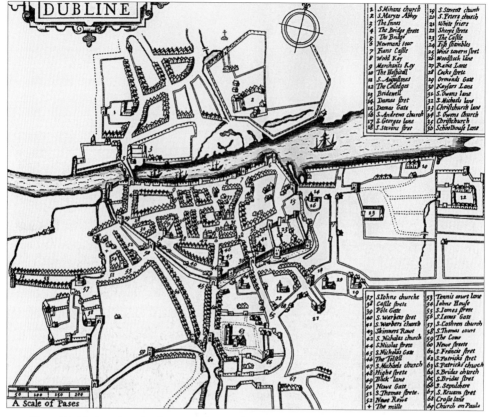

1	S.Mihans church	19	S.Stevens church
2	S.Maryes Abbey	20	S.Peters church
3	The Innes	21	White friers
4	The Bridge strete	22	Sheepi strete
5	The Bridge	23	The Castle
6	Newmans tour	24	Fish shambles
7	Barns Castle	25	Wnie tavern stret
8	Wodd Key	26	Woodstock lane
9	Marchants Key	27	Rame Lane
10	The Hospitall	28	Cocke strete
11	S.Augustines	29	Ormonds Gate
12	The Colledges	30	Kayfars Lane
13	Bridewell	31	S.Owens lane
14	Damas stret	32	S.Michaels lane
15	Damas Gate	33	Chrischurch lane
16	S.Andrews church	34	S.Owens church
17	S.Georges lane	35	Chrischurch
18	S.Stevens stret	36	Schoolhouse Lane

37	S.Iohns churche	53	Tennis court lane
38	Castle strete	54	Iohns House
39	Pole Gate	55	S.Iames strete
40	S.Warbers stret	56	S.Iames Gate
41	S.Warbers church	57	S.Cathren church
42	Skinners Rowe	58	S.Thomas court
43	S.Nicholas church	59	The Come
44	S.Nicolas stret	60	Newe strete
45	S.Nicholas Gate	61	S.Francis stret
46	The Talsell	62	S.Patricks stret
47	S.Michaels church	63	S.Patricks church
48	Highe strete	64	S.Brides church
49	Back lane	65	S.Brides stret
50	Newe Gate	66	S.Sepulchre
51	S.Thomas strete.	67	S.Keuam stret
52	Newe Rewe	68	Crosse lane
+	The mills	69	Church on Pauls

Map of Dublin by John Speed, 1610. (Courtesy of NLI/Dublin City Libraries)

From the Battle of Clontarf to the Normans

Following the Viking settlement, Dublin evolved into the Kingdom of Dublin. Despite a number of rebellions by the native Irish, it remained largely under Viking control until 1014, when Brian Boru, High King of Ireland, defeated them at the famous Battle of Clontarf. After this remaining Vikings were assimilated into the Irish way of life.

The Norman invasion of Ireland was launched from Wales in 1169. The King of Leinster, Dermot Mac Murrough, enlisted the help of Strongbow, the Earl of Pembroke, to help him conquer Dublin. Following Mac Murrough's death, Strongbow declared himself King of Leinster after gaining control of the city. In response to his successful invasion, and fearing that Strongbow would form a rival kingdom, King Henry II of England reaffirmed his sovereignty by mounting a larger invasion in 1171 and pronouncing himself Lord of Ireland. Henry's show of force was aimed as much at his own Anglo-Norman vassals as it was at the native Irish.[2]

King Henry II.

On arrival in Dublin, King Henry II then granted the city of Dublin to his faithful men of Bristol following its capture and on 15 May 1172, Dublin's first written Charter of Liberties was granted by Henry, Lord of Ireland, addressed to all his 'French, English, Irish and Welsh subjects and friends'.[3]

In 1177 Strongbow died in Dublin and was buried with great solemnity in Christ Church, where a monument to his memory is still on view. The same year Vivian, the Pope's legate, held a synod in Dublin, and therein published King Henry's title to Ireland, ratified by Pope Adrian (the first and only English pope). He announced that all who should withdraw their allegiance from Henry would be excommunicated. (Recent historians, however, have questioned the authenticity of the Pope's *Laudabiliter* as one of the justifications for Henry's invasion of Ireland.)[4]

2

HENRY II:
LIBERTIES OR
FRANCHISES?

The term 'The Liberties' is a very familiar feature in Dublin, but what exactly does it mean? The Liberties are not so called because they were ever free – in fact they had several masters – but because they lay outside the medieval city walls and so were not under the city's jurisdiction or control. The Archbishop of Dublin executed justice and levied dues in one part, the monks of St Thomas's Abbey another, and there were some lesser overlords. Those in control of The Liberties were granted certain privileges; the Archbishop, for instance, was entitled to have a boat on the River Liffey and to take salmon and other fish. He was also entitled to all the fines imposed on jurors for non-attendance at the King's Bench. The court of his Liberty was held in the Palace of St Sepulchre's (now Kevin Street Garda station) and the Archbishop himself tried and sentenced persons for offences committed within his Liberty.[1]

The ancient Liberties remained independent of the Lord Mayor and Corporation up to 1840. They were town lands united to the city, but still preserving their own system of local government.

How did these semi-independent royal government-mandated entities come into being, and to what extent did they retain their privileges and immunities that they enjoyed until well into the nineteenth century? Kenneth Milne in his excellent in-depth study, *Dublin Liberties 1660–1850*, shows that the four main Dublin Liberties were rooted in charters granted to ecclesiastics, the Archbishop of Dublin (St Sepulchre's), the prior of the Augustinian monastery of Thomas Court, and the two cathedral chapters.[2]

Liberty of Thomas Court and Donore

The origin of this liberty goes back to the founding of the Abbey of St Thomas in what is now Thomas Street, near St Catherine's church, in 1177. The founder was William FitzAldelm, deputy and kinsman of King Henry II. The church was dedicated to Thomas à Beckett (St Thomas the Martyr), who had recently been murdered in his cathedral at Canterbury by followers of the King. The church, which became a rich and powerful monastery, was for the use of the Canons of the Congregation of St Victor. In return for the support of the prior of the abbey, or to alleviate certain hardships suffered by Englishmen or the Church in Ireland, privileges were granted to the abbey. These allowed the abbey to have its own courts of justice, where it was allowed to try a limited number of crimes, mainly dealing with bad debts. The court-house was located in Thomas Court Bawn, off Thomas Street, while the jail was in Marrowbone Lane.[3]

In 1538, Henry VIII dissolved the monasteries. At this time the Abbey of St Thomas Court held 56 rectories, 2,197 acres of land, 67 houses, 47 messuages (houses and attached lands) and 19 gardens. Most of the land was in Meath and Kildare. These possessions were confiscated and distributed among several people, of whom Sir William Brabazon (ancestor of the Earl of Meath) and Richard St Leger were the major beneficiaries.

On 31 March 1545, Sir William Brabazon was granted the lands of the abbey, with all jurisdictions, liberties, privileges, and so on. This grant was confirmed in 1609 to Sir Edward, his son. In 1579 the city of Dublin claimed the abbey to be within the jurisdiction and liberty of the city, but they lost their case. From then on the head of the liberty was the Earl of Meath.

Liberty of St Sepulchre

The Liberty of St Sepulchre (also known as the Archbishop's Liberty) was under the jurisdiction of the Archbishop of Dublin. The headquarters of the Liberty was the Palace of St Sepulchre, located now where Kevin Street Garda station stands. This was originally constructed by John Comyn, the first Anglo-Norman Archbishop of Dublin, appointed in 1180. The name was suggested by the campaigns being waged by the Crusaders for the recovery of the Holy Sepulchre from the Muslims. Comyn was shortly after granted land by the monarchy for the See of Dublin, which provided the basis for the Liberty. The importance of the Liberty of St Sepulchre was enhanced by the fact that it consisted of a number of smaller Liberties, many of which lay outside the city or even county of Dublin. The Liberty of St Sepulchre in the city was, however, the principal Liberty.

As with the Abbey of St Thomas Liberty, privileges were granted to the Liberty (that is, to the archbishop and his successors) at various times and by various kings of England in return for his support. These rights and privileges were ended by the Manor Court of St Sepulchre Abolition Act 1856, the last such jurisdiction remaining in Ireland.

A courthouse and jail for the use of the Liberty were built in the early nineteenth century at the corner of Long Lane and Bride Street. Most of the prisoners were insolvent debtors. Much of the business of the court related to trading, fairs, and weights and measures.[4]

Milne points out that:

> Until modern times the lords of the larger Liberties, that of St Sepulchre and that of Thomas Court and Donore, exercised legal jurisdictions comparable to those of the Lord Mayor, and in all four Liberties they controlled the economic life of their territories (including the two smaller Liberties of St Patrick's Cathedral and Christ Church Cathedral) through their market juries and by administering the assize of bread, the provision of public lighting and fire-engines. The Liberties tenaciously maintained their privileges until the demands of an increasingly complex urban society became too much for them.[5]

Milne also notes:

> The Liberty and Ormond Boys frequently clashed (weavers versus butchers). This then led to the development of a law and order system to regulate crime, the dispensing of justice, courts, disputed jurisdictions, a legal system to oversee local government services, such as paving, sanitation, lighting, the right to hold markets and fairs and their supervision (the Kevin Street Market in the Liberty of St Sepulchre was the largest market south of the Liffey), the size, standard and quality of bread, water supply issues and problems of flooding, hazards of fire, payment for services through various taxes, e.g. hearth taxes, paving tax, foundling tax and many more.[6]

The main two Liberties are mentioned in Allen's Register of 1529, but without describing their exact location. In 1728 Charles Brooking published a detailed 'Map of the City and Suburbs of Dublin', which contained a description: the Liberty of St Sepulchre boundaries stretched from Bishop Street to St Stephen's Green, along Harcourt Street to Donnybrook, across Rathgar to Harold's Cross and back along Clanbrassil Street to Patrick Street. The Earl of Meath's Liberty ran west along the Coombe to Ardee Street, turning north towards Echlin Street, then along James's Street and Thomas Street to Meath Street, then through various smaller streets to Ash Street and back to the Coombe.[7]

In 1754 Roger Kendrick produced a map of the Liberty of St Patrick's and Thomas Reading followed ten years later in 1764 when he made a map showing the Liberty of Christ Church. In 1837 the Ordnance Survey started developing their maps, and that of Dublin published in 1840 showed all The Liberties, from the smallest (Christ Church Liberty, one acre two roods) to the largest (Earl of Meath's Liberty, 380 acres).

Riding the Franchises

There were those who quibbled at using the term 'Liberties' – according to a late nineteenth-century visitor to Dublin, the 'Franchises' and not 'Liberties' was the correct term. In fact the National Library of Ireland has a manuscript and map called: *Survey of The Liberties and franchises of Dublin City as ridden and perambulated every third year*, published in 1815, which seems to corroborate this view.[8]

'Riding the franchises' was a tradition that began in the Middle Ages and continued until the early nineteenth century. It involved the Lord Mayor of Dublin and his entourage, including representatives of the various guilds and other important citizens, parading in their regalia and finery around the boundaries that marked the city from The Liberties. Every so often they would stop and the Lord Mayor would bang his mace on a wall, signifying the boundary of his rule. This had the function of asserting his authority, protecting his territory and pointing to the authorities in the adjacent Liberties, the extent of the latter's rule: thus far and no further.[9]

But the use of the word 'franchises' to describe the local government system of royal administration is quite interesting. The Liberties need to be seen and understood in the context of the Anglo-Norman invasion of Ireland. The granting of so-called 'Liberties' by Henry II to the native Irish was in reality a contradiction. In fact the original lands they had enjoyed were sequestered by the invaders and handed back with stipulations that were called 'Liberties' with privileges. But these 'Liberties' and privileges were a step back from the freedoms and rights they previously owned and enjoyed before the invasion. The native Irish in these 'Liberties' were henceforth tenants of the English king and the 'Liberties' their rent books. In later years this policy was extended to other parts of Gaelic Ireland under the guise of 'surrender and re-grant'. The story of The Liberties area of Dublin then is also the story of Irish history and the overthrowing of that confiscation of the lands of Ireland. And some of the pivotal events in Irish history in this process took place in The Liberties.

3

THE MIDDLE AGES: BARBERS, BLACKPITTS AND THE BLACK DEATH

Dublin Castle, which became the centre of English power in Ireland, was founded in 1204 as a major defensive work on the orders of King John of England. Following the appointment of the first Lord Mayor of Dublin in 1229, the city expanded and had a population of 8,000 by the end of the thirteenth century. Dublin prospered as a trade centre, despite an attempt by King Robert I of Scotland to capture the city in 1317, though it remained a relatively small walled medieval town during the fourteenth century and was under constant threat from the surrounding Irish clans.

By 1400, however, many of the Anglo-Norman conquerors were absorbed into the Irish culture, adopting the Irish language and customs, leaving only a small area of Leinster around Dublin, known as The Pale, under direct English control.

Candles and Guilds

Medieval Dublin was a busy place. Many of the people who lived within the city walls worked at a trade or a craft and serviced the needs of the castle which was the centre of the city. They also paid taxes to the castle for the privilege of living within the city walls. Amongst the craftspeople who lived in the town, or just outside its walls in The Liberties, were goldsmiths, carpenters, smiths, butchers and fishmongers. There were also tanners, weavers, coopers, shoemakers, tailors, and bakers.

These craftsmen were organised into Guilds that were modelled on the self-help principles of the trade and craft guilds. A large number of such guilds came into existence throughout Europe in the Middle Ages. Most of the guilds were based around the High Street and St Audoen's church. One of most important was the Guild of Tallow Chandlers, Soap Boilers and Wax Light Makers that was founded in 1538 by a civic charter. Guild meetings were held at St Audoen's Arch. In medieval times candles were made by the simple process of repeatedly dipping a series of wicks on pieces of wood into melted wax until the desired thickness had been achieved. Candles would have been of great importance in the Middle Ages as a main source of light in churches, businesses and elsewhere. The old Dublin firm of Rathbornes Candle Makers were producing candles in Winetavern Street in 1488 and, now located in East Wall Road, Dublin, is still producing candles today.

Other important guilds included the Glovers and Skinners; the Weavers; the Brewers and Malters; the Felt Makers; the Smiths; the Tanners; the Tailors (who had their own Guild Hall on Winetavern Street and later at Back Lane); the Barber Surgeons (hence the red and white barber's pole signifying blood and bandages); the Coopers; the Cooks; the Bakers; the Carpenters; the Goldsmiths; and the Millers.

The Black Death

Like all medieval towns, Dublin was a dirty place. There were no sewers and rubbish was thrown into the streets. People did not have baths or showers regularly or even wash their clothes. There were rats and mice everywhere. Medieval towns were a perfect breeding ground for diseases and in 1348 the Bubonic Plague or 'Black Death' reached Dublin. The crowded conditions of the city allowed the deadly disease to spread like wild fire and it is estimated that around one third of the population was wiped out.[1] This was a common occurrence across Ireland and England and the Black Death led to the complete disappearance of some villages and towns as the population either died or moved away. Dublin, like the majority of other European cities, was large enough to survive the Black Death as it had a population of about 35,000 when the plague hit.

The victims of the Black Death inside Dublin were buried in mass graves, something that is reflected across many of the major cities in Europe. The graves were located in an area still known as the 'Blackpitts', but there has been some debate recently as to whether this refers directly to the graves of plague victims. It cannot be underestimated how much this set back the development of cities throughout Europe, including Dublin.[2]

The Black Death altered the balance of power in the city, which just before the disease was firmly in the hands of the Anglo-Normans, back in favour of the native Irish. The Black Death continued to return for most of the fourteenth century, and it meant that effective rule by the Anglo-Norman leaders was almost impossible. It was not until the sixteenth century that the English regained the full control of the city.[3] Consequently Dublin was seen as a potential hotbed of rebellion for many years to come.

4

FROM THE TUDORS
TO THE GEORGIANS

Silken Thomas and William Brabazon

Just off Werburgh Street in The Liberties at Ship Street Little, there is a series of wall panels (created by Grace Weir) depicting scenes from a very important event in Irish history – the attack by Silken Thomas on Dublin Castle in 1534. The plaque on the wall tells the story:

> In 1534, at the age of 21 years, 'Silken Thomas' of the Fitzgeralds of Kildare, laid siege to Dublin Castle from this vicinity. The rebellion failed and he was executed in London, together with all of his uncles (five), by order of Henry VIII. The fall of the House of Kildare was a major factor leading to the Tudor conquest of Ireland, which shaped the country we know today.

The Dissolution of the monasteries by King Henry VIII in the mid-sixteenth century and the accompanying Reformation had an enormous impact on The Liberties due to the concentration of cathedrals, churches, monastic houses and lands in the area.[1] In 1520 King Henry VIII abolished all religious orders in Ireland and in the 1530s gave the monastery of St Thomas's Abbey, and the land around it, one of the two major Liberties, to his vice-treasurer in Ireland at the time, William

Brabazon, who had been sent to Ireland in 1533. Furthermore, the monastery came with a large parcel of land in County Wicklow, known as Kilrotheric, on which the monks had built a retreat, farm and burial ground. This land, today the home of the Brabazons and Ardees who reside at Kilruddery House, extended to more than 22,000 acres and encompassed Bray Head and the Little Sugar Loaf. Over the years it contracted in size, but today it still comprises around 850 acres.[2]

In 1627 Brabazon's grandson, William, was made Earl of Meath. From then on the area was known as the Earl of Meath Liberties.

William Brabazon was buried in St Catherine's church on Thomas Street and is remembered in the naming of Brabazon Street, Brabazon Square, Brabazon Place and Brabazon Row and also Ardee and Meath Streets. Earl Street is named after the first Earl of Meath, Edward Brabazon, who was also the Baron of Ardee. The name is still being used to adorn dwellings even more recently with the Brabazon Hall and Brabazon Court blocks of apartments.

Reginald Brabazon, 12th Earl of Meath. The family fortunes blossomed when Henry VIII dispatched the Machiavellian Sir William Brabazon to Ireland as Vice-Treasurer. He established the family at Kilruddery in County Wicklow and his grandson was created 1st Earl of Meath in 1627. In 1539, Sir William Brabazon secured ownership of the Abbey of St Thomas, which stood between present day Thomas Street and the River Liffey. He converted the Abbey into 'Thomas Court', his home.

The Brabazon family, the Earls of Meath, have lived at Killruddery, near Bray, County Wicklow, since the early seventeenth century. The Brabazon pedigree commenced with Jacques le Brabançon, said to have lived about the eleventh century but almost certainly a legendary figure. The first of the family to settle in Ireland was Sir William Brabazon in the time of Henry VIII, who rose to the positions of Vice-Treasurer and Lord Justice.[3]

The Brabazon family had a huge impact on the development of The Liberties over the generations, in spheres ranging from water control, weaving, mills, the location of many business enterprises, health and housing, to name but a few. The 12th Earl of Meath (1841–1929) and his Countess were renowned for their philanthropic work. In 1876 the Earl of Meath owned 14,700 acres of land in

County Wicklow and 28 acres in Dublin City. They are remembered in many place names in The Liberties to this day.[4]

William Brabazon's influence and control over government finances at the time of the Reformation had an enormous impact on the subsequent history of The Liberties (and that of Ireland). Vice-treasurer and three times Lord Justice, he was described by historian Hiram Morgan as the prototype New Englishman – 'a hard man with sticky fingers'. He began the conquest of Gaelic Ireland by attacking the O'Moore and the O'Connor clans while St Leger (the Lord Deputy) was away in 1546. The Dissolution of the Monasteries, over which he had a major influence, presented an opportunity to overhaul government finances. However, Brabazon, St Leger, and other officials profited themselves by renting out confiscated land (dissolved monastic and confiscated rebel lands) at rates far below market values and leaving thousands of pounds of rent arrears uncollected. This massive fraud was not uncovered until three years after his death. When the widespread corruption was brought to light in 1556 St Leger was dismissed, tried and fined £5,000.[5]

The Exchequer itself gained very little extra revenue from the Dissolution of the Monasteries; the main beneficiaries were Lord Deputies Grey and St Leger, and treasurer Brabazon. However, 60 per cent of Irish monasteries and friaries remained undisturbed in the Gaelic and Gaelicised parts of Ireland. The Liberties, being in the Pale, and under direct English influence and control, was not so lucky, with the lands of the Abbey of St Thomas confiscated, as were the lands of the Franciscans on Francis Street, the Augustinians on Thomas Street, and both cathedrals. They all suffered hugely, and the legacy of this upheaval weighed enormously not only on The Liberties, but on Dublin and Irish life up until the present day.

On a broader scale, the Reformation itself was part of the conquest of Ireland that was gathering apace in the sixteenth century and would be legally and militarily complete with the surrender of Hugh O'Neill at Mellifont in 1603.

Gunpowder Plot?

The Tudor conquest of Ireland in the sixteenth century spelt a new era for Dublin, with the city enjoying a renewed prominence as the centre of administrative rule in Ireland. Determined to make Dublin a Protestant city, Queen Elizabeth I of England established Trinity College in 1592 as a solely Protestant university and ordered that the Catholic St Patrick's and Christ Church cathedrals be converted into Protestant cathedrals.

However, this move to turn Dublin Protestant and extend the conquest was also precipitated by the great gunpowder explosion in Dublin in 1597.

The background to the explosion was the English war against the Irish chieftains, the O'Neills and the O'Donnells, who were successfully waging a campaign during the Nine Years War. English soldiers and supplies were arriving in Dublin port and whether by accident or design, a number of barrels of gunpowder dramatically exploded in the heart of the old city, near Dublin Castle, killing over 100 people and destroying half the small city. Most damage was incurred to buildings in Cook Street, Fishamble Street, Bridge Street, High Street and St Michael's Lane.

The English government was particularly suspicious of the Catholic tendencies of the City Fathers despite their recognised loyalty to the Crown and the huge gunpowder explosion brought matters to a head. Consequently, moves were made to undermine not only the power of the Dublin aldermen, but also the privileges and independence of The Liberties, that had been guaranteed by charter for the previous 400 years. This move toward royal absolutism, however, was strongly and successfully resisted both within and without the city, particularly by The Liberties.[6]

The city had a population of 21,000 in 1640 before a plague in 1649–51 wiped out almost half of the city's inhabitants. However, the city prospered again soon after as a result of the wool and linen trade with England (much of it centred in The Liberties), reaching a population of over 50,000 in 1700.

As the city continued to prosper during the seventeenth century, Georgian Dublin became, for a short period, the second largest city of the British Empire and the fifth largest city in Europe, with the population exceeding 130,000. The vast majority of Dublin's most notable architecture dates from this period, such as the Four Courts and the Custom House. Temple Bar and Grafton Street are two of the few remaining areas that were not affected by the wave of Georgian reconstruction and maintained their medieval character.[7]

5

THE HUGUENOTS: WEAVERS AND DUTCH BILLIES

The expansion of Dublin ran parallel with the new brewing, distilling, textile and banking enterprises and by flourishing writing, publishing, and music endeavours in The Liberties. In the eighteenth century Francis Street and Skinners Row (Christ Church Place) were centres for Dublin's publishing and book auctions. The building of the Weavers' Hall in the Coombe, the construction of Marsh's Library at St Patrick's Close and Jonathan Swift's time as Dean of St Patrick's Cathedral, also illustrate a new confidence and growing prosperity.

Fishamble Street, in the shadow of Christ Church Cathedral, was the location for the first performance of Handel's *Messiah* in 1742. G.F. Handel had come to Dublin in November 1741 and stayed until the summer of 1742. This was an attempt to have a quiet year away from London, where his earlier success as an opera composer was dwindling under political and artistic opposition. Horatio Townsend, a barrister who practiced in Dublin, and who was known as a great authority on the works of G.F. Handel, detailed Handel's complete visit in a small book, *An Account of the Visit of Handel to Dublin*, published in 1852. While in Ireland, Handel gave a series of concerts. The New Music Hall had only just opened in Fishamble Street, one of the first concert halls built in Europe. His stay was a huge success and he praised the Dublin audiences and performers highly. The magnificent conclusion was the first performance of the *Messiah*, composed the previous summer.

Malton's eighteenth-century view of St Patrick's Cathedral with 'Dutch Billy' houses on the left. The sign refers to 'Cross Poddle' – the River Poddle flowed underground nearby. (Courtesy of Archiseek)

The present archway was the original entrance to the Music Hall. The building was a small steel assembly plant up to the late 1970s and it was demolished in the late 1990s.

Dutch Billies

French Protestants called Huguenots were granted religious toleration under the Edict of Nantes (1598), but in the late seventeenth century were subject to increasing persecution, culminating in 1685 in the revocation of the edict and their expulsion from France. The Huguenots were encouraged to move to Ireland due to an Act passed by the (then) Irish Parliament. A small Huguenot community already existed in Dublin by 1665, when a chapel in St Patrick's Cathedral was set aside for their use. A more substantial immigration, involving an estimated 10,000 persons, took place in the 1690s. They were skilled craftsmen who worked and worshipped in Dublin, particularly in The Liberties.[1]

They had a significant influence not only in The Liberties but in the wider Dublin also. D'Olier Street was named after Jeremiah D'Olier, Dublin High Sheriff in 1788 while Mercer Street and French Street show Huguenot influence. A Huguenot, David Digges La Touche and Nathaniel Kane founded Ireland's most historic bank in 1713. The Huguenots were to go on to have a very strong influence on the social and commercial life of Dublin for generations.[2]

In the late seventeenth century much planning, building and development started in order to house the Huguenot weavers who were moving into the area. Woollen manufacture was set up by settlers from England, while many Huguenots took up silk weaving, using skills they had acquired in their home country, France. They constructed their own traditional style of house, 'Dutch Billies', with gables that faced the street. Thousands of weavers became employed in the Coombe, Pimlico, Spitalfields and Newmarket and Weavers Squares.

When the Huguenots settled in the area they brought with them from France their fine skills and traditions. Their word was their bond and the saying 'as honest as a Huguenot' testified to their quality of integrity. The Huguenots brought an industriousness and prosperity to The Liberties. Over time their arrival gave the area a name for religious tolerance and the area became full of Protestants, Jews, and Quakers, as well as Catholics.[3]

The 'Dutch Billy' houses of The Liberties were a testament to these followers of William of Orange who settled in The Liberties. One of the finest examples of this kind of dwelling may be seen at 35 Kevin Street Upper, next door to St Patrick's Cathedral Grammar School (the former Deanery), which itself is a

'Dutch Billies' at New Row/Ward's Hill with tower of St Patrick's Cathedral in background, 1880s. (Courtesy of RSAI/Dublin City Council/Dublin Forums.ie/Damntheweather)

particularly unusual building. The front gables of the new apartment blocks along Lamb Alley, off Cornmarket, sport mock examples of Dutch Billies and there are hints of the influence on the front gables of the Iveagh Buildings.[6]

Dutch Billies were a rich architectural heritage in The Liberties. They were picturesque high gabled houses. The buildings were from time to time called Queen Anne, Dutch, Huguenot, Flemish, and were not just confined to The Liberties. However, many were to be seen in Weavers' Square, Newmarket, Warrenmount, Mill Street, Ardee Street, Marrowbone Lane, New Row, Blackpitts, St Patrick's Close, the Coombe, Sweeney's Lane, the old Molyneux House in Peter Street, Chamber Street, etc.

The Huguenots were industrious people and built the Weavers' Hall on the Coombe, beautiful houses, shops, schools and churches.[5] The Weavers' Hall was built by the Weavers' Guild in the Lower Coombe in 1682. In 1745 a new hall was provided, financed by the Huguenot, David Digges La Touche. In 1750 the Guild erected a statue of King George II on the front of their hall 'as a mark of their sincere loyalty'. The hall was demolished in 1965. The Huguenots also brought us the garden shears, several species of flowers, a florists club and our very first pineapples grown at Ward's Hill in The Liberties.[6]

They taught the people of Dublin to weave silks, tabinets and Irish poplin, which became the finest poplin in the world. They set up a hive of industry in this part of Dublin, which thrived. However, English woollen manufacturers felt threatened by the Irish industry, and heavy duties were imposed on Irish wool exports. The Navigation Acts of the seventeenth and eighteenth centuries were passed to prevent the Irish from exporting to the whole colonial market and effectively undermined the industry in The Liberties.[7]

In the eighteenth century a revival took place by importing Spanish wool into Ireland, which was helped from 1775 by the Royal Dublin Society, but the Rebellions of 1798 and 1803 (The United Irishmen Rebellion and Robert Emmett's Rebellion respectively), in which many weavers in The Liberties took part, and the economic decline that set in after the Act of Union, prevented any further growth in this industry in The Liberties.[8]

Similarly, the successful growth of the silk and poplin industries, which was supported by the Royal Dublin Society in the second half of the eighteenth century, was hindered by an act passed by the British government in 1786, which prevented the society from supporting any house where Irish silk goods were sold. When war was declared against France under Napoleon and raw materials were difficult to obtain, the silk weavers suffered greatly. The final blow came in the 1820s when the British government did away with the tariffs imposed upon imported silk products.[9] From this time on the fate of The Liberties was sealed and most of the once-prosperous houses became poverty-stricken tenements housing the unemployed and destitute.

The Huguenots had a cemetery in Peter Street, which no longer exists. The remains in all the graves were removed to Mount Jerome to make way for a car park for Jacob's biscuit factory. A plaque on a wall in Peter Street opposite the old Adelaide Hospital reads: 'From the 19th December 1711 this was the site of 'French Peters' the church and cemetery of the non-conforming French Huguenots until the remains were removed and re-interred in Mount Jerome cemetery in 1967'. There are also graves in Merrion Row near St Stephen's Green.[10]

Wide Streets Commissioners

The most important statutory influence on Dublin's growth in the eighteenth century was the Wide Streets Commissioners.[11] The Commission was set up by an Act of Parliament in 1757 to reduce city-centre congestion, and to widen and develop the thoroughfares of Dublin city centre. The work of the Wide Street Commission (1757–1851) had a lasting impact on the fabric of Dublin City and its built heritage. It helped create a city of fine public buildings, elegant streetscapes and residential squares. The framework of modern Dublin is largely their work.

The Wide Streets Commissioners were originally appointed under an Act of the old Irish Parliament in 1757 for the making of 'a wide and convenient street from Essex Bridge to the Castle of Dublin.'[12] This new street is the Parliament Street of today. Many other streets were subsequently laid out or enlarged and so we have the spacious thoroughfares of Thomas Street, which was widened at Cornmarket, Francis Street which was straightened out and Meath Street. Dame Street, Lower Abbey Street, Beresford Place, O'Connell Street, Westmoreland Street, D'Olier Street, Burgh Quay, Hawkins Street, which all benefited from the work of the commissioners.

Dublin grew dramatically during the eighteenth century, with the construction of many famous districts and buildings, such as Merrion Square, Parliament House and the Royal Exchange. Dublin was a city of magnificent balls, receptions and entertainments. There were exciting dinners with such unusual dishes as squab pigeon, stewed carp and venison pie and Mrs Delaney, a friend of Dean Swift, served her famous syllabub. There was the Smock Alley Theatre (later St Michael's church on Wood Quay) where Garrick and Peg Woffington appeared, and where the ladies and gentlemen in the audience were dressed in magnificent court costumes. The playhouses were lit with tallow candles and two soldiers with fixed bayonets stood like statues on the stage to keep the audience in control. The presence of the soldiers was intended to discourage riots, which sometimes occurred, particularly if the Trinity students were in the audience and sometimes in these unruly scenes there were more members of the audience on stage than in the auditorium.[13]

6

THE UNITED IRISHMEN:
THE WEARING OF THE GREEN

Thomas Street played a vital role in the events surrounding the 1798 and 1803 Rebellions. And it was a Liberties man, Richard Robert Madden (1798–1886) of Wormwood Gate, who wrote in the 1840s some of the first and finest histories of these rebellions and of their leaders.

Until 1800 the city housed an independent (though still exclusively Anglican) Irish Parliament (Grattan's Parliament), and it was during this period that many of the great Georgian buildings of Dublin were erected. By the late eighteenth century, Irish Protestants – mostly the descendants of British settlers – had been born in Ireland and saw it as their native country, and the Irish Parliament successfully agitated for increased autonomy and better terms of trade with Britain. From 1778 the movement to have the Penal Laws repealed, was gathering pace, pushed along by liberals such as Henry Grattan. Other factors however added a new urgency to the move for greater Irish independence.

Under the influence of the American and French Revolutions, some Irish radicals went a step further and formed the United Irishmen to create an independent, non-sectarian and democratic republic. United Irishmen leaders in The Liberties included Napper Tandy, Oliver Bond and Edward Fitzgerald. Wolfe Tone, the leader of the movement, was also from Dublin. The United Irishmen planned to take Dublin in a street rising in 1798, but their leaders were arrested and the city occupied by a large British military presence shortly before the rebels could assemble. There was some local fighting in the city's outskirts such as Rathfarnham, but the city itself remained firmly under control during the 1798 rebellion. Much of the significant activity took place in Wexford and Boolavogue was celebrated in song by the great Liberties writer and composer, P.J. McCall who lived at Patrick Street, in the shadow of the cathedral.[1] There is no doubt, however, that The Liberties featured prominently in the organising and planning of 1798 Rebellion.

Wolfe Tone and the Back Lane Parliament

In 1791, Theobald Wolfe Tone, William Rowan Hamilton, and Napper Tandy founded the Society of United Irishmen in Belfast. Wolfe Tone was born in Dublin in 1763 and became a lawyer. He was a Protestant, yet like many of the leaders of the United Irishmen he wanted to seek rights for his Presbyterian and Catholic countrymen. Under Wolfe Tone, the United Irishmen (which consisted of Protestants and Catholics alike) declared their belief in a peaceful future for Ireland in which Protestants and Catholics could live together in peace and with equality. They wanted to set up a French-style democratic republic in Ireland, which was independent of Britain.

In 1792 the Catholic Committee/Convention passed through the gates of Tailors' Guild Hall on Back Lane to discuss petitioning the Irish Parliament and the English King to relax the Penal Laws. It was to be a major step that culminated in the granting of Catholic Emancipation in 1829. Their gatherings gave the place the sobriquet 'The Back Lane Parliament'. The Dublin Society of the United Irishmen met here regularly and planned the 1798 Rebellion. Moreover, there were a number of prominent United Irishmen leaders based in The Liberties.[2]

Lord Edward Fitzgerald

Edward Fitzgerald was the fifth son of the Duke of Leinster. His ancestral home was the magnificent Carton Hall in Co. Kildare, and his Town House was Leinster House now the seat of our parliament (the Dáil). Lord Edward reached high rank in the English Army, and saw service in the American and West Indian colonies. Because of his family background, he was given a seat in the Irish Parliament, which was housed in what is now the Head Office of the Bank of Ireland in College Green, Dublin.

It did not take him long to realise that this was a puppet parliament. He became disillusioned with their policy rigging, and soon came to the notice of the United Irishmen. Because of his military experience, he was appointed head of their forces, and helped plan the Rebellion of 1798 with Robert Emmet, Wolfe Tone and Napper Tandy, Oliver Bond and others. However, due to the ever-present paid informer of the Crown in Ireland's long history of insurrection, Lord Edward was arrested in his hiding place at 151 Thomas Street (now the IAWS building opposite the entrance to Guinness's Brewery) prior to the date fixed for the rebellion. In resisting arrest he was severely wounded, and later died of his wounds in Newgate Jail. He was aged thirty-five. He is buried in St Werburgh's church, Werburgh Street.[3]

Napper Tandy and Napoleon

Napper Tandy lived for many years in the shadow of St Audoen's church on High Street. There was a plaque on his house before the developers demolished most of the street in the 1980s. In 1791, he helped Tone and Thomas Russell to found the Society of United Irishmen, and became the first secretary of the Dublin group.

In September 1798 he landed on the Donegal coast with the ship, the *Anacreon*, accompanied by a consignment of arms and French troops. Discovering that the rebellion had already failed, he set sail back to the continent where he was arrested in Hamburg and eventually extradited back to Ireland. At his trial he pleaded guilty to the charge of treason and was sentenced to be hanged, drawn and quartered. Fortunately for him, Napoleon Bonaparte interceded on his behalf and refused to sign a peace treaty, which had been agreed between France and Britain, unless Napper Tandy was released. His sentence was eventually commuted to transportation for life and then further reduced to exile. He was finally released into the care of his son and arrived at Bordeaux in March 1802 where he died the following year, aged sixty-three, and was buried with full military honours.

Napper Tandy. James Napper Tandy was one of the founding members of the Dublin branch of the United Irishmen. He lived at High Street near St Audoen's Church.

He is remembered to this day in the ballad 'The Wearing of the Green':

> ... I met with Napper Tandy, and he took me by the hand
> And he said, 'How's poor old Ireland, and how does she stand?'
> She's the most distressful country that ever yet was seen
> For they're hanging men and women there for the Wearin' o' the Green.[4]

Oliver Bond: Murder Most Foul?

Another United Irishman, Oliver Bond, was also associated with The Liberties. An impressive Dublin Corporation housing development, Oliver Bond House, is a reminder that he and his family lived in the area for many years. Oliver Bond Street links Bridgefoot Street to Lower Bridge Street via Mullinahack and Wormwood Gate.

A prominent United Irishman, he was born in Ulster about 1762. He commenced business as a wholesale woollen draper in Pill Lane (later called Chancery Street and behind the Four Courts). So well did his business thrive, that in 1786 he moved his business and family to a house at Lower Bridge Street, much larger premises. According to the historian, Gilbert, Bridge Street at the time was a thoroughfare 'chiefly occupied by merchants of wealth and eminence'. Five years afterwards he married the daughter of Henry Jackson, iron-founder, a leading member of the United Irishmen. He soon rose to be one of the most prosperous and respectable merchants in Dublin. He entered enthusiastically into Irish politics. However, in March 1793, he was committed to Newgate Prison, and fined £500, for inflammatory comments on the House of Lords. On his release in August he was presented with congratulatory addresses. In 1797 we find him exceedingly active in promoting the cause of the United Irishmen.

The meetings of the Leinster Directory (branch of United Irishmen) were usually held at his house and it was here, on 19 February 1798, that the famous resolution was passed: 'We will pay no attention to any measure which the Parliament of this kingdom may adopt, to divert the public mind from the grand object we have in view; as nothing short of the entire and complete regeneration of our country can satisfy us.'[5]

However, through the treachery of an informer called Thomas Reynolds, Bond's house in The Liberties was surrounded by the military on the morning of 12 March 1798 and he and fourteen members of the Leinster Directory were arrested.

Bond was tried and convicted on 24 July 1798. Prominent lawyers John Philpott Curran (father of Sarah Curran) and George Ponsonby defended him.

He was sentenced to death but it was commuted on appeal. He survived the commutation by only five weeks, dying suddenly in prison of apoplexy, on 6 September, aged thirty-six. However, there has always been a question mark over how he died, as he was of robust good health, and whether he was in fact murdered in prison. He was interred in nearby St Michan's graveyard. His family moved to the United States where Mrs Bond died in Baltimore on 15 September 1843.

Robert Emmet and Thomas Street

Robert Emmet (4 March 1778 – 20 September 1803) was an Irish nationalist and Republican, orator and rebel leader born in Dublin. He led an abortive rebellion against British rule in 1803 and was captured, tried and executed for high treason outside St Catherine's church, Thomas Street.

He came from a wealthy Protestant family who sympathised with Irish Catholics, namely their lack of fair representation in the Irish Parliament. The Emmet family also sympathised with the American Revolution. From a very early age Robert Emmett's political and social views were clearly defined.

After the 1798 Rebellion, Emmet was involved in reorganising the defeated United Irish Society. In April 1799 a warrant was issued for his arrest. He escaped, and soon afterwards travelled to the continent in the hope of securing French military aid. His efforts were unsuccessful, and he returned to Ireland in October 1802.

In March the following year, he began preparations for another rising with fellow revolutionaries Thomas Russell and James (Jemmy) Hope (of the Coombe). He began to manufacture weapons and explosives at a number of premises in Dublin, and in particular a depot just off Thomas Street at Marshalea Lane. He even invented a folding pike, fitted with a hinge, which could be concealed under a cloak. Unlike in 1798, the preparations for the uprising were successfully concealed, but a premature explosion at one of Emmett's arms depots killed a man and forced Emmet to bring forward the date of the rising before the authorities' suspicions were aroused.[6]

Emmet proposed an insurrection in Dublin with the goal of taking Dublin Castle. The rising went ahead on the evening of 23 July 1803. In a mood that Yeats later characterised as the 'delirium of the brave' Emmet led a crowd of Dublin 'Liberty Rangers' to attack Dublin Castle. Failing to seize the castle, which was lightly defended, the rising amounted to a large-scale riot at Thomas Street. He lost all control of his followers and in one incident, the Lord Chief Justice of Ireland, Lord Kilwarden, reviled as chief prosecutor of William Orr in 1797, but also the judge who granted *habeas corpus* to Wolfe Tone in 1798, was dragged from his carriage and hacked to death (despite

The execution of Patriot, Robert Emmet, Thomas Street, on 20 September 1803. Robert Emmet, born in Dublin on 4 March 1778, was an Irish nationalist and Republican, orator and rebel leader. He led an abortive rebellion against British rule in 1803 and was captured, tried and executed for high treason. (Courtesy of National Library of Ireland/Dublin City Libraries)

advising his assailants, 'I am Kilwarden'). Sporadic clashes continued into the night until finally quelled by the military at the estimated cost of twenty military and fifty rebels dead. There was also a skirmish in the Coombe but the event quickly petered out and Emmet fled to hiding in the mountains. He was arrested a month later. He was hanged in Thomas Street on 20 September and decapitated the following day.

According to the historian, G.A. Hayes-McCoy, 'the botched revolt of 1803 was a fiasco. Emmett's few hours fight was altogether an affair of the streets of Dublin, a wild night in The Liberties'. He added, 'The Liberties produced in 1803 an extraordinary urban guerrilla arsenal, brilliantly extemporised for a kind of street fighting that was never to occur in Ireland'.[8]

Emmet became a heroic figure in Irish history, the 'darling of Erin', and his story became the subject of stage melodramas during the nineteenth century, most notably Dion Boucicault's 1884 play *Robert Emmet*. Robert's friend from Trinity College, Thomas Moore, championed his cause by writing hugely popular ballads about him.

The 1803 defeat marked the end of the United Irishmen as a serious revolutionary conspiracy. Emmet's 'epitaph' speech from the dock is widely quoted and remembered. It became a classic of nationalist literature and one of the most celebrated patriotic speeches of the century, inspiring future generations of nationalists:

> Let no man write my epitaph; for as no man who knows my motives dare now vindicate them, let not prejudice or ignorance asperse them. Let them and me rest in obscurity and peace; and my tomb remain inscribed and my memory in oblivion until other times and other men can do justice to my character. When my country takes her place among the nations of the earth, then, and not until then, let my epitaph be written. I have done.[9]

His speech echoed around the world. Ireland's best-kept secret relates to the exact burial place of Robert Emmet.

The Role of Anne Devlin

Anne Devlin is a very important figure in Irish history. She was born in 1780 into a family holding strong nationalist views. While her family home was originally in Rathdrum, County Wicklow, she moved to Rathfarnham where Robert Emmet, who was residing in Butterfield Lane, knew her brother. She later became a confidante of Emmet, who had asked her to act as his house-keeper so as to deflect the attention of the authorities from the constant comings and goings in his house. She knew his plans and was particularly active in working with him at his depot off Thomas Street and after the 1803 Rising she was arrested and endured brutalisation in Kilmainham Jail for two years. But she never betrayed Robert Emmet's associates. Her importance and role in the Rising were reinforced by the fact that for the rest of her life she was under constant surveillance by the police.

In 1810 she married a Liberties carter, William Campbell, and they lived in a house behind John's Lane church for the next forty years. They had four children and she obtained a job as a washerwoman. On his death, living conditions for her and her children became worse, and she moved to dwellings at nearby Little Elbow Lane, off Gray Street, where she died in poverty a few years later in 1851. She was buried in Glasnevin Cemetery. Her headstone reads: 'To the memory of Anne Devlin (Campbell) the faithful servant of Robert Emmet who possessed some rare and many noble qualities. Who lived in obscurity and poverty and so died on 18th day of September 1851, aged 70 years.'

During The Liberties Festival of 2012 she was celebrated with a large-scale wall mural on the corner of Meath Street and Carman's Hall. The outdoor portrait was painted by the artist Maser.

Poverty and Plenty

Dublin was also renowned for its squalor and the numbers of beggars on the streets. 'Ireland itself is a poor country, and Dublin a magnificent city; but the appearances of extreme poverty among the lower people are amazing', wrote Benjamin Franklin after a visit to the capital in the early 1770s.[10]

In 1798, Merrion Square, immediately adjacent to Fitzwilliam Street, was one of the main city bases for peers and Members of Parliament. After the upheaval of the Rebellion of that year came the Act of Union, and with the Union the large-scale desertion of the city by those associated with parliament. The grand mansions of the nobility became less viable. Some were sold, some were converted for other uses, and many became tenements. Leinster House, the grand town house of the Duke of Leinster and anchor of development in this part of Dublin had by 1812 slipped into a state of sad neglect and was sold in 1815 to the Dublin Society.

The ending of the Irish Parliament and the extension of control from England after the Act of Union did not bring renewed prosperity, as had been promised. Dublin stagnated and did not industrialise in the same manner as Belfast or the northern cities of industrial England. The bulk of the city's people lived a pre-carious existence in high-density, poor-quality housing, surviving on the low incomes earned from casual labour. Ill health was endemic and mortality rates extremely high. The nationalist Dublin Corporation proved singularly incapa-ble of successfully addressing the poverty that spilled all around the city. The emergence of the trade union movement spoke eloquently of looming crisis.

The Liberties and Dublin's industrial heartland. A view across the rooftops at St James's Brewery, c. 1906-13. (Courtesy of Guinness Archive, Diageo Ireland, GDB.BR14.0014.24)

7

FROM DANIEL O'CONNELL TO THE IRISH TRICOLOUR

The Penal Laws

The Penal Laws (1695-*c*.1793) which forbade Irish Catholics to practice their religion and other draconian measures to deprive them of all civil life, education and ownership of the land of Ireland, were strictly upheld and those caught evading the laws could expect to suffer very unpleasant consequences.[1] However, Catholics in The Liberties managed to survive somehow, notwithstanding repeated alarms, which closed up churches in The Liberties for months at a time, sent the clergy scurrying off to safer quarters, and kept the Catholic archbishop, Edmund Byrne, principally occupied in studying how to keep himself invisible.

One notorious 'priest-hunter' was Edward Tyrrell who swore before the Privy Council in 1712 that he believed that 'Edmund Byrne's papers are kept in the house of one Byrne, a cooper, in Francis-street', but of the archbishop's personal whereabouts he was unable to produce any evidence. The archbishop had managed to escape to Borris, his home parish, Another priest-hunter of 'popish priests', an Italian called John Garsee, was principal witness at the trials of five priests in 1710. The priests were convicted of saying Mass and wearing vestments and were sentenced to be transported. Some of the Franciscan priests in Francis Street church were betrayed by a Spaniard posing as a priest.

The priests were tried, found guilty and transported to Van Dieman's Land.[2]

In 1788 the Dominican priest, Dr John Thomas Troy was made Archbishop of Dublin and he was enthroned in the Pro-Cathedral, Francis Street. The music was conducted by Giordani, who had come to Dublin in 1772 and who acted as musical director of Francis Street pro-cathedral for many years.

With the relaxation of the Penal Laws and the granting of Catholic Emancipation in 1829 opportunities much improved for Catholics and this

Illustration of 'The new Roman Catholic Church, Francis-street, Dublin' From the *Dublin Penny Journal*, Volume 1, Number 27, 29 December 1832.

was reflected in a spate of church building in the nineteenth century. The great era of church building came after the Synod of Thurles in 1854 and in particular thanks to the advent of Cardinal Cullen who did much to promote Catholic interests. Consequently, The Liberties witnessed a surge in church-building with St Nicholas of Myra in Francis Street, St Catherine's in Meath Street, John's Lane in Thomas Street and Adam and Eve's on Merchant's Quay. All were built in the second half of the nineteenth century. Also, the Christian Brothers opened their first Dublin school in The Liberties.[3]

Souperism

Proselytism and Souperism were huge issues during and after the Great Famine of the 1840s in The Liberties, with much competition among Catholic and Protestant clergy for the souls of the large concentration of people living in the area. Such were the huge numbers living in The Liberties, partly as a result of the influx by people fleeing the effects of the Famine, that it was like a city within a city.

In the early 1840s a census was made of the parish of St Nicholas of Myra, Francis Street. Dr Flanagan, the parish priest, calculated that it contained 35,000 people, of whom 6,000 were Protestants or other denominations, and the rest Catholics. There were 200 girls in Warrenmount School, and

400 boys with the Christian Brothers in Mill Street, and there were four orphan societies.[4]

The opening up of soup kitchens to feed the poor during the Famine years by groups such as the Quakers was very laudable but a source of anger and bitterness. There were many instances of aid being provided by Protestant groups on condition that the recipients renounce their Catholicism and/or make their name more English-sounding. This led to the phrase 'taking the soup' and the word 'Souperism', which to this day is very emotive. It was a bitter issue at the time, the more so because it helped fuel the antagonism between Catholic and Protestant.[5]

It was in this context that religious orders were encouraged to open up convents, monasteries and schools in The Liberties. In 1856, with the help of Miss Margaret Aylward, an orphanage, St Bridget's, for the rescue of children exposed to the dangers of Proselytism, was opened.[6]

The Foundling Hospital at James's Street (later South Dublin Union and St James's Hospital), which opened in 1704 and closed in 1835, saw 56,000 Catholic children becoming Protestant. Because of this, Canon Edward McCabe, parish priest of St Nicholas of Myra church 1856–1865, 'set to work to stop this mischief' and prevent a similar exodus in the post-Famine Liberties. It was reported that he organised a Mission and 'to such a pitch of excitement and indignation were the people roused when they heard the doings of the "soupers" that for the last fortnight of the Misson the Parish might have been said to have been in a state of siege.'[7] This attitude was helped by the street ballad-singers who lived in the Coombe and the surrounding area, and recounted in strident tones and Coombe dialect the valiant efforts of Mrs Smyley (Protestant) and her friends. Much rioting took place and the windows of Bride Street Protestant church (St Werburgh's) were shattered. A report spread that the 'soupers' were going to retaliate with an attack on Francis Street church and 200 police were drafted in and 2,000 volunteers among the parishioners mounted a guard to defend it. This prevented a major sectarian battle. The practical outcome of the rather vigorous crusade was the consolidation of St Brigid's Orphanage, the opening of a Catholic Ragged School in Park Street, off the Coombe, and the expansion of the Holy Faith Convent in the Coombe.[8]

A massive increase in the numbers of religious orders influenced all levels of Catholic social life and religious practice in the nineteenth century. The number of nuns in Ireland, which stood at 120 in 1800, had risen to 3,700 by 1870. Teaching orders of brothers, particularly the Irish Christian Brothers, also substantially increased in number. Through their work in schools in particular, these Church personnel had a powerful influence on the youth and did much to ensure the dominance of a strict Catholic ethos. That, combined with stricter rules governing religious practice, the 'Devotional Revolution' (the introduction of many devotions such as devotion of the Sacred Heart, annual novenas to Our Lady of Good Counsel in John's Lane, visiting the seven chapels at Easter, tridiums, confraternities, sodalities, temperance groups and much more) and the power of the 'Mission' in the second half of the nineteenth century (visiting Order priests to a parish such as the Redemptorists and Jesuits), did much to solidify Catholic Church control of the life of the people of The Liberties and elsewhere.[9]

The story of the nineteenth century is one of the steady erosion of the power of the Protestant ascendancy. Catholic Relief Acts in the last two decades of the eighteenth century repealed many of the Penal laws, which discriminated against Catholics. In the aftermath of the Act of Union in 1800, Catholics continued to fight for the right to hold political office and having secured this 'Catholic Emancipation' in 1829 under the strong leadership of Daniel O'Connell, used it to claim a measure of municipal power in Dublin city. Dublin remained a colonial capital, but as the century progressed, the Catholic professional and business classes took control of city government.[10]

End of The Liberties?

The commission of enquiry reports of the 1830s into the local jurisdictions in towns, including Liberties, found that they were:

> ... remnants of the feudal policy in which they originated, the object of which was to make a powerful individual, or ecclesiastical corporation, responsible for the good order of a particular district which was their private property. But ... whatever may have been their utility in former days, it appears evident that they are productive of great present inconvenience, and that these manorial jurisdictions are not suited to the altered circumstances of modern times.[11]

The old systems of local administration (including The Liberties) were regarded as obstacles to the reforms necessary with the introduction of Catholic Emancipation in 1829 as well as parliamentary reform in general. The old medieval jurisdiction system stymied wider participation in local government politics. In 1835 there were five Liberty jurisdictions in Dublin: St Sepulchre's; Thomas Court and Donore; the Liberty of the Dean of St Patrick's; the Manor of Glasnevin or Grangegorman and the Manor of Kilmainham. The administration of the city was radically altered by the Municipal Corporations (Ireland) Act of 1841, and during the following twenty years the area controlled by the Corporation was increased by the abolition of The Liberties.[12]

By the 1850s the rights and privileges of The Liberties were extinguished. The erection of a fountain at the junction of Thomas Street and James's Street

Browsing outside clothes shop near Winetavern Street, 1953. (Courtesy of National Library of Ireland)

in 1898 and the official opening ceremony by the Lord Mayor of Dublin signified, according to Kenneth Milne of Christ Church Cathedral, 'the closure of a feature of Dublin life that was almost as venerable as the city itself, the distinctive role of The Liberties'. He added: 'They have kept their hold on the city's folk memory through the continuing sense of place experienced by those who live and work there.'[13]

1848, The Liberties and the Best-known Symbol of Irish Nationality

The man who introduced the national flag, the Tricolour, to Ireland, was a Huguenot silk-weaver who lived in Francis Street in the nineteenth century. He was called Edward Hollywood and it was he who created the first Irish tricolour.

He was born in 1814, was a leader of an early trade union for artisans and a member of the nationalist independence movement, the Young Ireland movement. In 1848, he travelled to Paris as part of a three-man delegation (with Young Irelanders Thomas Meagher and Smith O'Brien) to pass a message of congratulations from Ireland to the new Second French Republican government. He was inspired by the French tricolour to weave an Irish equivalent. He returned to Ireland with a flag based on France's red, white and blue emblem, given to him by the French government. It was the famous green, white and gold (orange) flag.

His republican tricolour – featuring green to represent the Gaelic tradition, orange to represent the followers of William of Orange, and white to represent peace between them – was later adopted as the flag of the Irish Republic in 1916 and by the Irish Free State which succeeded it in 1922.

Edward Hollywood died in 1873. His grave in Glasnevin Cemetery was only discovered in early 2012.[14]

8

FORGED IN THE SMITHY: POVERTY AND TENEMENTS

Swift, Whitelaw and Stephens

In 1729, Jonathan Swift's *A Modest Proposal*, or to give it its full title, *A Modest Proposal for Preventing the Children of Poor People from Being a Burden on Their Parents or Country, and for Making Them Beneficial to the Publick* was written as a reaction to the appalling poverty he witnessed daily in The Liberties. He wrote in a sarcastic, abrasive style designed to encourage reform of social evils.

Swift famously proposed that the dire conditions of the starving Irish could be alleviated by getting them to sell their well-fattened one-year-old children to the meat market. This would accomplish several important social aims, such as providing an income to impoverished parents, allowing the well-off to demonstrate their gastronomic expertise and greatly improving the economic situation of Ireland as a whole.

Less than 100 years later, James Whitelaw of St Catherine's church on Thomas Street (appointed rector in 1788) also wrote on the same theme. He was a compassionate pastor with a strong social conscience and his record of the appalling state of the people of The Liberties is still, 200 years after it was written, shocking and a terrible indictment of the conditions under which many of the teeming masses in The Liberties lived. He took a census of the city in 1798,

Blackpitts in 1913. (Courtesy of National Archives of Ireland, RSAI, Darkest Dublin Collection, No. 10.)

revealing the poverty and the squalid living conditions of many of its inhabitants especially amongst the weaver families of The Liberties. It was a place of disease, poverty and filth worse than that seen in most English cities.

In 1798 Revd Whitelaw described The Liberties:

> The streets are generally narrow; the houses crowded together; the rears of back yards of very small extent, and some without accommodation of any kind. Of these streets a few are the residence of the upper class of shopkeepers or others engaged in trade; but a far greater proportion of them, with their numerous lanes and alleys, are occupied by working manufacturers, by petty shopkeepers, by labouring poor, and beggars, crowded together to a degree distressing to humanity. Ten to sixteen persons, of all ages and sexes, in a room, not fifteen feet square, stretched on a wad of filthy straw, swarming with vermin, and without any covering, save the wretched rags that constituted their wearing apparel. A single apartment in one of these truly wretched habitations rates from one to two shillings per week, and to lighten this rent two or even four families become joint tenants. Under such circumstances it is not extraordinary that I should have frequently found from thirty to forty individuals in a house.[1]

However, it was not only in small apartments that the problem of overcrowding, lack of privacy, disease and destitution arose. Some eighteenth-century houses that fell out of fashionable use were subdivided and rented out, or simply not

divided at all, and filled with any tenants who would pay. The subdivision of buildings into tenements really commenced in the late seventeenth century and was
widespread by the end of the eighteenth century. A four-room-plus-garret Dutch
Billy might have been split into as many as five or six rooms, each let separately and
many with their own exit to a street, yard or alley.

The Revd Whitelaw was also attached to the Cork Street Fever Hospital, where
on one day he administered the sacrament separately to six patients in the last
stages of malignant fever. He died in 1813, a victim of the illness he contracted
from those to whom he ministered.

Despite some late nineteenth- and early twentieth-century housing improvements in The Liberties, at the turn of the twentieth century nearly a quarter of
the population lived in one room. A building with 100 inhabitants usually had
just two toilets, and two thirds of the tenements were considered unfit for human
habitation. State provision for the poor of Dublin was very limited. Most of the
available relief came from charitable organisations, most of them run by the
Churches. Nevertheless, most of the city's poor lived on a monotonous diet of
bread and tea.

Pimlico resident, the writer James Stephens, captured these conditions in
his classic work, *The Charwoman's Daughter* (1912). It was the first novel to
deal with life in Dublin's tenements. He grew up in the tenements in the late
1800s, was orphaned and later found work as a clerk. The story he wrote is
about Mary Makebelieve and her mother who live in a one-roomed tenement
flat. By day her mother cleans the houses of the Dublin rich, while Mary makes
observations as she walks through the city. Stephens gives a vivid picture of the
Makebelieve's home: the dark room, the dirty window, the decaying wallpaper,
the carrying of water up five flights of stairs, the crippling poverty:

> Mary Makebelieve lived with her mother in a small room at the very top of a
> big, dingy house in a Dublin back street. She knew every crack in the ceiling,
> every spot of mildew on the ancient wallpaper was familiar, at night-time the
> cockroaches came rattling, the grime of many years had encrusted the glass
> of the window, the chimney pots of next door continually hurled jays of soot
> against her window, and water had to be carried from the very bottom of the
> five-storey house up hundreds and hundreds of stairs to her room ... she dis-
> liked having to use too much water ...[2]

James Stephens does not simply focus on the squalid social realities. These are
transmogrified and offset by the fairyland image of Dublin that he creates for
Mary Makebelieve filled with sunlight, wonderment, magic and possibilities. Yet
the story carries the imagination into the not-so-makebelieve reality of life for
many living in The Liberties.

Shawled women waiting on the pawnshop to open. (Courtesy of Dublin.ie Forums/Jimmymac)

'Unfit for Human Habitation'

By far the worst tenements in The Liberties were in Francis Street, the Coombe, Chamber Street, Engine Alley, Cork Street and Kevin Street (where Iveagh Trust buildings are today). Dublin Corporation described them in the early years of the twentieth century as 'unfit for human habitation'.[3] Decay had set in to these old buildings, abandoned by their former residents who moved to new suburbs in the burgeoning Pembroke and Rathmines Townships. Gradually streets such as Chamber Street, Francis Street, Meath Street, and the Coombe, amalgamated into slums.

Life in the slums was raw and desperate. In 1911 nearly 26,000 families lived in inner-city tenements, and 20,000 of these families lived in just one room. Most families were dependent on intermittent casual labour; three out of five workers in The Liberties were unemployed. Remarkably, many one-room tenements in The Liberties did not just house a family, but that family also took in members of their extended families as tenants.

Poverty, unemployment, appalling living conditions – these were the facts of life for most of the mothers in The Liberties, and many died before their time. Mothers looked old while still young in years. They were often also the breadwinners and mainstay of the family. Many men, in an age of rampant authoritarian patriarchy, escaped from reality and lived practically full-time in the many pubs in the area.

A plaque on Nicholas Street states:

> They had seven children and decided this was enough. One day after Mass, she arrived home and told her husband that the priest said no one of childbearing age should stop having children. Sometime later she had another. Both she and the baby died during the birth. They were buried together.[4]

The most prevalent disease in the Dublin slums at this time was tuberculosis (TB), which spread through tenements very quickly and caused many deaths amongst the poor. A report published in 1912 claimed that TB-related deaths in Ireland were 50 per cent higher than in England or Scotland, and that the vast majority occurred amongst the poorer classes. Overall, the death rate in Dublin per thousand was 22.3; in London it was just 15.[6]

Interior of a Liberties tenement flat c. 1913. A young child sleeps in a metal bed while her sister stands at the door. A chamber pot is visible in the corner; a crude toilet in the yard might have to be shared by up to forty people. (Courtesy of UCC Multitext Project Irish History)

Poverty was perpetuated in Dublin by the lack of occupational opportunities for unskilled workers and the poor condition of the housing. Dublin Corporation employed men to inspect dangerous buildings, but disasters still took place. Tenements owned by Mrs Ryan on Church Street, for example, collapsed in 1913, killing seven people. In Kevin Street in The Liberties, a tenement house collapsed killing two people.

The death rate in the city was not helped by the unsanitary conditions in the tenements, where livestock were kept in dairy yards, cattle yards and down side-alleys. Drainage was little better than rudimentary and the majority of meat eaten in the city came from beasts slaughtered in small private slaughter-houses in The Liberties. Offal and other substances lay on city streets despite being forbidden in a series of acts, such as the Nuisance Acts, through the nineteenth and early twentieth centuries.

'Massacre of the Innocents'

In a booklet published in 1914, called *Poverty in Dublin*, trade unionist John Hughes noted that 'a considerable proportion of Dublin citizens are habitually without the essentials of decent living'. For Hughes, Dublin was the happy hunting ground of social reforms. There was no lack of reports, official and unofficial, on its health and sanitary conditions, the condition of its housing and its slums, and the exploitation of labour. He called the statistics of infant mortality, 'the massacre of the innocents', because of the excessively high rate. He was also critical of the divine dictum which he had heard so many times from Church people: 'the poor you will always have with you', i.e. the Catholic Church viewed poverty in Dublin as being deplorable yet unavoidable.[5]

In The Liberties, many families were forced to put their children to work selling wares on the streets. A 1902 report dealing with the problem of the thousands of children street-selling, noted that in one in six cases, one or both parents were dead. Others were from homes riven with illness, drunkenness or unemployment. Help for some destitute children came from Mrs Smyly's Homes and Schools, eleven of which were based in the city. The Coombe Ragged School was run for young Protestant boys, and the Dublin Working Boys Home and Harding Technical School operated on Lord Edward Street and was intended for boys working in the city who did not live with their parents.[6]

There were also several penitentiaries for children across the city, including High Park Reformatory for Girls, most of whom were committed for petty theft. And for all manner of reasons, boys could also be sent to prison or to industrial schools such as the one in Artane.

Women tried to make money as dealers selling fish (Mary of Coombe Place a replica for Molly Malone), flowers (Frances of Pimlico Cottages), old clothes, pigs, fruit (Mary of Francis Street) and much more, on the side of the streets. Women worked at home, or with other women, to make various items such as bags, hats, vests and dresses, and worked in laundries and parlours of fine houses or with rag-a-bone merchants. Some worked in factories as weavers of wire (Annie of Chamber Street), and in the fields which still lay in parts of the city. Some were forced to turn to prostitution on the streets or in brothels in The Liberties, and they, too, ended up in Mountjoy Prison.[7]

Charwomen were a widespread feature of Dublin and this was the main occupation for many Liberties women from the tenements in the first half of the twentieth century. (Courtesy of Dublin.ie Forums/Jimmymac)

A photograph was taken around the turn of the century showing the clothes hanging out of windows and drying in front of the houses in Pimlico. That they had the luxury of a pole to hang out their clothes made them the envy of the slum.

Charities attempted to fill the gaps left by the state. As a response to the appalling conditions in The Liberties area two centres were established that are still going strong 100 years later.[8] The first is the Society of St Vincent De Paul's Back Lane Shelter (c.1915) and the second is the Little Flower Centre (called the Penny Dinners c. 1911) opposite St Catherine's church in Meath Street.[9] Dublin's oldest charity, The Sick and Indigent Roomkeepers Society, founded in Dublin in 1790, offered assistance without religious or moral intent, from its house at 2 Palace Street. Mostly, though, people struggled to survive through their own informal networks, with generations of the same extended family and their in-laws living together in few rooms. The unemployed, the elderly and the infirm, as well as those who had lost spouses or parents, were supported by the able.

The Liberties supported a number of pawn shops, offering immediate relief to those in distress. Interest was high, however, and it was not unknown for people to have to pawn essential clothing, boots and work-tools, so worsening the cycle of poverty.

Workhouses such as the South Dublin Union at James's Street, dealt with all manner of social problems from destitution, to old age, illness and abandonment. Workhouses accommodated people who were in need of short-term relief from homelessness, but they also housed those who were permanently destitute. Families were generally separated by gender into different wards on entry and were required to work around the house or the grounds, as was the case at the South Dublin Union that was known as 'the Poor House'. Workhouses were also the inappropriate homes for many who suffered from long-term mental illness, becoming de facto asylums.

The Royal Visit of 1911

Some older residents will remember stories of the Royal visit to Dublin and The Liberties in 1911. Locals prepared for the visit of King George and Queen Mary by decorating the streets with flags and other colourful decorations. Dublin Castle provided accommodation for the Royals and the King and Queen received a warm welcome in The Liberties. In fact it was one of the most

King George V and Queen Mary entertained by the children at Myra Hall, 1911

The 1911 Royal visit to The Liberties. King George and Queen Mary entertained by the children of Myra Hall. (Courtesy of Liam O'Meara's book *The Bayno*, The Liberty.ie/Tessa Fleming and the National Library of Ireland)

spontaneous and heartfelt in all of Dublin, according to contemporary news-paper reports.

On the first day the King and Queen went to the 'Iveagh Play Centre' on Francis Street. The Guinness Trust had established this centre, which also provided free breakfasts on Sundays for the poor children of the parish. Children were taught physical education, basket weaving, lace making, singing and dancing. King George and Queen Mary acknowledged the warm and friendly welcome from the massive crowd as they arrived.

Children from surrounding schools were selected to sing and dance for them and four barefoot girls, Lillie Lawlor, May Lawlor, Bridget King and Annie Boyle made a presentation of bouquets to the royal contingent. Both the King and Queen enjoyed the performance, clapping to the entertainment as the young children sang and danced.

As the carriage pulled off, one woman was almost killed in her rush and desire to get to the carriage to see the Royal couple. She fell beneath the horse's feet but a nearby constable grasped her and pulled her from the danger.

Queen Mary also paid a visit to the old Coombe Hospital. The route from Dublin Castle to the hospital was through Christ Church Place and Thomas Street. The Queen asked if she could visit the new Pembroke wing of the hospital, opened just days previously, but the Matron did not want her to as no special carpet had been laid or decorations hung. The Queen laughed and hitched up her skirts and tripped across the courtyard to the new wing. The Royals also visited St Patrick's Cathedral.

On 12 July, the King and Queen departed Dublin. Among the many places they visited in Dublin, the Royals' wish to spend time in The Liberties prompted *The Irish Times* to pronounce that 'in King George the Dublin poor have a warm friend'![10]

After the visit King George donated £1,000 to the poor people in the area, which included the Iveagh Play Centre itself. Within two years the centre recorded 4,000 children coming through its doors. It was a part of daily life in The Liberties. In 1915, the play-centre closed and on its last night, 918 people attended. The centre moved to Bull Alley, one of the oldest streets in The Liberties.

Rosie Hackett of Jacob's Biscuits

The Royals had barely departed when on 22 August 1911 3,000 workers at Jacob's biscuit factory withdrew their labour in pursuit of a pay claim. Many of these workers lived in The Liberties. Jim Larkin said the conditions for the bis-cuit makers were 'sending them from this earth twenty years before their time'. A contemporary description of the strikers, although not exactly sympathetic to their position, shows clearly how ready workers were to support each other in times of strife:

The greater number of the employees of Messrs. Jacob, biscuit manufacturers, were on strike yesterday. The strike originated on the previous evening in the secession of the bakehouse hands to the number of 350. This was subsequently followed by the stoppage from work of 140 men employed by the New Row branch of the firm. The men on strike paraded yesterday morning in the vicinity of the works, and in sympathy with them a number of girl employees came out at an early hour.

A procession of the strikers was then formed, and moved round the block of buildings, which constituted the factory. A great deal of excitement in vent of the strike spirit was manifested and the ranks of the strikers being reinforced by many without work to do, there was a continued state of turmoil in the streets ... Shortly after noon, some 3,000 girls who were employed in packing and other branches of the firm's business reinforced the strikers. These latter formed in professional order and moved about .... The output was largely at a standstill, though the machinery continued in motion. The girls admitted that they themselves had not struck from any grievance to themselves, but only out of sympathy with the men.[11]

One of the first women to come out in sympathy with the men was Rosie Hackett, a young messenger for the company, who had joined the Irish Transport and General Workers Union in the previous year. Two weeks after the successful Jacob's strike, Rosie was one of the founder members of the Irish Women Workers Union, set up to protect women in the face of the appalling conditions in which many of them were expected to work.

The 1913 Strike and Lockout

The Dublin Lockout of 1913 was a major industrial dispute between approximately 20,000 workers and 300 employers, which took place in Dublin. The dispute lasted from 26 August 1913 to 18 January 1914, and is often viewed as the most severe and significant industrial dispute in Irish history. By September nearly 20,000 workers were locked out or on strike and workers and their families faced increased hardship. Central to the dispute was the workers' right to unionise.

Prior to the advent of trade unionism in Ireland, unskilled workers lacked any form of representation. Furthermore, there were many more unskilled labourers in Dublin than there were jobs for them. Thus unskilled workers often had to compete with one another for work on a daily basis, the job generally going to whoever agreed to work for the lowest wages.[12]

In August 1913, when the tram workers struck, Rosie and her fellow workers from Jacob's again mobilised in support of the pickets and they gathered in

O'Connell Street on 31 August for a rally against the employers. She was in the crowd that the police baton-charged, resulting in terrible injuries to the workers. Such was the ferocity of the attack on the striking workers that the day became infamous as 'Bloody Sunday'. On the following Saturday, three Jacob's workers were sacked for refusing to remove their ITGWU badges and Rosie was one of the organisers of the supporting strike which began immediately afterwards. The employers retaliated by locking out all the workers and Rosie began a period of tireless work, bringing together the members of the IWWU to provide physical and moral support for the strikers throughout the city.

The lockout eventually concluded in early 1914, when the calls for a sympathetic strike in Britain from Larkin and Connolly were rejected by the TUC. Most workers, many of whom were on the brink of starvation, went back to work and signed pledges not to join a union. The ITGWU was badly damaged by its defeat in the Lockout, and was further hit by the departure of Larkin to the United States in 1914 and the execution of Connolly for his part in the Easter Rising in 1916. However, the union was re-built by William O'Brien and Thomas Johnson and by 1919 its membership had surpassed that of 1913.

As a result of her efforts during the Lockout, Rosie was not re-employed by Jacob's, and instead, she took up a full-time post as Clerk to the IWWU. She was involved in the 1916 Rising and was arrested for the part she played but it is as a stalwart trade unionist that she will be remembered. Rosie Hackett died in 1976, after giving more than sixty years of service to the trade union movement.

Although the actions of the ITGWU and the smaller UBLU were unsuccessful in achieving substantially better pay and conditions for the workers, they marked a watershed in Irish labour history. The principle of union action and workers' solidarity had been firmly established; no future employer would ever try to 'break' a union in the way that William Martin Murphy attempted with the ITGWU.[13]

The Marrowbone Lane Play

Robert Collis was a paediatrician working in both the National Children's Hospital and the Rotunda in the late 1930s. He was appalled by the conditions of the poor in The Liberties, and wrote a play, *Marrowbone Lane*, for the Gate Theatre, which exposed the shocking reality of tenement life.[14] Marrowbone Lane links Cork Street to Thomas Street via Pimlico.

The actress Shelah Richards, who played Mary in this production, was one of the leading lights of the Abbey Theatre Players and the mother of the novelist Jennifer Johnston. The play, dealing with life in the slums, was initially rejected by the Abbey but was played by the Gate in 1939, and revived in 1941.

It was set on the top floor of a tenement house in Marrowbone Lane. A young girl from Mayo marries into a tenement family and is shocked by the world of grinding poverty her ne'er-do-well husband has brought her into, which endangers the life of her baby.

As a reaction to the play, the Marrowbone Lane Fund was set up to relieve the conditions of the poor in the tenements. Collis used some money from this fund to found the National Cerebral Palsy Clinic (now Enable Ireland) and he was one of the physicians who encouraged the young Christy Brown to overcome his disabilities. He was also very active in bringing Jewish orphans to Ireland after the end of the Second World War and was one of the first physicians to arrive in Bergen Belsen concentration camp. Collis wrote a second play, *The Barrel Organ* (a feature of Liberties life for many years), but his main concerns were with medical and social causes.

From Barrell Organs to Boot Funds

The harsh conditions endured by the working classes intensified during the Second World War. Neutral Ireland, now in a state of Emergency, experienced severe shortages of food and fuel. *Marrowbone Lane* was revived in 1941 resulting in a public appeal through the Dublin Rotary Club to help alleviate poverty. Moved to action by the appeal, Hilda Tweedy wrote to numerous friends in February 1941:

> What is your dream of Ireland. What does the story of Marrowbone Lane mean to you? Are you satisfied that you are doing all in your power to build the kind of world you wish your children to live in? Alone we can do little, together we can rouse public opinion to remove some of the blots on our civilization.

Following her appeal a petition was sent to the government to ration all essential foods in order to control prices and suppress black market sales. The petition caught the attention of the national press who dubbed it 'the Housewives' Petition'.[15]

But *Marrowbone Lane* did have an impact on public awareness and led to a number of progressive initiatives. The Catholic Social Services Conference, for example, was set up involving a combination of over forty charities pooling their resources and experience to tackle poverty, shortages of food and clothing. Bewleys helped to feed malnourished children. The St Vincent de Paul Sunshine Fund offered holidays to deprived children in Balbriggan. Lastly, the Irish Housewives Association was established by Hilda Tweedy in 1942.

'Galloping Consumption' and the Emergency

During the war years the rate of deaths due to TB (widely known as 'Galloping Consumption') rose substantially, reaching a peak in the period 1942–1945, with an estimated 147 deaths per 100,000 of the population being attributed to some form of the disease. In regional terms Dublin and its environs suffered the highest mortality rate, and the number of deaths was consistently above the national average.

The Sick and Indigent Roomkeepers Society, which worked in The Liberties, noted in a report in 1943 that the epidemic was a growing problem. They, and charities such as the St Vincent de Paul Society noted the numerous requests for money to help pay for infants' funeral expenses, or to help people emigrate. Constant references were made by these charities to poor people being transferred to Crooksling TB Sanatorium on the outskirts of Dublin. There were also cases of children in The Liberties losing both parents to the disease and consequently ending up in orphanages. The Royal Irish Academy of Medicine, in a report in 1941, blamed bad housing, lack of fresh air, and shortages of fresh

Liberties children in the late 1940s. (Courtesy of Dublin.ie Forums/cosmo)

food as the major causes of the rising mortality. A paper of the Statistical and Social Inquiry Society of Ireland in 1941 showed that life expectancy was almost ten years higher for a baby boy born in Connaught than for one born in Dublin. The society also showed the link between tuberculosis and poverty, overcrowded housing and poor living conditions – exactly describing many of the tenements in The Liberties.[16]

In 1942 Dublin's famous Lord Mayor, Alfie Byrne (known as the 'shaking hand of Dublin' as he was always shaking everyone's hands) called a conference to discuss the problem and representations were made to the government with a view to tackling the problem of lack of footwear on children and clothing for the poor. Although the *Evening Herald* had introduced its 'Herald Boot Fund' to help tackle the issue, it was not until 1944 that a government 'Footwear Regulations Scheme' was launched which provided free footwear to all children of persons in receipt of public assistance.

The Emergency, by bringing all these social issues to the forefront, accelerated social, health and other legislation and led to the establishment of government ministries to tackle these endemic problems including the Departments of Social Welfare and Health.

'Lugs' Branigan

Nor surprisingly in these terrible and harrowing living conditions, violence was at times a feature of life in The Liberties. It was fuelled by a number of factors: poverty, unemployment and alcohol. The so-called 'Animal Gangs' of the 1930s and 1940s from The Liberties regularly fought pitched battles in Baldoyle and Tolka Park with similar 'Animal Gangs' from inner city areas around Gardiner Street and Sheriff Street and also from the northside of the city. At one time Marrowbone Lane residents banded together to fight and defeat the local marauding Animal Gang.

The term 'Animal Gangs' came to the public's attention in 1934 in the media following court cases and referred to a gang in Corporation Street in the city centre who had emerged out of the printers' strikes of that year and were mainly street newsvendors, but the term then came to be applied to any gang causing trouble in those decades.

The Animal Gangs are a staple of Dublin folklore, remembered by some as Robin Hood figures who protected the poor, and by others as brutal thugs whose nickname reflected their savagery. Some of the gang members in The Liberties were weavers and carried tools of the trade on the street. And some of the north inner-city gangs were young dockers who carried large hooks that they used during their work. Other weapons included blades hidden in peaked caps or potatoes! At one time in The Liberties it was said that an animal gang ruled Meath Street and around the Coombe area before Garda James 'Lugs' Branigan broke them up.[17]

James Christopher Branigan, better known as Lugs Branigan or Jim Branigan (6 January 1910 – 22 May 1986) was a well-known member of the Garda Síochána, as well as an Irish boxer, boxing referee and to some, a folk and urban legend. Born in No. 1 James Street, which was part of St Kevin's Hospital (South Dublin Union) in 1910, James Branigan became a well-known figure in Dublin, both for his interest and participation in the boxing scene, but also due to his long career with An Garda Síochána.

He was born to John Alick Branigan, an official of South Dublin Union, and Ellen Branigan (*née* Kavanagh). James witnessed the shooting of a British soldier during the 1916 Rising when the area saw heavy fighting. He was educated at Basin Lane Convent and James' Street Christian Brothers School.

He joined the Gardaí in June 1931 and took up physical exercise after barely passing the physical requirements. He was stationed in Kevin Street Garda station in 1936 and was known for using physical force against petty criminals, which he admitted to doing to avoid excessive paperwork. Garda Branigan distinguished himself during the violent disturbances of the 'wild' forties in Dublin and became well known after a violent Animal Gang pitched-battle which subsequently became known as the 'Battle of Baldoyle' where one person died. Branigan sometimes acted as an unofficial social worker, as he was close to people on his beat. He was promoted to detective Garda in July 1958 and Garda sergeant in December 1963 and put in charge of a mobile riot squad unit, in which he remained active until his retirement. It was called Prevention and Detection of Street Nuisances Unit, also known as 'Brano Five Team', who were called out to any trouble spots in Dublin. This unit became well known around the night spots of Dublin, such as dance halls and cinemas, where 'tough justice' was meted out to any transgressors.

Stories of mistreatment, rough or tough justice surrounded Garda Branigan and his squad, and the sight of his Bedford van was feared on Dublin's late night streets. His individual heavy-handedness, strength and fearlessness drew much attention, with his personal notoriety growing over the years. He believed his outspoken personality had been held against him by senior Gardaí, preventing his further promotion. An oft-repeated story, has Detective Branigan giving culprits the choice of a 'box to the face' or a day in court. Commenting in court after one notorious incident when a criminal bit him on the bottom during an arrest, he said: 'He was worse than the Balubas. At least they cook you first.'[18]

Detective Branigan enjoyed the respect of the community, the judiciary and those he prosecuted and sometimes he was appointed as a bodyguard to visiting celebrities. When Richard Burton and Elizabeth Taylor came to Dublin to make the film *The Man Who Came in From the Cold* (part of it filmed in Cork Street) he was assigned to take care of them.

The origin of his nickname 'Lugs' is disputed, but it is commonly believed that it was assigned to him by a Dublin criminal in the 1940s due to his cauliflower ears, a condition most common among amateur wrestlers, rugby players, mixed martial artists and grapplers. This writer will also vouch that it was a nickname he disliked.[19]

9

THE 1916 RISING
AND THE LIBERTIES

The Liberties played a key role in the 1916 Rising, as it was the site of several rebel outposts that saw some of the fiercest fighting. The main insurgent force under 1916 Proclamation signatory, Eamonn Ceannt, was based in the South Dublin Union (now roughly St James' Hospital) but there were also outposts in the Mendicity Institute (Usher's Quay), Jameson's Distillery (Marrowbone Lane), Watkins Brewery (Ardee Street) and Jacob's biscuits factory (Bishop Street).

Not only that, but James Connolly, one of the leaders of the Rising, had lived at 54 Pimlico and then in a cottage off Weavers' Sqaure. He also had rooms in Thomas Street, a few doors from Chadwick's Builders Supplies, from where he developed his ideas for a Labour Party and a big trade union. There can be no doubt that seeing the poverty of Dublin at first hand in the area would have inspired him. William T. Cosgrave, born in James's Street, opposite the South Dublin Union, was also involved in the Rising.

Michael Mallin

Another 1916 Rising leader, Michael Mallin, was born and raised in The Liberties. He is remembered to this day in the Dublin Corporation flats, Michael

Mallin House, between Thomas Street and Swift's Alley, just behind the Vicar Street music venue.[1]

Born on 1 December 1874 in a tenement in The Liberties, his father John was a ship's carpenter and his mother Sarah a silk winder who had worked in England before losing her job because of her support for the Manchester Martyrs. Michael was the eldest of six children who survived to adulthood; five died in childhood due to the poor living conditions in The Liberties tenements. While Mallin's mother had republican sympathies, many of her siblings were involved in the British military. Michael was interested in music from a young age and just before his fifteenth birthday, in 1889, he was convinced to join the regimental band of the Royal Scots Fusiliers. He signed up as a drummer boy for twelve years' service. In 1896 he was sent to India where he contracted malaria. Mallin returned to Ireland at the end of 1902 and soon married. He found work as a silk weaver and joined the Dublin Silk Weavers' Union, and before long he became secretary of the union. In 1913, Mallin was heavily involved in a strike by weavers at Atkinson & Co. poplin factory in Hanbury Lane, just behind Thomas Street. This was the factory in which Mallin was employed and by the time of the strike almost the entire workforce had been unionised. On 12 March 1913, around 120 men went out on strike over pay and conditions. The strike was resolved to the union's satisfaction.[2]

Mallin's family meanwhile had run a small grocery shop in Meath Street during this period, which helped sustain the family during the twelve weeks of the strike. Perhaps owing to the bitterness of the strike, Mallin left Atkinson's shortly after its conclusion. He continued working in the shop, but as the Great Lockout of 1913 developed, the family was forced to close it. Workers who were locked out or on strike could not afford to spend money in the shop. The following year he joined the Irish Transport and General Workers Union (ITGWU) and subsequently the Irish Citizen Army (ICA). James Connolly soon appointed him Chief of Staff of the ICA because of his military and musical background as well as his organisational skills.

In 1916 he was appointed to command the insurgents' garrison at Stephen's Green (with Countess Markievicz as his second-in-command). Under attack from British forces, Mallin and his soldiers fell back to the College of Surgeons where they were pounded by machine guns for days. He would have continued fighting except that the surrender order came through from Pearse and Connolly on 30 April. He was executed by firing squad at dawn on Monday 8 May 1916. Before his death Mallin said: 'I am satisfied I have done my duty to my beloved Ireland.' His wife Agnes Hickey, his three sons and two daughters, the younger who was not born until four months after his death, survived him.[3]

The South Dublin Union

During the uprising the 4th Battalion, consisting on the day of only about 120 Volunteers (out of a normal strength of 500), under Commandant Eamonn Ceannt occupied the South Dublin Union, James's Street, because of its pivotal position commanding one of the main routes for Crown forces into the city.[4]

The Union was built as a workhouse in the middle of the nineteenth century. In 1916 it housed about 3,200 of the poor and elderly and a large quota of doctors, nurses and ancillary workers. Nurse Margaretta Keogh was accidentally shot dead in the course of the fighting.

As indicated, the South Dublin Union was in a strategic position as it overlooked Kingsbridge (now Heuston) railway station to the north and controlled the route from Richmond Barracks and the Royal Hospital (military headquarters) leading to the city centre. It consisted of a complex of buildings serving a variety of functions, including living quarters, an infirmary, a hospital and churches; it was laid out in streets, alleys and courtyards and was set in fifty acres of green space surrounded by a high stonewall. The main cluster of buildings opened onto James's Street; there, Ceannt established his headquarters in the night nurses' home. He deployed his men at appropriate points, displaying considerable tactical judgment.[5]

Ceannt also occupied three outposts, assigning a captain and about twenty men to each: Captain Seamus Murphy to Jameson's Distillery in Marrowbone Lane to the south east; Con Colbert to Watkins' brewery in Ardee Street to the east; and Captain Thomas McCarthy to Roe's Distillery in Thomas Street. Lily O'Brennan, sister of Eamon Ceannt's wife, Áine, was one of a number of Cumann na mBan members who joined the garrison at Marrowbone Lane on Easter Monday.[6]

In the fighting at South Dublin Union Richard O'Reilly was one of first casualties on the insurrectionists' side; another brother was also in the SDU, but two further brothers were in the British Army. One of his brothers later observed, 'That day there were two of us fighting for England, two of us against'.[7] The volunteers in Marrowbone Lane were bypassed by the British and it is claimed they were even able to stage a ceili!

The most intense fighting was on Monday and Tuesday. On Thursday large forces of the military pressed home the attack, but were forced to withdraw late that evening, both sides having suffered losses proportionate to their numbers. By that stage General Lowe had decided to concentrate his attention on the GPO and the Four Courts. News of the general surrender order did not reach Commandment Ceannt until Sunday.

Con Colbert

Born Cornelius Colbert in Monalena, Limerick in 1888, Con Colbert was raised in Athea in the same county. His family moved to Dublin when he was thirteen. He went to CBS North Richmond Street and later worked as a baker in Kennedy's. He was a fluent Irish speaker and was passionate about Irish history. He was present on 16 August 1909 when Fianna Éireann was founded at 34 Lower Camden Street. He became a captain and was given charge of a city branch.

Colbert headed an IRB circle composed of Fianna boys. He was elected to the Executive of the Irish Volunteers and became Captain of F Company, 4th Battalion. Pearse called him 'the gallant Captain Colbert' and asked him to drill the St Enda's boys at his school in Rathfarnham.

A dedicated Pioneer, Colbert was known not to drink or smoke and even gave up dancing during Lent. There was a joke in Na Fianna: 'Colbert swore last night, he called a man a pick axe.'[8] He first commanded Watkins Brewery on Ardee Street, and then moved to the Marrowbone Lane distillery. He assumed command of the whole garrison upon its surrender on Sunday, 30 April 1916. He famously moved the piece of white paper that was being pinned to his chest for the firing squad to aim at saying 'would it not be better nearer the heart'. He was executed on 8 May 1916 in his twenty-eighth year. Limerick railway station is named Colbert station in his honour.[9]

Jacob's Factory and 1916

The National Archives building stands on the site of the former Jacob's biscuit factory, a Dublin institution from the 1850s until it was destroyed by fire in 1987. The factory was another of The Liberties sites that played an important role during the Rising. The 2nd Battalion, under Commandant Thomas MacDonagh, occupied Jacob's biscuit factory on Bishop Street.

Thomas MacDonagh was a native of Tipperary, born in 1878 and spent the early part of his career as a teacher. He moved to Dublin to study, and was the first teacher on the staff at St Enda's, the school he helped to found with Patrick Pearse. MacDonagh was well versed in literature, his enthusiasm and erudition earning him a position in the English department at University College Dublin and his play, *When the Dawn is Come*, was produced at the Abbey theatre.

He was appointed director of training for the Irish Volunteers in 1914, later joining the IRB. MacDonagh was appointed to the IRB military committee in 1916 and became commander of the 2nd Battalion of Volunteers[10]

Thomas MacDonagh was married to Muriel Gifford and they had two children Barbara and Donagh. Muriel was tragically drowned a few months after his execution. His sister-in-law, Grace Gifford, married Joseph Plunkett shortly before Plunkett was executed in Kilmainham.

When MacDonagh laid down his arms at the time of surrender, he said he 'would give anything to see Muriel once more'. When somebody offered to go for Muriel, he declined, not wanting his wife to see and remember what the area looked like during defeat.

He was executed at 3.30 a.m. on 3 May. His wife had not been able to reach him, but his sister, a nun, was able to see him shortly before his death.

The Jacob's company's annual report for 1917 noted that production resumed in the factory after four or five days. With the ending of the First World War, full working capacity returned to the factory in 1919, when supplies of raw materials such as sugar were reported to be back to their 1915 level.

One noteworthy volunteer in Jacob's was Michael Molloy. He was the printer of the Proclamation of the Irish Republic. Interestingly, it is because of typographical errors in the wording of the proclamation that its originality, authenticity and value are tested. There are very few copies of the original proclamation available. Molloy was later a compositor for many years with *Independent Newspapers*.[11]

Outcome of the Rising

The executions of the leaders of the 1916 Rising had a huge impact in Ireland and did much to change public opinion in favour of the Rising. This change in attitude from one that initially frowned on the actions of the men, to one of outright support changed the political landscape, by ushering in Sinn Fein, ousting the old Irish Parliamentary Party and boycotting attendance at the House of Commons. The War of Independence followed from 1919 to 1921 which culminated in the Anglo-Irish Treaty of 1921 that created the Irish Free State.

In 1922, William T. Cosgrave, born at 174 James's Street, across the road from the South Dublin Union where he had been in action during the Rising, became President of the Executive Council of the Irish Free State, a role he kept until 1932. He helped steer the newly independent Ireland along the rocky road to democracy in a very challenging period during the ten years after the achieving of independence.[12]

Sadly, of the seventy-seven Republicans executed by the Irish Free State government in the ensuing Civil War (June 1922 – May 1923), the first four were from The Liberties. It has been claimed that the intention of the government initially was to execute Erskine Childers but it believed that this would be counter-productive. Consequently, four Liberties young men (they were barely out of their teens) were executed and not long afterwards, Erskine Childers suffered the same fate.

10

THE WOOD QUAY CAMPAIGN
AND THE KNIGHT

It may appear at first glance that Vikings were unwelcome visitors to our shores (and in fact were defeated at the famous Battle of Clontarf in 1014) but it has to be remembered that they gave us much. Everything from their craftsmanship to their trading techniques and their hunting skills was new to this land and was carried on in varying forms long after the Vikings were defeated in battle. They also left behind a treasure trove of magnificent artefacts that tell us so much about who we are and where we came from. Arguably the most famous find of all was that at Wood Quay in Dublin in the 1970s.[1]

Before the building of the office blocks we now see, as in many other parts of Dublin, beautiful houses and buildings of several hundred years vintage were bought up, in this case by what was then known as Dublin Corporation, and demolished, in anticipation of the building of a new headquarters.

In 1975, after many years of planning, Dublin Corporation announced it would build its new civic offices on the site but the excavations that followed revealed a massive Viking settlement with thousands of artefacts intact along with a section of the old city wall. This precipitated the enormous reaction from the public in the late 1970s to 'Save Wood Quay', such was its historical importance and significance for the history of the early years of the city of Dublin.[2]

Controversy arose in 1977 when conservationists led by Professor F.X. Martin and including Liberties campaigner John Gallagher, sought more time for excavation than had been allowed. The builders however carried on regardless and bulldozed much history and heritage away. The excavations of the Wood Quay site, however, carried on and many treasures were saved by the archaeological work that continued until 1981. New evidence was revealed about the Viking and later medieval settlements in Dublin. This evidence included the Viking earthen defences, wattle-and-daub houses, and part of the city's medieval stone wall. Also revealed was evidence of land reclamation and successive wooden waterfronts from the tenth to the thirteenth centuries (hence the name 'Wood Quay'). Land was reclaimed from the River Liffey using wood as building blocks.)

The site was particularly well preserved, with layer upon layer of material (e.g. housing) surviving which had not been destroyed by different generations. Among the artifacts found was jewellery, including pendants of Baltic amber and glass, objects of carved walrus ivory, an antler comb case, gaming counters, and worked leather items all providing evidence of Viking craftsmanship. Another key find was a thirteenth-century pewter pilgrim's flask in the shape of a ship. Some of the Wood Quay finds are on now on display in the National Museum in Kildare Street in Dublin city centre.[3]

Irish Government Stance on Wood Quay

According to a Wood Quay Memo in the Irish State Papers that were recently opened, the Irish government described Wood Quay as 'the medieval equivalent of a modern municipal dump' and said very few of the objects found were 'of intrinsic merit or importance'.

The 1978 memo was prepared by a senior civil servant for Táiniste George Colley to update the Cabinet on the Wood Quay controversy. It claimed that preserving the Viking site would involve 'an unjustifiably high level of public expenditure, perhaps as high as £5 million in compensation to Dublin Corporation alone'. It also said Wood Quay 'would not rank highly in most archaeologists' priorities, if resources on the scale required for preservation of that site were freely available'.[4] The memo was written in September 1978, before a Friends of Medieval Dublin protest march, which attracted up to 20,000 people. The protestors seized the site. A few days earlier, Dr T.K. Whitaker wrote a personal letter to Taoiseach Jack Lynch warning that building civic offices over Viking remains could do irreparable damage to Ireland's reputation.

Senator Whitaker noted that some Dublin Corporation members were 'now conspicuously silent where their own interests are involved'. He said he had no personal knowledge of what lay at Wood Quay but the evidence given by so many experts at the High Court impressed him. But if Wood Quay was of national and international importance 'I think it would do irreparable harm to the Government's and Ireland's reputation if we were to destroy rather than conserve' the senator wrote. 'We would appear uncaring and uncivilised.'[5]

'Save Wood Quay', September 1978

The battle to save Wood Quay was arguably the largest showing of people-power ever seen in Ireland as thousands joined protests to try and halt the development. Many well-known personalities joined members of the public on protest marches and sit-in occupations of the site. It all ended in sadness, however, as the development eventually went ahead.

The Wood Quay campaign of the late 1970s and early 1980s was not merely of interest to Irish people; it also generated huge interest from leading international scholars who were appalled by the decision to destroy the archaeological remains of what was regarded as one of the most important Viking sites in Europe.[6]

F.X. Martin and Wood Quay

Two individuals stand out in the campaign to protect and preserve the Wood Quay Viking site. Professor F.X. Martin OSA (1922–13 February 2000) was an Irish cleric, historian and activist, based with the Augustinian community in John's Lane, Thomas Street. Born in County Kerry Fr Martin was raised in Dublin and later joined the Augustinian Order. In 1959 he joined UCD's History Department, where he quickly established a glowing reputation among his students for the clarity and wit of his lectures and his warmth and accessibility as a person. In 1963 he was appointed head of UCD's Department of Medieval History.

In 1966 he organised a series of television lectures which were subsequently published as *The Course of Irish History*, probably the most widely read popular history of the country. In 1976 he was elected chairman of the Friends of Medieval Dublin, and this led him into the campaign for which he is best remembered: Save Wood Quay. He became a leading member of the struggle to save the historic Wood Quay archaeological site in the late 1970s and early 1980s. Professor Martin led the campaign but ultimately he failed to prevent the erection of the Civic Offices, despite appeals to both the courts and public opinion, but he did gain an invaluable delay, which allowed excavations on the site to be concluded.[7]

John Gallagher and the Battle for Wood Quay

Standing side-by-side with Fr Martin was John Gallagher. Local history is one of the many passions of John Gallagher and he is a sponsor of The Liberties Heritage Projects. John is also an active conservationist and preservationist and he was on An Taisce's council for a number of years. He was elected Deputy Lord Mayor of Dublin in June 2007.

John was born in 1933 in the Weavers' Alms House beside the Weavers' Hall in the Coombe. His father was Michael Gallagher who worked in the despatch department of Jacob's biscuit factory in Bishop's Street. His mother was Eileen Garvey from Newmarket. John went to school in St Nicholas of Myra primary school and later to Francis Street CBS. Even from an early age John was enmeshed in local community work. He assisted Sister Rita in the convent next door to his house in her charity work. Sister Rita used to give parcels or bread, tea, sugar and butter to the elderly poor who lived locally and John delivered these parcels to those who could not come to the convent to collect them. As a result John became highly aware of the poverty in the area and he also became familiar with all aspects of tenement life.

At that time St Bridget's provided a breakfast room for workers and when they were going home in the evening they were given half a loaf to feed their families at home. The poverty was intense at that time and John remembers children scrambling for crumbs at the end of the empty biscuit tins when they were being exchanged in the local shops (biscuits were sold loose in those days).[8]

From an early age John was very aware of the development being done which was damaging the city's cultural heritage and he became a great supporter and leader of many campaigns over the following years. As a member of An Taisce he was involved in securing an archaeological dig at the Tailors' Hall which was carried out by Professor O'Riordan and where important Viking finds were made. And when Fr F.X. Martin launched his campaign to save Wood Quay, John Gallagher was one of the first to get involved. He later refused the summons ordering him to exit the excavation and subsequently became one of the last to occupy the site.

A Tribute to John Gallagher

Tonight we have come to celebrate
John Gallagher of the Coombe.
A guardian of city and people
in times of joy and of glum.

He's a Liberties man he's a free man,
    not fettered by fear or foe.

He never once missed a meeting
of the 'corpo' in the old days.
Now his labours are rewarded;
they have garlanded him in gold.

He's a Liberties man he`s a free man,
    not fettered by fear or foe.

He loves every stone of The Liberties,
    every cobbled yard and alley.

He campaigned for the Vikings of Wood Quay,
    was at every sit – in and rally.

He's a Liberties man he's a free man,
    not fettered by fear or foe.

I think every cell of his body
must house a city archive.
He could grow you the family tree
of every family dead or alive.

He's a Liberties man he's a free man,
    not fettered by fear or foe.[9]

(Courtesy of Liberties poet, Christine Broe)

11

BOOTS, BREWS, BISCUITS AND THE GOLDEN TRIANGLE

Dublin, unlike Belfast in the north, did not experience the full effect of the Industrial Revolution and as a result, the number of unskilled unemployed was always high in the city. Industries like the Guinness brewery, the Powers and Jameson distilleries, and Jacob's biscuit factory, provided the most stable employment – and they were all based in The Liberties.

According to John Gallagher, resident, local Dublin City Councillor and activist in The Liberties, 'During the period 1800 to 1900 it was fairly wealthy around the Coombe. Guinness's Brewery and Jacob's biscuit factory were employing around 8,000'.[1]

One of the indispensable advantages of The Liberties in terms of industrial activity was easy access to water. Waterpower was vital for industrialisation in a country largely devoid of coal and iron and the area was blessed with three watercourses, the Poddle, the Dodder and the Camac (ably helped in later years by the Grand Canal and the Vartry Reservoir), that were crucial to the location of brewing, milling, distilling, weaving, and dyeing. And the established industries encouraged other ancillaries e.g. engineering, malting, tanning etc.

The River Poddle was the main supplier of water to the city from earliest times. It was augmented later with water from the Dodder river. Wooden and lead pipes (and iron pipes in the late nineteenth century) along water courses below James's Street and Thomas Street were important channels for bringing

Checking the quality of the stout in the huge vats in Guinness's Brewery, James's Street, in the 1940's. (Courtesy of Diageo/Guinness's Brewery; Dublin.ie Forums/dan1919breen)

the water to the city. In 1721 the city basin was constructed at James's Street and this was supplied by the Poddle to hold ninety days' storage. In 1865, with the opening of the Vartry Reservoir in the Dublin Mountains, Dublin was able to use fresh water instead of canal water.[2]

Tanning: Winstanleys

The Back Lane/High Street excavations carried out in 1962–1963 show that substantial trades and crafts were practiced from the tenth century onwards. The tanning craft became highly developed over the centuries and one of the largest quality shoe factories emerged in Back lane. Winstanley was a major employer (over 500) and enjoyed an international reputation for exporting quality leather shoes, mainly into the UK, until the late twentieth century. In addition to this, many clothing factories, including Doreen in Cork Street and Glen Abbey in Patrick Street, operated in this locality though they have long since closed.

'Nurses and Curses': Brewing and Distilling

The great supply of water, coupled with the fact the monks of the Abbey of St Thomas and the Augustinians of John's Lane had their own mills, and aided by the fact that grain came to the city via Thomas Street, facilitated the early and subsequent development of brewing and distilling.[3]

George Roe & Co. began in 1757 when Peter Roe bought a small distillery on Thomas Street in Dublin. In fact, it was two years after Peter Roe established the Thomas Street Distillery that Arthur Guinness set up his famous St James's Gate Brewery across the street. Given that they were close neighbours, and that they shared the complementary callings of producing a fine whiskey and a fine stout, one would readily assume that they shared professional admiration for one another. Apparently, that was not so. Over the years, generations of the Guinness family considered their stout to be the 'nurse of the people', while they considered spirits (e.g., Roe whiskey) to be the 'curse of the people'.[4]

In 1804 there were approximately thirty brewers listed in the *Dublin Directory* as being located in The Liberties. There were breweries in James's Street, Thomas Street, Thomas Court, the Coombe, Watling Street, New Row, Pimlico, Blackpitts, Cork Street (site of old chimney still there), Mill Street, Ardee Street, and Meath Street. There were also distilleries in James's Street, Thomas Street, Marrowbone Lane, Watling Street and Bridgefoot Street. Over the years, however, the number of breweries declined so that by the end of the nineteenth century Guinness and Watkins in Ardee Street, and the City of Dublin Brewery in Blackpitts/Fumbally Lane were the only survivors (although greatly expanded). Watkins survived until the middle of the twentieth century. The building is still there in Ardee Street and the names on the old adjacent streets, such as Watkins Buildings are a reminder of its importance.[5]

1759: The Year of the Guinness

The sights, sounds and smells of the Guinness brewery at St James's Gate in Dublin have been part and parcel of The Liberties for nearly 250 years – ever since Arthur Guinness himself first secured a 9,000-year lease on 4 acres of ground in 1759 for an annual rent of £45, including water rights. The brewery has expanded substantially since then and now occupies 64 acres on either side of Thomas Street, stretching down to Victoria Quay on the River Liffey. It was from here that the Guinness barges transported kegs of stout downriver to the *Lady Patricia* and *Lady Gwendolyn*, moored at City Quay. The vast brewery has its own theatre and swimming pool, as well as the tracks of a narrow-gauge railway that once served the site. It still has its own power station to fuel the production

A view across the cask yard, St James's Gate Brewery, c. 1906-13. Guinness was one of the city's 'outstanding employers'. (Courtesy of Guinness Archive, Diageo Ireland, GDB.BR14.0014.18)

of over 50 million barrels (nearly 83 million hectolitres) of beer – including Guinness Extra Stout, proudly brewed at 'James's Gate Dublin'. At one stage, the brewery employed as many as 5,000 people and, although the number has fallen to a fraction with the onset of automation, Guinness remains the largest employer in The Liberties.[6]

Early Days

Dublin emerged as the main centre of brewing in Ireland in the eighteenth century; the city provided the largest market for beer, which was costly to transport. When Guinness was established in 1759 it had to compete with sixty other commercial brewers in the Dublin area. There has been a brewery on the site of Guinness's brewery since 1670. In 1715 the owners were the Rainsfords and they transferred their business to Paul Epinasse, who subsequently transferred it to Arthur Guinness in 1759 and the brewery became known as the St James's Gate Brewery, taking its name from the nearby James's Gate. Ten years later, on 19 May 1769, Guinness exported his ale for the first time, when six-and-a-half barrels were shipped to Great Britain.

The excise duty on beer was abolished in 1795, reducing costs. The quality of Irish barley, malting techniques, and brewing methods were all improving, enabling Dublin and Cork brewers to eliminate British imports. In 1810 Cork's Beamish & Crawford was the largest brewer in the country, followed by Guinness in The Liberties. Soon Ireland became a net exporter of beer. Guinness exported half its output by 1840, a trade that expanded dramatically with the growth of the British railway network. The railways also opened up the Irish rural market. Output in Guinness's grew in the second half of the nineteenth century and the industry in Ireland as a whole became more centralised in the larger urban breweries. At the turn of the century The Liberties brewery of Guinness's produced about three quarters of the total output and 96 per cent of exports. Guinness was by this time one of the seven largest companies in the world and its huge turnover made brewing by far the most important industry in the fledgling Irish Free State after the War of Independence.[7]

Stout and Porter

Guinness is sometimes believed to have invented stout. This, however, was not the case as the first known use of the word stout in relation to beer appears in a letter in the Egerton Manuscript dated 1677, almost fifty years before Arthur Guinness was born. 'Stout' originally referred to a beer's strength, but eventually shifted meaning toward body and colour. Arthur Guinness started selling the dark beer porter in 1778. (The name 'porter' came from porters in the Billingsgate Markets in London who liked the taste of the product.) The first Guinness beers to use the term 'stout' were Single Stout and Double Stout in the 1840s. Throughout the bulk of its history, Guinness produced only three variations of a single beer type: porter or single stout, double or extra and foreign stout for export.

Already one of the top three British and Irish brewers, Guinness's sales soared from 350,000 barrels in 1868 to 779,000 barrels in 1876. In October 1886 Guinness became a public company, and was averaging sales of 1,138,000 barrels a year.[8]

By 1914, Guinness was producing 2,652,000 barrels of beer a year, which was more than double that of its nearest competitor Bass, and was supplying more than 10 per cent of the total UK beer market. By the 1930s, Guinness had become the seventh largest company in the world.

Guinness has also been referred to as 'the black stuff' and as a 'Pint of Plain' – referred to in the famous refrain of Flann O'Brien's poem 'The Workman's Friend': 'A pint of plain is your only man.'[9]

1930s image of Fermenting House/Guinness's Brewery in the heart of The Liberties. (Courtesy of Diageo/Guinness Brewery; Dublin.ie Forums/Pele)

The Guinness Storehouse is located in the heart of the brewery complex. The Storehouse is laid out over seven floors and shaped internally like a pint glass. The seven floors are given over to a complete history of the Guinness family and the story of the famous product. The bottom floor shows the method of brewing and previous Guinness advertisements, while the seventh floor of the Storehouse is taken up by The Gravity Bar, which features an almost 360 degree view of Dublin.

Roasting, Boiling and Mashing – The Guinness Process and Aroma

The two main brewery smells derive from the Guinness-making processes of roasting the barley, boiling of the wort and hops and mashing the malt with water. You can smell the unmistakable odours across the city; it's not unpleasant either, but kind of comforting and as some Dubliners say, it is the smell of home to them.

According to author Anto Howard (and resident in the Tenters area of The Liberties) in his book, *Slow Dublin*:

> I can sometimes get the faint whiff of the brewery from my front garden. There are two distinct smells. The first is a strong and harsh yeasty odour ... I find bracing and challenging, like a good cheese. The other, rarer and fainter, is a much mellower, rich roasted-coffee fragrance with a hint of warm bread about it. It smells like pure pleasure.[10]

Working in Guinness's Brewery, James's Street, in the 1940s. (Courtesy of Dublin. ie Forums/dan1919breen)

However, other residents have mixed views on the various aromas. For one it is an intrinsic part of The Liberties with 'that gorgeous smell'. For another, 'I used to live in a Guinness cottage in Pimlico, and it was really strong especially during the summer months. I wouldn't be a huge fan of the smell but it does bring back some happy memories'. Another resident declares:

Most of the time it's not too bad. In fact I quite like it. Much better than the slaughter house opposite my school when I was growing up. Down Island Street, it's wicked bad though, and around Mother's Tank Station ... Jesus, when I used to have to walk past there to get to Thomas St. – I nearly retched some mornings. Is the other side to a night on the black stuff.

Still another resident prefers the boiling of the hops to the roasting of the barley: 'I wouldn't drink it and I live beside the Guinness brewery but I do love the smell of hops from it every Tuesday.'[11] A Tenters resident recalls the family coming home through the Phoenix Park and as the car approached The Liberties, her father used to say to her 'Hold your nose, June'! There was such a strong, even harsh, yeasty smell 'that the car would nearly need to be fumigated'![12]

The Golden Triangle

In 1886 there were three major distilleries in The Liberties: John Powers' John's Lane Distillery; George Roe Distillery, Thomas Street (the largest distillery in Europe in 1887, the site of which was subsequently taken over by Guinness's Brewery in 1949); and W. Jameson of Marrowbone Lane. They (along with the other Jameson's in Bow Street) were part of what was known as 'The Golden Triangle' such was their importance. There were also a number of smaller ones such as Millars. And then there was Gilbeys, one of the major suppliers and distributors of whiskeys in Ireland.[13]

Gilbeys of Thomas Street

Gilbeys had premises at 118 Thomas Street as well as Talbot Street, South Circular Road, Lower Dorset Street, and several other locations around Dublin. Whiskey sales were on the rise in the late nineteenth century. A big turning point was noted at a general meeting of the Dublin Distillers Company in 1898 when Gilbeys sold 357,501 gallons of Irish whiskey, against 301,876 gallons of Scotch. It was felt that when Dublin whiskey was sold to the public there was great demand and that the people preferred it. Gilbey's Thomas Street business was the main supply outlet from 1886 when they opened there. This shop front is now well hidden behind a seemingly constantly changing business premises, but its former location is still a reminder of The Liberties important role in the business and commercial life of Dublin.[14]

George Roe Distillery: 1757–1923

The history and legacy of the George Roe Distillery is very interesting. Roe's annual output had in some years reached the enormous quantity of 2 million gallons – twice as much as the John Jameson Distillery and probably the highest output of any distillery in the world at that time. Yet, talk to anyone today about the George Roe Distillery or George Roe whiskey and you draw a complete blank. This distillery closed in 1926 and nobody seems to remember it or its whiskey. Its whiskey, however, is still available as Cherry Whiskey.

Located in the 'golden triangle' of distilling in Dublin, it was also the biggest of all the Dublin distilleries, covering an unbelievable 17 acres, extending all the way to the Quays by the river Liffey. The entrance was on Thomas Street, more or less opposite the entrance to Guinness's Brewery and was most striking. Alfred Barnard, who undertook a tour in 1889–1891, visiting over 110 breweries in Britain and Ireland in order to produce *The Noted Breweries of Great Britain and Ireland,* compared it to a French Chateau with its ivy-covered walls and flowerbeds. You could enter the premises in Thomas Street and by means of bridges and gangways you could keep almost under cover throughout the entire complex. Unfortunately, Barnard did not include a drawing of the distillery in his book, leaving us with only our imagination as to how it could have looked.[15]

Whiskey from the Dublin Mountains

Peter Roe had originally bought a small Distillery in 1757. Its location was of paramount importance with water from the nearby Vartry in abundance for the distilling process. During the eighteenth and early nineteenth century, several members of the Roe family operated different distilleries in Dublin. George Roe inherited the Thomas Street and Pimlico distilleries and quickly expanded, buying up premises and land as the business grew. George Roe's two sons, George and Henry, inherited the family firm in 1862 and during the next twenty years the distillery reached its peak. So successful were they that Henry gave £250,000 – easily more than €2.5 million in today's money – for the restoration of the nearby Christ Church Cathedral. Both men were eventually knighted, a testament to their standing in Victorian Ireland.

The Finest Dublin Pot Still

At the time of Barnard's visit, the distillery was not only the biggest, but also one of the best-equipped distilleries in the world. There were eight pot stills, holding from 12,000 to 20,000 gallons and five powerful engines. The Mill in St Patrick's Tower, which contained eight pairs of stones, could grind 1,500 barrels of grain a day and the sixteen fermenting vats each had a capacity of 40,000 gallons. The cooperage and stables extended over 2 acres and there were Smiths', Engineers', Fitters' and Carpenters' Shops on site. The storage warehouses could hold 23,000 casks, representing upwards of 1,250,000 gallons of whiskey and the company also owned large warehouses at Mount Brown capable of holding another 6,000 casks. Two hundred men were employed by this distillery and the whiskey produced was Dublin Pot Still of the finest quality. It was shipped to all parts of the world, in particular to Canada and Australia, and to the United States.

In 1891, the distillery was starting to feel the effects of cheap blended Scotch whiskies and joined forces with the DWD Distillery in Jones Road and the William Jameson Distillery in Marrowbone Lane. Their combined output had the potential of reaching 3.5 million gallons; however, this proved more of a downfall than an advantage. Not only was cheaper blended Scotch taking over many of Ireland's traditional pot still whiskey markets, worse trading conditions were to come with American Prohibition in 1919 and Ireland's War of Independence and Civil War. The Dublin Distillers Co. Ltd, as the consortium was known, entered the twentieth century with vast over capacity and far too much stock. The Thomas Street and the Marrowbone Lane Distilleries appear to have closed in 1923, but it took another twenty years for stocks to be disposed of.[16]

The distillery buildings appear to have been demolished in stages, starting with those closest to the Liffey to make way for housing. Some of the top part of the site was taken over by Guinness who demolished it further to make way for car parks and office buildings. The only reminder today is St Patrick's Tower in the Digital Depot complex.

From Hearts to Gold:
John's Lane Distillery (John Power & Sons) 1791–1974

Powers Gold Label is a unique brand of Irish whiskey. Originally a pure pot still whiskey, it is now produced from a blend of pot still and grain whiskey. It is one of the most popular Irish whiskeys sold in Ireland, selling over 6 million measures per annum.

James Power was originally a coaching innkeeper on Thomas Street. It is unlikely that he could have known how successful his new business would become when, in 1791, he converted his inn into a small distillery. By 1800, James was joined in the business by his son John. Originally known as James Power & Son, by 1809 the business name was changed to John Power & Son, with James remaining in charge. The business continued to grow successfully and in 1823 John Power boasted of a 500-gallon still with an annual output of 33,000 gallons of whiskey per year. This was the start of something big and within another ten years the company's yearly output had increased to over 300,000 gallons.

This success had benefits for a family that within one generation had risen from innkeepers to members of Dublin's high society. John Power was knighted and became High Sheriff of Dublin. Because of his celebrity he was chosen to lay the foundation stone for the O'Connell Monument in Dublin's city centre.

In 1871, the distillery was rebuilt in classic Victorian style, occupying almost 7 acres. It was one of Dublin's most impressive sights and employed approximately 300 people. John Power & Son continued in their success and became one of the largest Irish whiskey distillers. Powers was the first Whiskey Company to sell their product in miniature bottles called 'Baby Powers'. The importance of their influence in government facilitated changes to the distilling law in order to produce this innovation. The last member of the Board with the Power name was Sir Thomas Talbot Power. After his death in 1936, ownership remained in the family through his sisters. Powers remained a leading player in the industry until 1966 when they merged with the only two remaining distillers in the Irish republic, Cork Distillers Company and their long time rival, John Jameson & Son.[17]

From Baby Powers to Gold Label

The Powers were noted breeders of shire horses and in the premises in Thomas Street there were large stables and even a 'horse hospital' for any horses that fell ill. There were also engineering shops, sawmills, carpenters, coppersmiths and fitters. Barnard noted that the water used in the distillery was principally from the Vartry Reservoir and that some of the old-fashioned customers sent two empty casks with their order – one to be filled with Powers' whiskey, the other to be filled with water from the Vartry Reservoir, in order to reduce their whiskey with the same water as had been used in the making of the spirit.

The distillery had its own fire department, manned day and night by a team of eight men and the alarms were connected through the exchange to the city Fire Brigade. In case of fire, the water supply would come from the Vartry, the Grand Canal and the Royal Canal. The distillery also had its own stationary horizontal double-acting fire engine, capable of throwing 800 gallons of water per minute through eight lines of hose to a height of 150ft.

In 1866, John Power & Son began bottling their own whiskey, which was unheard of in Ireland, as it was usually sold in the cask. A gold label was added to the bottle and it was from this that the whiskey got its name, 'Powers Gold Label'.

The Powers distillery was a founding member of the Irish Distillers Group and ownership of the company remained with the family until 1966. The distillery installed a column still in 1961, which they used primarily for the production of gin and vodka, but which was also used to experiment with producing grain whiskey for blending. They were instrumental in persuading the Irish Distillers Group to move from focusing on pot still whiskeys to blended whiskeys. The distillery finally closed its doors in 1974, when the Irish Distillers Group decided to move all its production, including that of Powers Whiskey, to the Midleton Distillery in Cork, where Powers (and Jameson) Whiskey continues to be distilled. Interestingly, the still house in the new distillery in Midleton with its interconnecting pot stills and column stills was modelled mainly on that of the John's Lane distillery.[18]

From Chimney Stacks and Pot Stills to Art College

So what has become of the distillery complex itself? Most of it unfortunately has been demolished, some of it even before the closure and the move to Midleton. In 1980 Ireland's National College of Art and Design bought most of the site and the Counting House, a magnificent building on Thomas Street which was used as offices, still stands today. The Great Still House with its five pot stills that gleamed 'like burnished gold' has unfortunately vanished, but three pot stills were spared and can still be seen today, outdoors, in the college's Red Square. Part of the original Kiln building is still distinguishable from its circular shape and houses the college's library upstairs. Two of the original five Engine Houses have survived, the most notable being Engine House No.5 with its beam engine of 250hp manufactured by Turnbull, Grant and Jack of Glasgow in 1886. The double-faced clock, admired by Barnard, set in the wall of the Engine House can still be seen today. Only the smaller of the original two chimney stacks has survived (95ft); the taller stack, which stood at 120ft, was demolished for safety and insurance reasons, shortly after the college acquired the site.

Fortunately, the vestiges of the John's Lane Powers Distillery today are now protected structures, so they are likely to remain as a testament to this once great distillery. The College of Art and Design is not open to visitors; however, they are most amenable, and will accommodate anyone who wants to visit what is left of the distillery.[19]

Millars Distillery and the Classic Dublin Sipping Whiskey

Adam Millar & Co. was a firm of Dublin whiskey bonders, which was located on the opposite side of Thomas Street, where part of the Digital Hub is now based. Millar's Blended Irish Whiskey was created in 1843 as a premium Irish whiskey and was successfully marketed until the 1970s. Millar's Special Reserve was renowned as a classic Dublin sipping whiskey. The traditional method of drinking such a whiskey was to sip it neat or to accompany a pint of stout. Cooley's distillery bought them out in 1988 but the name Millar is still evident (on close inspection) on the front entrance brickwork to the Digital Hub.

'A Small Jemmy' – William Jameson and the Marrowbone Lane Distillery

The Marrowbone Lane Distillery was founded in 1750 and taken over by John Stein of Kennetpans in 1780. Around 1800, the famous distiller John Jameson's son, William, who was married to one of Stein's daughters (Isabella), joined his father-in-law's Marrowbone Lane Distillery. William's new venture was to be short lived as he died within a few weeks of becoming a partner. It is thought that he was a victim of Typhus or Relapsing Fever, which raged through The Liberties and elsewhere at the time.

William's share was passed on to his brother James, who eventually assumed total control of the distillery in 1820 after buying out John Stein. Despite family ties, the Bow Street and Marrowbone Lane Distilleries were nothing but business rivals.

To meet demand, Jameson enlarged the distillery with an investment of £100,000 (approximately £20 million) taking the site to an incredible 14 acres, which produced 900,000 gallons of whiskey annually by means of four old pot stills with the capacity of 18,000, 12,000, 11,000 and 9,000 gallons. It had the largest Mash House in the United Kingdom or Ireland with a capacity of 100,000 gallons.

The distillery had nine bonded warehouses, which regularly would contain in excess of 20,000 casks, plus four other out warehouses, which held another 7,000 duty-paid casks. As with all distilleries of this period it was self-sufficient. The distillery had a total staff of over 200 employees. The cooperage alone took up one acre and employed thirty men; it had its own carpenters, painters, engineers and smithy on site. The stables were the size of cavalry barracks with their own horse hospital.[20]

In more recent times the Marrowbone Lane Distillery was linked to the Easter Rising of 1916. Con Colbert was captain of the Forth Battalion and was in charge of a force of more than 100 rebels at this distillery when it surrendered on Sunday 30 April 1916.

The distillery sadly closed in 1923 but the name Jameson lives on as one of the best selling Irish whiskeys in the world. 'A small Jemmy' is one of the classic Liberties terms for a small Jameson's whiskey. Another one is 'a ball of malt', meaning an Irish blend, not a single malt. Or, 'A drop of the craythur'. A pint of stout and a ball of malt is what Flan O'Brien's The Brother used to order. As did Tim Finnegan in the famous ballad: 'He'd a "drop of the craythur" every morn.'

Jacob's Biscuits, Mr Figgerty and 'Dear Frankie'

The National Archives building stands on the site of the former Jacob's biscuit factory, a Dublin institution from the 1850s until it was destroyed by fire in

1987. All that remains today to remind us of the world-famous Jacob's biscuit factory on Bishop Street/Peter Street are the words 'W & R Jacob & Co Ltd' on two of the original building blocks that were retained, and also the word 'Offices' on another on the lower walls of the National Archives building.

The name of W & R Jacob is synonymous with Dublin biscuit making. The business was founded by two brothers of a Quaker family, William and Robert Jacob, in Waterford in 1851, and shortly afterwards the business moved to Peter's Row/Bishop Street in Dublin. The Dublin factory's dramatic involvement in the 1913 Lockout is renowned, as is its pivotal role in the 1916 Easter Rising.

In the 1970s, Jacob's merged with Boland's Biscuits to form Irish Biscuits Ltd and moved to Tallaght, Co. Dublin. Jacob's impact on the social and economic life of Dublin and The Liberties, and indeed further afield, is profound. Its famous biscuits were, and still are, found in shops and on tea-tables in every corner of Ireland and abroad. It has been said that its crackers and fig-rolls are stuff made of legend. And to be a 'Jacob's Girl,' working in the factory was indeed an honour! There were thousands of them from The Liberties working there for many years; The Liberties was the heartland of the Jacob's workforce for generations.[21]

Figs and Crackers

Kimberley, Mikado & Coconut Creams were biscuits launched by Jacob's in 1881. Kimberley, a mallow sandwiched between two ginger-flavoured biscuits, was topically named after the famous diamond mine in Australia. Mikado, topped with stripes of mallow and jam and sprinkled with coconut, was named after the famous opera by Gilbert and Sullivan. Coconut Cream, originally spelt 'Cocoanut Cream' was one of a series of similar products. All mallows products were originally hand-piped using an icing bag.

George N. Jacob (son of William B. Jacob, the founder) visited the USA in 1884 and brought back to Ireland ideas to develop Ireland's first cracker. By the end of 1884 Jacob's had invented and perfected the Cream Cracker, which became synonymous with the company. The oven, which was imported from the USA, proved unsuitable, and they reverted to their own adaptation of an existing oven. Jacob's Cream Crackers were launched in early 1885. The famous Club Milk sandwich biscuit was launched by Jacob's in 1919 and remains a popular favourite to this day.

Exporting to England and Wales has been an important part of Jacob's since the early days. By the end of the century Jacob's biscuits were well known around the globe. In 1886, a depot and Sales Office was opened in Liverpool, while the first London-based salesman was appointed. Other depots opened shortly after in London and Manchester.[22]

World Wars and Turf

Jacob's supported the two Word War efforts in a number of a different ways. They produced biscuits in packets and other suitable containers for the troops and Jacob's sent a 4-ton Leyland lorry to be used by the Red Cross in France at a time when transport was in short supply. Jacob's offered allowances for male employees who joined the army during the First World War and 388 workers enlisted, of whom twenty-six were killed and many wounded. In 1941 Government policy halted exports to Northern Ireland, Britain and overseas; this business was transferred to the UK company base. Gas supply was limited to a few hours a day and so Jacob's made use of turf to provide power for the factory and in 1944 the company leased and worked a turf bog to source supplies.[23] Jacob's were also forced to introduce rationing of deliveries due to raw material shortages.

Outside the Jacob's factory, Bishop Street. (Courtesy of Jacob's Fruitfield; Dublin.ie Forums/Jimmymac)

'Dear Frankie': the Frankie Byrne Radio Show

In January 1961 Telefís Éireann was launched in Ireland. Jacob's sponsored various radio programmes to advertise its product range. In the same year Harry Thuillier presented *Come Fly with Me* on Radio Éireann during which he interviewed people travelling on Aer Lingus flights. From 1963 Frankie Byrne (Jacob's Public Relations Officer) presented an agony-aunt programme on Radio Éireann entitled *Women's Page* and she started reading listeners' letters with the famous words, 'Dear Frankie'. It was renowned for its use of Frank Sinatra recordings (particularly 'Strangers in the Night') between items and was sponsored by 'the people who make better biscuits better everyday'. The programme continued until 1985. To attract a younger audience Jacob's also sponsored a music programme on Radio Luxembourg.

By 1962 Jacob's were sponsoring the Jacob's TV Awards. For ten years, the awards were televised from the Jacob's factory with Jacob's employees on duty to host the elite of the Irish entertainment world. By 1969 Radio Awards were included in the presentations.[24]

The Jim Figgerty Mystery

In 1962 the Irish public became aware that a person named Jim Figgerty was missing. Ads began to appear in all national and regional newspapers seeking his whereabouts. A massive television campaign followed. On the hunt for the guarded secret of how Jacob's gets the figs into the Fig Rolls, Jim became a national icon that remains a classic part of Jacob's and Irish advertising history to this day.

Today, Jacob's is a brand name for several lines of biscuits and crackers. Jacob Fruitfield Food Group owns the brand name in the Republic of Ireland and in the United Kingdom it is owned under license by United Biscuits.

12

STAIRWAYS TO HEAVEN: LANDSCAPE OF SPIRES

Easter in The Liberties was once a time for the tradition of 'doing the seven chapels'. This meant saying the Holy Thursday prayers at the seven local Catholic churches. These churches were the church of the Immaculate Conception ('Adam & Eve's'), St Michael's on Merchant's Quay (originally the site of the famous Smock Alley theatre and latterly again a theatre with the original name), St Catherine's of Meath Street, the Augustinian John's Lane church, St Nicholas of Myra, St James's and St Audoen's. Churchgoers would visit all seven churches in that one evening. 'There was nothing else to do at that time,' said Sadie Doyle, a local resident who has lived in The Liberties all her life, adding that the 'tradition is long gone'. Another tradition also gone but one that used to attract thousands of parishioners regularly was the confraternities and sodalities – though it was not always accepted. One local recalls that in the 1950s, at the height of the Catholic Church's influence in Ireland, he was standing at a street corner with some friends when they were approached by the parish priest who asked them if they going to attend the sodality meeting the following Tuesday. The reply given by one of the friends was: 'Yes, Father, I will, when you can tell me how many daughters Adam and Eve had.'[1]

Although the outside of these churches in The Liberties may appear to be plain and grey, John's Lane excluded, the interiors are often very decorative and beautiful. Many of these churches contain work by world-renowned stained-glass artists and are highly praised by architectural historians. Two of the churches – St Nicholas of Myra and John's Lane – have stained-glass windows designed and produced by the renowned Irish artist and book illustrator Harry Clarke.

Some of the churches of The Liberties are also unusual in that they are crowded in by houses or other buildings which prevent one from seeing the totality of the church. John's Lane is an example. In order to appreciate the impressive front façade, one of the best views is from Chadwick's yard across Thomas Street. Likewise with St Catherine's on Meath Street, where the front entrance is just feet from the road itself. It is nearly impossible (but not quite!) to appreciate the front or any elevation of this church.

Confusing Cathedrals

One of Dublin's earliest archbishops, John Comyn, an English cleric who was appointed by the king to succeed Archbishop Laurence O'Toole (deliberately, so as to help extend Anglo-Norman influence in Dublin), wished to be outside the control of the city so he built his palace on what is now the site of Kevin Street Garda station (Liberty of St Sepulchre), and began the new church of St Patrick, which was dedicated on St Patrick's Day 1192. It was raised to the status of a cathedral in 1216. However, Christ Church Cathedral continued to operate just up the hill and confusion reigned for many years over the status of both cathedrals. This problem was not resolved until 1872 when Christ Church was made cathedral for Dublin alone and St Patrick's became the national cathedral for all Ireland.[2]

Some of Dublin's finest churches are to be found in The Liberties and we will take a circular route to view these landmarks.

The Brewer's Church: St Patrick's Cathedral

St Patrick's Cathedral is one of Ireland's finest, largest, best-known and most-visited ecclesiastical buildings. The cathedral is today the National Cathedral of the Church of Ireland (a church of the Anglican Communion). James Malton stated at the end of the eighteenth century, 'It is not a rich style of Gothic architecture. Yet it is on the whole a large and respectable pile of building, and might, with some care and expense, be a real ornament to the City', which, as we can see today, it is. This is a beautiful, massive cathedral, a grandiose interior with gorgeous stained-glass windows, ancient battle colours from various wars including the Boer and Crimean, the seats of the Knights of St Patrick and the most attractive little pews.

St Patrick's Cathedral is steeped in history. Built in honour of Ireland's patron saint, the cathedral stands adjacent to the famous well where tradition has it St Patrick baptised converts on his visit to Dublin. The well was beside the River Poddle and the river still runs under St Patrick Street near the cathedral. To commemorate his visit a small wooden church was built on the site. The stone which had marked the well was found in 1901 and is now kept inside the cathedral.[3]

A View of St Patrick's Cathedral from St Patrick's Park.

Over the centuries as the elements, religious reformation, and persecution took their toll the cathedral fell into disrepair. Between 1860 and 1900 the Guinness family carried out a full-scale restoration. Some people took umbrage at this involvement by the brewing family in the restoration and St Patrick's became known as 'the brewer's church'. However, without the vital help from the Guinness family St Patrick's would not have survived until today.

There are many monuments and memorials located around the cathedral. Some of the most famous include Jonathan Swift, Dean of St Patrick's, Douglas Hyde, the first president of Ireland, and the blind harpist Turlough O'Carolan, the last Irish Bard. It is also the resting place of the Duke of Schomberg, King William's second-in-command who was killed at the Battle of the Boyne.

Minot's Tower

The building of the large north-west tower of the cathedral is attributed to the fourteenth century Archbishop of Dublin, Thomas Minot, who occupied the see from 1363 to 1375. The cathedral's graceful spire is an addition from 1769.

The first public clock in Dublin was placed on Minot's Tower in 1560. The tower was restored in 1897 by Lord Iveagh under the supervision of the renowned architect Sir Thomas Drew. It is well known to Dubliners both for its clock, which unusually for institutional clocks, tells the correct time, and as the home of the cathedral's bells which have for long been an integral part of Dublin life. The tower contains the largest ringing peal of bells in Ireland – fifteen in all. The two-faced clock at one stage controlled a now disused carillon, which was last played in the 1950s. This instrument, made in 1878, had seven religious tunes on the one drum. In its heyday, the carillon played 'Adeste Fideles' ('O Come

All Ye Faithful') twice at noon, and 'Martyrdom' twice at midnight. Other tunes played were Rousseau's 'Dream' and the 'Sicilian Mariner's Hymn'.

The north face of the tower has an interesting figure of a carved head over-looking St Patrick's Park, which possibly dates from the period of King Henry II. It was uncovered when some work was being done on the tower in 2008 and they decided to leave it exposed. Whether it is an image of Archbishop Minot or some king is still debated.

The Knights of St Patrick

From 1783 until 1871 the cathedral served as the Chapel of the Most Illustrious Order of Saint Patrick, for the members of the Knights of St Patrick. With the dis-establishment of the Church of Ireland in 1871 the installation ceremony moved to St Patrick's Hall, Dublin Castle, but the heraldic banners of the knights at the time of the move still hang over the choir stalls to this day. There are also flags and banners of various army regiments containing Irish soldiers.

From 1666 French Huguenots used the Lady Chapel for their services. The Lady Chapel became known as L'Eglise Française de St Patrick during this time. The Lady Chapel continued as a Huguenot chapel up until 1816.

Door of Reconciliation

When you visit St Patrick's Cathedral, you will see a door inside with a hole cut into it. The origin lies in a famous incident during a feud between two promi-nent Irish families, the Ormonds and the Kildares, in 1492. At one point, Sir James Butler, the Earl of Ormond, took refuge with his followers in the chapter house (this is where the cathedral staff lived) of the cathedral. After a while, Gerald Fitzgerald, the Earl of Kildare, came to realise that the feud was non-sense and tried to make peace. In order to prove that no villainy was intended and that his wish for reconciliation was genuine, he cut a hole in the door and thrust his arm through. In doing this, of course, he was placing himself at the mercy of those inside, who could easily have cut it off. He need not have wor-ried: Butler grasped his hand warmly and his peace overtures were accepted. This is where the phrase 'to chance your arm' derives from.[4]

The Choir School was founded in 1432 and many of its members took part in the very first performance of Handel's *Messiah* in 1742. The manuscript is on display in a glass case in the cathedral.

Dean Swift

The most famous person associated with St Patrick's is Dean Jonathan Swift (1667–1745) who was the Dean of St Patrick's Cathedral from 1713 to 1745. There is a plaque on the wall marking the site of his birthplace at 7 Hoeys Court off Werburgh Street but it is situated on the wall around the corner at Ship Street where the 'Forty Steps' connects Dublin Castle to Castle Street. This is possibly an appropriate location as it was said that he liked to be fit and that he ran up and down the steps several times each day. Swift was greatly loved by ordinary Dubliners and when he died it took two days for them to file past his coffin. Few people in Irish history obtained such a wonderful hold over the people and the somewhat riotous artisans of The Liberties as did Dean Swift.[5]

He wrote many books, but his best-known work is *Gulliver's Travels*, published in 1726, a large portion of which he wrote at Woodbrook House in County Laois. As with his other writings, the *Travels* was published under a pseudonym, the fictional Lemuel Gulliver, a ship's surgeon and later a sea captain. Some of the correspondence between printers Benjamin Motte and Gulliver's also-fictional cousin negotiating the book's publication has survived. Though it has often been mistakenly thought of and published as a children's book, it is a great and sophisticated satire of human nature based on Swift's experience of his times. *Gulliver's Travels* is an anatomy of human nature, a sardonic look at how we see ourselves. It challenges its readers as to whether it has adequately characterised human nature and society. Each of the four books – recounting four voyages to mostly fictional exotic lands – has a different theme, but all are attempts to deflate human pride.[6]

Though many thought of Swift as a remote and difficult character he was in fact a most charitable individual. Whenever he walked the streets of The Liberties he made sure to fill his pockets with coins to give to the poor and to street beggars. Time and time again he showed his care and deep concern for the people of The Liberties, and agitated on behalf of the weavers and starving families. He has been described as the 'absolute Monarch of The Liberties and King of the Mob'.[7]

In 1729, Swift published *A Modest Proposal for Preventing the Children of Poor People in Ireland Being a Burden on Their Parents or Country, and for Making Them Beneficial to the Publick*, a satire in which the narrator, with intentionally grotesque logic, recommends that Ireland's poor escape their poverty by selling their children as food to the rich: 'I have been assured by a very knowing American of my acquaintance in London, that a young healthy child well nursed is at a year old a most delicious nourishing and wholesome food...' Following the satirical form, he introduces the reforms he is actually suggesting by deriding them:

> Therefore let no man talk to me of other expedients ... taxing our absentees ... using [nothing] except what is of our own growth and manufacture ... rejecting ... foreign luxury ... introducing a vein of parsimony, prudence and temperance ... learning to love our country ... quitting our animosities and factions ... teaching landlords to have at least one degree of mercy towards their tenants ... Therefore I repeat, let no man talk to me of these and the like expedients, 'till he hath at least some glympse of hope, that there will ever be some hearty and sincere attempt to put them into practice.[8]

It was while he was in the deanery that he wrote the famous *Drapier Letters*, published by Swift under the pseudonym 'M.B. Drapier', that consisted of seven pamphlets attacking Wood's Halfpence. The background to the controversy (1722–25) was an Englishman, William Wood, who was given a patent by the King's mistress, the Duchess of Kendall, to supply Ireland with copper coin. Instead, the coin was to be made from a cheap metal, and Wood could therefore share the profits with the duchess. The scheme provoked hostile reaction, pamphlets and popular demonstrations. Swift was outraged and wrote his pamphlets in the form of letters and signed M.B. Drapier. He pointed out that to buy a quart of ale you would need to pay for it with thirty-six halfpences.[9] Moreover, the tone of the pamphlet hinted strongly of Ireland's political subordination to England. In the fourth pamphlet, 'To the Whole People of Ireland', he argued that Ireland had a right to be governed by laws of her own making. Swift then was part of that determined defence of Irish against English interests and gives the controversy an honoured place in the development of Irish patriotism.

The government prosecuted the printer of *Drapier's Letters* and offered a reward for the name of their author. Although everybody in Dublin knew Swift had written the letters, not one person informed on him. Eventually the halfpence were withdrawn in 1725 and Swift became the hero of Dublin. The rejection of the patent also meant that the English government could only manage Ireland's affairs with great difficulty and had to depend on local power brokers.

Dean Swift, by his *Drapier Letters*, written in the character of a plain shop-keeper, at once became the leader and spokesman of the local population. He was held in such high esteem that there is a story that a crowd, which had assembled near St Patrick's Cathedral to watch for an eclipse of the moon, dispersed at once on hearing a message from the dean that the eclipse had been postponed by his orders.

He died in 1745, and in his will he bequeathed his entire estate to found a hospital for 'fools and mad' and on 8 August 1746, a Royal Charter was granted to St Patrick's Hospital, at the edge of The Liberties, by George II. Following from his experiences as a governor of the Bedlam hospital in London, Swift intended the hospital to be designed around the needs of the patient and left strict instructions on how patients were to be treated. The first psychiatric hospital to be built in Ireland, it is one of the oldest in the world and still flourishes today as one of the largest and most comprehensive in the country.

His grave is located in the cathedral, in the south aisle, near his beloved 'Stella', Mrs Esther Johnson. Swift's epitaph that may be seen over the door of the robing room was hailed by W.B. Yeats as one of the best of all time. It is translated 'Swift has sailed to his rest; he lies where furious indignation can no longer rend his heart'.

St Patrick's Cathedral, c. 1900. (Courtesy of NLI, LROY 759)

The great charm of St Patrick's Cathedral rests on its association with Swift. 'The Cathedral is merely his tomb', wrote Sir Walter Scott, who could see nothing but the Dean's 'dark saturnine face' in every corner of the church. His gigantic personality effaces all minor personalities except that of Stella.[10]

A Sham?

Former president of Ireland, Mary McAleese, described the theme of her Presidency as 'Building Bridges'. She incurred criticism, however, from the Catholic Archbishop of Dublin Desmond Connell for taking inter-church communion in St Patrick's Cathedral in December 1997. The Cardinal generated a furore and huge controversy when he called her action 'a sham' and a 'deception'. The then Taoiseach, Bertie Ahern, said it was ironic that 'the church was condemning an act of reconciliation and bridge-building between the denominations'.[11]

Christ Church Cathedral – The Heart of Medieval Dublin

Continuing up the hill we come to Christ Church Cathedral. Lying within the old city walls, the cathedral is officially claimed as the seat (cathedral) of both the Church of

Ireland and Roman Catholic archbishops of Dublin (it is also strongly associated with one of Dublin's first archbishops, St Laurence O'Toole (1162–1180)). In practice, since the English Reformation of the sixteenth century, it has been the cathedral of only the Church of Ireland's Archbishop of Dublin. Though nominally claimed as his cathedral, the Catholic Archbishop of Dublin uses St Mary's in Marlborough Street, Dublin as his pro-cathedral (acting cathedral). Before that the Catholic archbishop's seat was St Nicholas of Myra church in Francis Street.

Christ Church Cathedral is located in the heart of medieval Dublin, next to Wood Quay at the top of the hill overlooking the city. However, a major dual carriageway separated it from the original medieval street pattern which once surrounded it, with its original architectural context at the centre of a maze of small buildings and streets. As a result the cathedral now appears dominant in isolation behind new civic offices along the quays.[12]

The building that can be seen today is older than Dublin's other Church of Ireland cathedral, St Patrick's. It is believed that it started off as a small wooden church built around 1030 for Dublin's first bishop, Dúnán by the Viking King Sitric Silkbeard. Despite being within the city walls it later became part of one of the four main Dublin Liberties.

The wooden structure was replaced with a stone one by Archbishop Laurence O'Toole, in 1172, in the Romanesque style we see today. Many changes were added to the cathedral since, but by the 1800s it had fallen into disrepair. As is the case with St Patrick's, a wealthy Dublin man came to the rescue and donated £230,000 to restore it. The name of this man was Henry Roe and he made his money by distilling whiskey in nearby Thomas Street. Henry Roe turned the cathedral into the building Dubliners know today but while the outside was much changed, the inside stayed pretty much as it was in the Middle Ages. Following its restoration, a new thoroughfare was cut in the vicinity of Christ Church, and although it was named 'Lord Edward Street', a local witticism at the time was 'Roe Row'.[13]

Tales from the Crypt

Inside the cathedral one can see steps leading down to the crypt, a huge underground room running the whole length of the building. The crypt dates from the twelfth or possibly late eleventh century, and is not only one of the largest medieval crypts in either the UK or Ireland, but also the oldest structure in Dublin. It is a forest of heavy rough-stone pillars, which carries the weight of the cathedral and central tower.

The crypt contains various monuments and historical features, including the oldest known secular carvings in Ireland: two statues that until the late eighteenth century stood outside the Tholsel (Dublin's medieval city hall, which was demolished in 1806). Also on view are the tabernacle and set of candlesticks which were used when the cathedral last operated (for a very short time) under the 'Roman rite', when the Catholic king, James II, having fled England in 1690, came to Ireland to fight for his throne and attended High Mass in the temporary restoration of Christ Church as a Catholic cathedral. The 'Chain Book' is also preserved in the cathedral and it contains the laws of the city and reports of annual fairs in medieval times.[14]

The crypt contains other historical artifacts which have survived here simply because they were in no one's way! This includes a set of stocks, formerly in Christ Church Place, made in 1670 and used for the punishment of offenders before the Court of the Dean's Liberty (the small area under the cathedral's exclusive civic authority). Offenders were locked in the stocks for the prescribed period while 'friends' often pelted them with rotten fruit or vegetables! Another item of interest is the cat and the rat, the one presumably chasing the other, that were trapped in an organ pipe in the 1860s and became mummified. According to a local wit, 'Egypt might have Tutankhamen but Ireland has Tom and Gerry!'[15]

Strongbow and St Laurence

Many people and stories are connected with Christ Church Cathedral, including Laurence O'Toole, the first Archbishop of Dublin and patron saint of the city. His heart has been preserved in the cathedral for centuries (though unfortunately it was stolen in early 2012). He invited Augustinian monks to live beside Christ Church and the remains of some of their houses can still be seen inside the grounds of the cathedral.

King Henry II of England attended the Christmas service at the cathedral in 1171 during the course of his Irish expedition. This was the first time Henry received Holy Communion following the murder of Thomas à Beckett by Henry's knights in Canterbury. In the 1180s, Strongbow and other Norman knights helped to fund a complete rebuilding of Christ Church in stone.

Inside the cathedral is the tomb of Strongbow, the Norman knight who came to Ireland on the invitation of the King of Leinster, Dermot MacMurrough. Strongbow married MacMurrough's daughter, Aoife and himself became King of Leinster in 1171. It is said that this was the beginning of the rule of the Normans in Ireland. The figure on his tomb shows a knight with a shield dressed for battle. His hands are joined and his legs crossed. The current tomb of Strongbow is actually a memorial brought in at a later date as the real one was vandalised.

One of the strangest events ever to take place in Christ Church happened in 1487. The English were fighting over who should be their king. In order to win this quarrel, some of them found a ten-year-old boy called Lambert Simnel who looked very much like the princes who were kept in prison by the English king. They gave him fine clothes and jewels and crowned him King of England in

Christ Church Cathedral. Many important Irish lords and nobles attended the ceremony. When the lie was discovered Lambert was dismissed and sent to work in the king's kitchen but his life was spared.[16]

Spirits Below and Spirits Divine

The west door of the cathedral opens onto St Michael's Hill and Winetavern Street, which run down to the River Liffey. This was once a street of tall, crooked houses, many of them actually taverns or pubs. Dublin's narrowest house occupied a site here for many years. In the sixteenth century, such was business booming, that the owners of the taverns moved gradually into the crypt of the cathedral and set up business there! A wit of the day commented: 'Spirits above and spirits below, Spirits divine and spirits – of wine'! However, the Earl of Wentworth heard about the carousing going on below 'whilst we above are serving the high God'. He then ordered the removal of the tavern and issued an ordinance decreeing, 'that no person presume to make urine against the walls of the said church'.[17]

A charming covered bridge, added by Street in 1875, connects the cathedral to the old Synod Hall, which now holds the Viking multi-media exhibition 'Dublinia'.

For Whom the Bells Ring

The tower of Christ Church Cathedral contains the world's greatest number of full-circle, ringing peal of bells hanging in a single tower, nineteen in all. It probably has at least one ringing bell from its foundation. By 1440 there were known to be three great bells in the tower; however, on 11 March 1597 an accidental gunpowder explosion in one of the nearby quays damaged the tower and caused the bells to crack. The effects of this blast also damaged the tower of St Audoen's church nearby. In 1670 six new bells were cast for the tower from cannon gun metal. These were augmented to eight in 1738 and then to twelve in 1878. The most recent augmentation was in 1999 when an additional seven bells were added to the ring, giving a grand total of nineteen bells, a world record for bells rung this way. Although this does not produce a diatonic scale of nineteen notes, it does uniquely provide a choice of combinations: three different twelve-bell peals (in the keys of B, C# and F#) as well as fourteen- and sixteen-bell peals. They are rung by the Society of Bell Ringers, one of Dublin's oldest organisations, founded as far back as 1670. The 'Ringing Master and Master of the Tower' lead the bell-ringing work. For generations, Dubliners celebrated (and continue the tradition) by ringing in the New Year.[18]

In the Shadow of the Cathedral: Hell!

For many years locals knew the lane behind the cathedral as 'Hell'. There are many stories about this unusual description. One such story related how some of the judges and barristers in the nearby Four Courts (old courts that were near the cathedral) used to live in the area and the heavy sentences passed on some of the poor unfortunates whose lives were quickly extinguished, resonated with people so much that over time the area was known as 'Hell'. Other stories concerned its nearness to Copper Alley and Winetavern Street with their brothels and taverns. It was the exclusive reserve of criminals, lepers, murderers and outcasts, where the ghost of Darky Kelly, a famous brothel-owner, had been spotted many times. She was burnt alive as a witch to end a notorious life.[19]

Philip Dixon Hardy in a letter to the editor of the *Dublin Penny Journal* in 1832 described his experience of walking through 'Hell' on his way to the Four Courts:

I remember, instead of turning to the right down Parliament-street, going, in my youth, straightforward under the Exchange and up Cork-hill, to the old Four Courts, adjoining Christ Church cathedral. I remember what an immense crowd of cars, carriages, noddies, and sedan chairs beset our way as we struggled on between Latouche's and Gleadowe's Banks in Castle-street – what a labour it was to urge on our way through Skinner-row – I remember looking up to the old cage-work wooden house that stood at the corner of Castle-street and Werburgh-street, and wondering why, as it overhung so much, it did not fall down – and then turning down Fishamble-street, and approaching the Four Courts, that then existed, through what properly was denominated Christ Church Yard, but which popularly was called Hell.

This locale of Hell, and this representation of his satanic majesty, was famous in those days even beyond the walls of Dublin. I remember well, on returning to my native town after my first visit to Dublin, being asked by all my playfellows, had I been in Hell, and had I seen the devil. Its fame even reached Scotland, and Robert Burns, in his story of 'Death and Doctor Hornbook', alludes to it when he says – 'But this that I am gean to tell, / Which lately on a night befell / Is just as true as the dell's in hell, / Or Dublin city.'

As Hell has not now any local habitation in our city, neither has the devil – but I can assure you, reader, that there are relics preserved of this very statue to this day; some of it was made into much-esteemed snuff-boxes and I am told there is one antiquarian in our city, who possesses the head and horns, and who prizes the relic as the most valuable in his museum.

The 'Grandest' and 'Finest': St Audoen's

After the Reformation the majority of parishioners remained loyal to the Catholic Church, and in 1615 a new Catholic parish of St Audoen's was estab-

St Audoen's RC Church from Back Lane, c. 1959, seen through a gap in the streetscape caused by the demolition of houses on High Street. (Courtesy of Archiseek)

lished. This is the reason for having two St Audoen's churches in the area (and two St Catherine's, and two St James's). However, the Catholics were obliged to hold their services in secret, mainly in nearby Cook Street. Later in the century celebration of Mass was forbidden and bishops and priests deported, imprisoned or executed. This troubled period for Catholics lasted until the beginning of the nineteenth century.

The Catholic Church of St Audoen's on High Street was built between 1841 and 1846 to the design of Patrick Byrne, who also designed nearby St Paul's Church on Arran Quay and the church of the Immaculate Conception (Adam and Eve's) on Merchant's Quay. A central dome positioned over the crossing of the nave was the main external feature of the church until it collapsed in 1880 and was replaced with a flat roof. Lunette windows high above the walls and next to the coffered ceiling light the interior. The walls are constructed of Black Calp and are best appreciated from Cook Street from where their sheer bulk dominates the area and the medieval City walls. Because of its steeply sloping site, the church has a double level crypt to the rear.[20]

Maurice Craig in his book *Dublin 1660–1860* describes St Audoen's church as 'the last, as it is the grandest monument of the classical tradition in Dublin church building'. Writing of the interiors of nineteenth-century Dublin churches he says 'the finest is undoubtedly Byrne's masterly St Audoen's, High

Street (1841–46)'.[21] The parish priest, Revd Patrick Mooney, (1859–67) completed the delicate and much-admired internal plastering and built the splendid Walker organ.

In 1899 Irish architect George Ashlin added the front portico with its Grecian pillars, statues, piazza and railings to the church. The statue on Our Lady's Altar is the work of Peter Bonanni of Rome and won a gold medal at the Dublin Exhibition in 1853. The pulpit is richly carved and was used for the first great Mission conducted in Ireland. A series of arched windows high up on the interior walls are worth viewing. The interior retains much of its early elegance, with fluted Corinthian pilasters, cornices and high-level windows, and the coffered ceiling with barrel vaulting.

The back of the building looks quite grim and overpowering when viewed from Cook Street where it seems to tower endlessly above the old city wall. A unique feature of the church is the holy water fonts at the main door. They are large seashells, used first as garden ornaments and converted to a more sacred use in 1917. The giant clamshells were donated by a Pacific-Sea captain as a gift to his brother, the parish priest at the time. The great bell of the church won the Gold Medal on of the Royal Dublin Society and is named the 'Liberator' in honour of Daniel O'Connell of Catholic Emancipation (1829) fame. The firm of James Spendi cast it. Devotion to St Anne has been associated with St Audoen's for over 600 years and the present church is the national shrine of the saint.[22]

St Audoen's (C of I)

Situated on the north side of High Street, the principal street of medieval Dublin, adjacent to the Catholic church of St Audeon's, with parts of it nestling up against its towering walls, we have the Protestant St Audoen's church. This historic church is a national monument. This is a most unusual church, in that, firstly, it is invisible from the street, except its impressive clock and bell tower, and secondly, in order to access it, one has to walk down quite a number of steps – it is nearly an underground church. In plan, St Audoen's is roughly a rectangular building with long twin aisles.

The attractive and unusually located St Audoen's Park, in front of the official entrance to the church, was a former graveyard. One of its gates is called Fagan's Gate because Fagan's Castle/Tower was located near this site. From this park one is able to walk the old battlements of the ancient wall of the medieval city of Dublin.

When the church was built it was named after St Audoen, who was the bishop and later patron saint of Rouen, in Normandy, France. On his death on

St Audoen's Ruins, High Street, c. 1900. (Courtesy of National Library of Ireland)

24 August 684, Ouen was buried in Rouen, and a great church was built on the site in the succeeding centuries. The Dublin church of St Audoen's was built between 1181 and 1212, while John Comyn was the first Norman Archbishop of Dublin. However, a ninth-century grave slab, now housed in the church porch, suggests that there may have been an even older church structure on the site. The Guild of St Anne was established in 1430 in St Audoen's.

One of the leading politicians of his time, Sir Roland FitzEustace, Lord Portlester, founded a private chapel in St Audoen's dedicated to the Blessed Virgin Mary. A cenotaph, erected in 1482 by Sir Roland commemorating both himself and his wife Margaret, shows their recumbent effigies. The Portlester Tomb, now housed in the tower, would have been a focal point of his chapel. The tower loft also contains the six bells, three of which have been in use since 1423 (except for the period 1898–1983) and are thus claimed to be the oldest still-used church bells in Dublin. The bells also rang out at curfew time and in times of communal danger. The tenor was tolled each evening at 8 p.m. and was known locally as 'the old cow'. The present clock came from St Peter's church, Aungier Street, after the church was demolished in the early 1980s.[23]

Many members of Dublin's leading municipal families of the sixteenth, seventeenth and eighteenth centuries were buried in St Audoen's and some of their memorial monuments, both elaborate and modest, still survive. United Irishmen, Napper Tandy and Oliver Bond, were both wardens of the church in the late eighteenth century. Tandy was baptised in the church on 16 February 1738. The recently restored seventeenth-century wall monuments of the Sparke and Seagrave families, as well as one of the former Lord Mayor of Dublin, Thady Duff, on the north wall are splendid examples of what the lost monuments probably were like. These commemorative monuments date from 1600 to 1630 and depict members of the families at prayer. There is much detail and the fashion of the era and bowls of exotic fruit, including pineapples, illustrate the wealth of the families. The skull and crossbones at the base of the images are softened with the addition of angels' wings.

Nearby, the stained glass of the east window, dating from the 1848 restoration, portrays the Three Castles of Dublin Corporation's Coat of Arms. From an early age St Audoen's was one of the chapels of Dublin Corporation and the clergy of the church acted as chaplains to the Lord Mayor until the end of the nineteenth century.

The now blocked Foundling's Door of St Audoen's tells the story of how impoverished women of The Liberties could leave their babies in a basket in the door which revolved inwards. The children were then placed in orphanages by the Church.

St Audoen's Ruins, High Street, c. 1900. Notice the pointed turrets on tower, since removed. (Courtesy of National Library of Ireland)

A fine late-Romanesque font stands inside the doorway. A baptismal font, beside the main aisle, dates from 1190 and was re-discovered during the restoration. The gothic arches and windows are a particular feature. The large colourful organ, with the old bellows and bishops' mitres painted on the pipes, sits intrusively near the altar, rather than in its original home near the back of the church.

Opposite the entrance to St Anne's Chapel, the remains of a cobbled lane were revealed during excavations. This ran from the direction of High Street towards St Audoen's Arch, the thirteenth-century gateway in the City Walls. The medieval town of Dublin would have been traversed by such lanes, some of which are still in use, particularly leading off Thomas Street. This one in particular, however, was uncovered during excavations in 1991–2 and is the only example in Dublin in its original state.

Dublin Corporation in 1880 condemned the St Audoen's church tower and would have demolished it had it not been for the public outcry. It was subsequently restored, but without much regard for the original design and four picturesque miniature spires, one on each of the corners of the top of the tower, were not replaced.

According to a notice in the church, the removal of the cross from the small spire on top of the tower by Archbishop Charles Cobbe (1743–1765) provoked a satirical verse, which is attributed to Jonathan Swift:

> Christ's Cross from God's house,
> Cursed Cobbe has pulled down
> And put in its place
> What he worships – the Crown.

Lucky Stone of The Liberties

Between the back of the church and its official entrance, there is the Luck Stone perched up against a wall in a cell-like circular passageway. This is a late ninth-century grave slab adorned with a Greek-style cross. This stood outside the tower of St Audoen's for centuries. It was rumoured to have a supernatural guardian, because, despite being removed a number of times, it has always returned to its rightful place. In 1308 a marble cistern was erected in Cornmarket to provide the citizens of Dublin with their first public water supply (alcohol/beer was hitherto deemed safer to drink). The Lucky Stone was set up beside the cistern so that all who drank the water might have luck. Local merchants believed that success in business depended largely on making a daily visit to touch the stone. In 1826 people from outside Dublin stole the Lucky Stone. However, during the theft, the stone became heavier and heavier until the horse collapsed under the weight and the thieves dumped the stone on waste ground. Later, when workmen attempted to smash it, the stone moaned and rolled. It was set in its present position in the 1860s and it is said the ghosts of clergymen still walk the passageway to protect the stone.[24]

Entrance to Hell: The Forty Steps

Between the two St Audoen's churches we have the famous Forty Steps – the passageway between the interior of medieval Dublin to the area that stretches from Christ Church to St Audoen's church known as 'Hell', the location of brothels and shady taverns.

'A Poem in Stone' – The Remarkable John's Lane

The soaring tower and spire of St John's Lane church on Thomas Street is one of the great landmarks of Dublin. It is unusual in that the tower is rectangular rather than square in shape. Officially known as St John the Baptist and St Augustine, the church's popular name comes from the time when it was forbidden to practice Catholicism and parishioners had to use a clandestine chapel in the adjoining John's Lane. The present building was constructed between 1862 and 1911.

It is unquestionably one of Dublin City's most outstanding pieces of church architecture. John Ruskin (1818–1900) writer, critic, artist and philosopher, who heralded the Gothic Revival movement in Britain, called the church 'a poem in stone'.[25]

Even by Dublin standards the story of John's Lane is a remarkable one. It begins about 1180, with Aelred the Palmer, a Norman living in Dublin. Grateful for a safe homecoming from an arduous pilgrimage to the Holy Land, he founded a monastery of Crossed Friars under the Rule of St Augustine who would also manage a hospital close-by. The monastery was dedicated to St John the Baptist and stood just outside the old Dublin city walls. Just as today the John's Lane steeple is one of the stand-out landmarks in the city, so in medieval times the tower of John the Baptist, or the Magdalen Tower as it was called, at the New Gate caught the eye of every visitor to Dublin. It was sited almost exactly where the present high altar is now positioned. The church is served by members of the Order of St Augustine (known as Augustinians) who have been in The Liberties and Dublin in one way or the other since those early days.[26]

In the middle of the nineteenth century the Augustinians decided to build a new church and the architect Edward Welby Pugin was selected. In this work his partner and brother-in-law George C. Ashling, assisted him. His father was Augustus Welby Pugin (1812–52) one of the chief revivers of Gothic architecture and ecclesiastical art in Britain and Ireland. The design was in the style of thirteenth-century French Gothic, influenced no doubt by Pugin's French Huguenot background. Michael Meade, JP of Great Brunswick Street (now Pearse Street) was the initial contractor and he also built the O'Connell Monument and Vault in Glasnevin Cemetery.

In 1874, with the roof and tower in place, the church opened for public worship. It took until 1895 before the entire exterior was complete and the opening took place on 15 December of that year.

The Fenian Connection

It is said the church was built by the Fenians many of whom were bricklayers and labourers on the job. They even say the pagan John O'Leary was the clerk of works! The building of John's Lane church was begun when many of the senior citizens of the congregation could still vividly recall the events of 1798 and the trial of Robert Emmet in 1803. Many of the men who laid the stones we see today and who laboured on the site, met by night at the house of their foreman, Denis Cromien, in Pimlico to drill in the use of arms and learn the ways of revolution. Cromien came from Carnew, Co. Wicklow and from a family dedicated to Fenianism. His two brothers, Joseph and Laurence, served prison sentences as political prisoners, but he himself avoided arrest.

Highest Steeple in Dublin

In this age of statistics the following may be of interest. John's Lane church is 165ft long and 93ft wide and the nave is 65ft high. The nave columns, which were chosen for their strength and slenderness, are of Cork red marble. The steeple is the highest in the city by virtue of its geographical location and is an impressive 223ft high. Its massive bell-tower holds ten bells weighing almost 6 metric tonnes.[27]

The monastery behind the church is a fine red-brick five-storied building. A feature of its entrance doorway is an ornate biblical-message carving. Along the cobbled lane we look up at the three towering chimneys. Directly below them the date '1878 A.D.' is crafted in blue bricks and at each side is a cross, also crafted in blue bricks, against the red-brick background.[28]

The 1916 Connection

It is also worth noting that the bell-tower has twelve niches for statues of the apostles; the man commissioned to carve these was James Pearse, father of the 1916 Rising patriots Padraig and Willie. One of his assistants was Edmund Sharpe, who later on became expert in the trade and sculpted the beautiful white Carrara marble high altar and the shrine to Our Mother of Good Counsel. The carved detail in front of the main altar is a masterpiece and well worth a closer look.

Across the road from the church at No. 50 Thomas Street, another 1916 leader, James Connolly, founded his Irish Republican Socialist Party.

The Harry Clarke Windows

Apart from the magnificence of the building itself, one of the most striking aspects of John's Lane is the beautiful stained-glass windows. Walking into the church is like going into a forest glade with the light breaking through in lovely colours, so graceful are the pillars and the soaring Gothic arches and so magical the light from the windows. There are four different schools of stained glass represented here.

Pride of place goes to the three windows from the Harry Clarke studio. On the right-hand side going towards the altar the fourth window along is a Harry Clarke. Next to it, just outside the Shrine to Our Lady of Good Counsel is a beautiful window by Michael Healy, a contemporary of Harry Clarke. It represents the major events in the life of St Augustine; the rich colours of this window can really only be seen in full splendour on a sunny summer's morning. The five windows in the apse are the work of Mayers of Munich, noted for the detail in the faces. Looking at them from left to right we see St Patrick baptising Aengus, King of Munster. Behind, we see the Rock of Cashel, seat of the Kings of Munster. Next is St Thomas of Villanova, a Spanish Augustinian famous for his love of the poor. Beside him stand St Augustine and St John the Baptist, joint patrons of the church. Then we have St Nicholas of Tolentine, an Italian Augustinian famous for his devotion to the souls in Purgatory. The last of the five windows depicts St Monica receiving the cincture and passing it on to St Augustine.

The three windows at the Sacred Heart altar are the work of Earley & Son and show us:

1. Jesus appearing and revealing the secrets of his Sacred Heart to St Margaret Mary
2. Jesus saying 'Come to me all you who labour and are burdened, and I will refresh you'
3. Jesus saying 'Let the little children come unto me ...'

Coming back down the church there are a further two Harry Clarke studio windows, the first one at the Shrine of St Rita. Now, go and stand directly in front of the main altar and look down the church to the great window over the entrance.

Like the apse windows, it is the work of Mayers of Munich and is best seen as a complete unit. There are two rows of saints represented. The arch overhead is aflutter with angels' wings.

We have to remember that up to recent times, stained glass windows were called 'the poor man's Bible', teaching the Christian story to those who could not read.

A Mosaic of Images

Due to the brilliance of the windows, soaring arches and graceful pillars, the mosaics in this church sometimes do not get the attention they deserve. Particularly worthy of mention are the two at the Shrine of Our Lady of Good Counsel; the one nearer the outside is one of only two Nativity scenes in the church. The inner, near the altar, is of the Annunciation. It is very similar in style to the Nativity mosaic.

There are some fine mosaics in tile and glass at the Sacred Heart Altar and also at the St Rita of Cascia Shrine. And don't forget to look down; the floor of the sanctuary and both side-altars is an intricate lacework of beautiful tiling with the traditional Augustinian logo/crest depicted in front of the high altar.

Dublin's Most Popular Shrine?

Of the three main shrines in John's Lane church the most popular is dedicated to Our Mother of Good Counsel. There are also the shrines of St Rita of Cascia and the Sacred Heart. The Mother of Good Counsel Shrine – sited to the east of the high altar – is the longer established having been erected in 1898. In 1884 Monsignor Dillon arrived in John's Lane from Rome and urged the community to adopt devotion to Our Lady of Good Counsel. The devotion in its present form goes back to the original shrine at Genazzano in Italy in the fifteenth century.

The Devotion soon became hugely popular with Dublin people and 'special custodians' called Knights of the Shrine were appointed in 1885 to look after the shrine. In May 1900 Dublin's Archbishop Walsh gave his sanction for the establishing of a confraternity of Knights of the Shrine.[29]

John's Lane was the home for many years of Fr F.X. Martin, the leading figure in the efforts to save the Viking remains on nearby Wood Quay from being built over for the civic offices of Dublin Corporation (now Dublin City Council).

Another Augustinian priest, Fr Malachy Cullen, wrote a booklet called *Little Saints of The Liberties*, on all the great mothers of The Liberties and their sheer hard work, courage and determination to bring up their families – 'God's aristocrats', he called them.[30] Padraig Daly is not only an Augustinian priest, but also a poet. And while based in John's Lane he wrote many poems that captured different aspects of the colourful life in The Liberties.[31]

Adam and Eve's Merchant's Quay (Church of the Immaculate Conception)

Evoked by James Joyce in the opening passage of *Finnegan's Wake*, Adam & Eve's with its great green copper dome, like John's Lane and St Audoen's, is a major landmark on the Dublin skyline. The great church we see today was built by James Bolger in 1834 on the spot where the Penal Laws era chapel of St Michael had once stood. Before the Reformation in the 1530s the Franciscans had long been established in The Liberties, particularly in Francis Street on the site of St Nicholas of Myra church. However, they were evicted from there by the Penal Laws, but despite that they continued their ministry in secrecy in the back room of a tavern on Winetavern Street/Cook Street which was affectionately known by the locals as 'Adam and Eve's' to hide the true nature of the activities. Even when the present church was opened by the Franciscans under its official name, people continued and continue to call it 'Adam and Eve's'.

Like so many churches in the area Patrick Byrne designed it in a classically inspired Romanesque style. Over the years it has been modernised and an entrance was opened on Merchant's Quay (its main entrance hitherto had been on Cook Street, and not easily visible on the principle thoroughfare).[32]

St James's Church and the Liberator

James's Street has two churches, both called after St James and practically opposite each other at the Thomas Street end of James's Street. The Church of Ireland one closed its door in recent years. Given the extent of the cemetery behind the church (extending to Usher's Quay) it is not hard to imagine that this was once a large parish.

Daniel O'Connell, the Liberator, laid the foundation stone of the Catholic St James's church in 1844, after being asked to do so by its first parish priest, Fr George Canavan. Over the main door are two corbel heads: one is the Liberator, wearing an Irish crown; the second is of the first parish priest. The parish is an old one, having been established in 1724, which is connected by tradition with the start of the medieval pilgrimage to the shrine of St James of Compostela (Santiago De Compostela) in northern Spain. This was one of the major pilgrimages of Christendom, and one of the most popular in medieval Ireland. The pilgrims' passports were (and still are) stamped there before undertaking the pilgrimage.

During the 1916 Rising, the priests of the parish attended the needs of the signatories of the Irish Proclamation in Kilmainham Jail. Joseph Mary Plunkett, hours before his execution by firing squad at the age of twenty-eight, was married in the prison chapel to Grace Gifford, a Protestant convert to Catholicism. The chalice and ciboria used at their wedding Mass are kept in the church.[33]

The Grand Canal Basin, used by the barges to transport stout from the nearby Guinness brewery, was behind the church, but has been filled in, leaving only a reminder in the name, Basin Street.

In between these two churches there is an obelisk fountain with sundials. As Catholics were forbidden to say prayers in the Protestant graveyard any time there was a mixed-marriage funeral, the funeral cortege had to walk around the fountain three times saying the funeral prayers before the remains were consigned to the grave in the cemetery.

'The Finest Classical Façade of any Church in Dublin' – St Catherine's, Thomas Street

St Catherine's (Church of Ireland) church is situated on a very elevated location, almost on the site of the Abbey of St Thomas. St Catherine's was originally built in 1185. Called a 'sober classic' by John Harvey, the present church was designed by John Smyth in 1760–69, and replaced an earlier ruined church.

St Catherine's is a galleried church (a type common in Dublin from the late seventeenth century). The interior, which is about 80ft by 50ft, is remarkably imposing, and has been called the 'finest classical façade of any church in Dublin, a superbly virile composition in Roman Doric' by architectural historian, Maurice Craig. The pews and the front of the gallery are of carved oak, highly varnished. The organ is large and ornamented, and there are two handsome galleries, one on each side of the organ, for the parish children. The altar stands in a recess, beautifully decorated with stuccowork, and has a handsome arched ceiling, also richly ornamented. Architects Curdy and Mitchell restored the church in 1877 and during the following decade architect James Franklin Fuller undertook a full reordering, during which the old box pews were replaced with open ones.[34]

The church closed in 1966 due to a decrease in the local population and it was de-consecrated the following year. For a period it was used by Dublin Corporation for exhibitions and concerts. After a period of decline, and later of refurbishment, St Catherine's was re-consecrated and has been the place of worship for the Anglican 'CORE' church (City Outreach for Renewal and Evangelism) since then.

The Brabazon Vault

The crypt contains the remains of several of the Brabazon family (the Earls of Meath), long associated with The Liberties. The vault below the chancel holds the remains of the first four Earls of Meath. The original William Brabazon was buried there but there are no monuments to him in the crypt.

In 1803 the church was the site of Robert Emmett's execution – and a plaque commemorating this has the following inscription: 'Robert Emmet, who died in the cause of Irish freedom on 20 September 1803 outside this church'. The funerals of the Young Irelanders, some of the Fenian leaders and patriot Thomas Ashe, stopped here for a moment on their way to Glasnevin Cemetery.

Another plaque bears an inscription to William Mylne (1734–1790), architect and engineer, who with 'uncommon zeal... formed, enlarged and established on a perfect system the waterworks of Dublin.'

The churchyard and cemetery lie to the rear of St. Catherine's. Originally dating from 1552, burials here ceased in 1894. The cemetery is now a small public park.[35]

St Catherine of Alexandria, Meath Street

St Catherine's Catholic church stands as a local landmark near the entrance to Meath Street coming from Thomas Street and was built between 1852 and 1858. St Catherine of Alexandria is the patron saint of philosophers and many are to be found in the area! She was an Alexandrian (Egypt) martyr of the fourth century, who was killed bound to a spiked wheel, with which she is always depicted. Hence the name of the well-known firework - Catherine's Wheel. The original church was on Dirty Lane (Bridgefoot Street) but with the easing of the Penal Laws it moved to Meath Street, seen as a more suitable location. It is quite an ornate church with inside timbered roof, fine stained-glass windows and very elaborately laid out, with massive arches along the aisles. The great east window and west window are most impressive.

It is a beautiful mid-Victorian gothic church. The architect chosen to build it was James J. McCarthy a prolific designer in the nineteenth century who was responsible for many gothic churches and religious buildings in Ireland during the expansion of the Catholic Church in the decades following Catholic Emancipation in 1829. At the time it was built it was noted as 'one of the most important edifices erected in the Dublin metropolis'.[36]

St Catherine's has a fine collection of stained glass and a nationally important collection of stone and marble works. Of particular interest is the high altar window (1862) by the English artist Frederick Borff, a former Anglican priest who was received into the Catholic Church in 1852. He studied ecclesiastical art in Munich before setting up a partnership in Dublin and forming the firm Borff, Beeley & Co.

Of interest are the tall imposing buildings flanking the church, including one serving as the Presbytery.

Patriot Kevin Barry Remembered

Few who visit the church are aware that they are being silently observed from above by a young Republican martyr who was executed during the War of Independence that followed the 1916 Rising. When the church was being renovated in the 1920s a decision was made to place facial impressions of the country's litany of saints at the base of each of the plaster ribs extending up to the ceiling.

They are all there, including St Patrick and St Brigid; yet when it came to St Kevin of Glendalough they were, seemingly, unable to find a suitable image of the man to put up on the wall. The parish priest of St Catherine's had Republican sympathies and knew Kevin's father and this facilitated the placing of Kevin Barry's image in the church. Fortunately there had been a death mask of Kevin Barry after his execution, which provided a suitable compromise. He is the one without the beard.

Like a Scene from the Blitz

In early 2012 there was a major fire at the church after which the parish priest Fr Niall Coghlan said the historical church was 'like a scene from the Blitz' and would cost millions to repair. Rebecca Moynihan, a local City Councillor who lives near the church, said the fire would be a blow to the local community. 'It is

Interior of Meath Street Catholic Church in the early twentieth century. (Courtesy of National Library of Ireland)

a church that is kind of central to the heart of The Liberties and the social life of The Liberties. Many older members of the community use it every day and every Sunday it is still packed out. It's one of the busiest churches in the city', she added. However, in true Liberties spirit, members of the Parish Council involved in St Catherine's said that hundreds of volunteers had come forward immediately to offer their help with the determination that the community would get together to clean up the fire damaged church and get it open again as soon as possible. One of the Parish Council said: 'It will be sorted ... we will build it back up and whatever damage is done will be fixed.' The fire brought out the very best in The Liberties community. One commentator said, 'It is a place where sorrow in one house, is sorrow in every house, and joy in one house is joy in every house. It is a place where everyone knows one another.'[37]

Dublin's Hidden Treasure – St Nicholas of Myra Church

The site on which the present St Nicholas of Myra church is built in Francis Street appears to have been a place of worship from at least the twelfth century, when a timber church existed there. A stone church or monastery that followed the demolition of the timber building was built in 1235 for the Franciscan order by Archbishop John Comyn, successor to Archbishop Laurence O'Toole. The Franciscans remained here for hundreds of years. Following the sixteenth century Reformation its days were numbered and the monastery and lands were confiscated.

In the early eighteenth century, the Franciscans, who had managed to re-acquire their confiscated lands, planned to build a church on the site. The imprisonment of a succession of Dublin bishops during the Penal times delayed building until 1829, the year of Catholic Emancipation, when Fr Matthew Flanagan was parish priest. Archbishop Patrick Russell built the present church as the main church for the archbishop of Dublin. It was built in celebration of Catholic Emancipation in Ireland.[38]

The designer of the church was the architect of Russborough House, John Leeson. The building of the church began in 1829 and the main building was opened in 1834 and dedicated in 1835. The portico and bell tower were added in 1860. Above the bell tower, a twin-faced clock is provided in a copper-covered timber-framed cupola. In its heyday, the clock struck on the hour, utilising the large bell in the belfry below

The opening of a new Catholic church was to become an important social event attended by many from the wealthy and influential sections of Dublin society, indicating a general acceptance of the Catholics' role in contributing to public architecture. 'A very fashionable congregation' which included several

Standing outside St Nicholas of Myra Church, Francis Street, late 1940s. Notice the boy playing marbles beside the footpath. (Courtesy of Dublin City Public Libraries)

Protestant families attended. The music was selected from Masses by Haydn and Mozart, and members of the band of the 1st Dragoon Guards supplemented the orchestra.[39]

John Hogan and Harry Clarke

The building is a fine late Georgian church and classical in conception, with an Ionic portico, pediment, bell-tower and cupola. Inside the colourful church there is a splendid decorated ceiling and a fine altarpiece. One of the interior windows has an image of St Thomas à Beckett, after whom Thomas Street is named. The side altars are decorated with gesso reliefs of the Last Supper and the Marriage of Joseph and Mary, based on Perugine's painting, one by John Hogan and one by Smyth, two distinguished Irish artists. Two marble angels flank the impressive High Altar, built in Italy, also the work of Hogan. Above the tabernacle is the beautiful Pieta, unique in Hogan's oeuvre, and it had the effect of establishing his reputation as a major sculptor in Rome.

Above the sanctuary, the ceiling is decorated with a circle depicting the twelve apostles and the four corners contain pictures of four of the early Fathers of the Church: St Gregory the Great, St Ambrose, St Jerome and St Augustine. The ceiling of the nave is highly decorated with Celtic designs and Christian symbols. Two panels are of particular interest: one depicts the arms of the Isle of Man, reminding us of links with this parish, and the other commemorates the foundation of the Legion of Mary in Myra Hall in 1921. The Nuptial Chapel contains a stained-glass window by Harry Clarke depicting the Marriage of Mary and Joseph.[40]

Santa Claus and Dublin

There is also a somewhat humorous depiction of the life of St Nicholas of Myra or Santa Claus. St Nicholas, a bishop of the third or fourth century, of a town, in present-day Turkey, is depicted in stained glass with three golden balls/bags and an anchor at his feet. The golden bags are a reference to Santa Claus. The anchor can be seen as an indication of the Saint's patronage of the people of Dublin during its seafaring times and as a link to St. Patrick's Cathedral's Myra chapel provided in 1038 by the Danish king to oversee Norsemen returning from their travels.

From 1783 to 1967, when the Coombe Hospital was at its original location nearby, the births of all Catholics born there were registered in this church. Registers for the church began in 1742. Early registers contain baptismal entries for the Isle of Man since the Isle of Man was part of the Archdiocese of Dublin when the church was a pro-cathedral of the city.[41]

Waiting at the gates of St Nicholas of Myra Church, Francis Street, 1957. (Courtesy of Dublin City Public Libraries)

In 1534 Silken Thomas amassed his troops here before an abortive attempt to march on Dublin Castle.

St Luke's Church

The ruins of this church are situated on St Luke's Avenue in the Coombe. The parish of St Luke's was created in 1707. The church was designed by Thomas Burgh and built by John Whimrey in 1714. Many Huguenots of French connection settled in the area around the Coombe and the graveyard was originally a Huguenot place of burial. The parish of St Luke's was united with St Nicholas Without (outside the city walls) in 1862. An almshouse fronted the church called the Widow's House of the Parish of St Nicholas Without and St Luke's. This name is still visible on the building along the Coombe just past the St Luke's Avenue and Deane Street junction. The almshouse closed in the early 1980s and the church itself closed in 1975. Unfortunately both buildings were destroyed by fire in 1986 and only the shell of the church and almshouse remain.

In 2002 the new Cork Street/Coombe relief road carved through the historic site of St Luke's, separating the church from its former main entrance on the Coombe. However, the alignment of this new road through the middle of this site has resulted in a radically new and visually prominent setting for St Luke's. There is an arched gateway at the back of the church connecting onto Newmarket Square.

The Moravian Church, Kevin Street

Situated directly on Kevin Street, opposite the public library, is a large building with tall stained-glass windows. This building has the unusual name of 'The Moravian church' and took its name from a Protestant sect called 'The Moravian Church', sometimes called 'The Unity of the Brethren'. The Moravians had settled in Eastern Germany in the eighteenth-century but came originally from Moravia (hence their name) and Bohemia in the present-day Czech Republic.

The Moravians believed in spreading the message of the Bible to different countries, so in 1746, one of the most famous Moravian preachers, John Cennick, came to Dublin to talk about his faith. He was very charming and many Dubliners came to hear him speak. At first he preached to people outside, then he moved to a hall in Skinner's Alley (Christ Church Place) in The Liberties and eventually built the Moravian church in Kevin Street in 1760 to cater for growing numbers. Masking the earlier meetinghouse, the present building was built in the early twentieth century as a church hall.

On the upper front of the building is a carving of the Lamb of God holding a flag, which is the symbol of the Moravians. The church was closed for religious services in 1959 and the organ is now used in the chapel of Blackrock College.[42]

St Werburgh's Church

St Werburgh's church, Werburgh Street, is arguably Dublin's very best Georgian church. It is quite difficult, however, to obtain a proper vista of the exterior of this splendid church, so it is important to walk down the hill of Werburgh Street past the former Labour Exchange to get a good perspective. The original church on this site was built by the Normans in 1178 and named after the King of Mercia's daughter, Barbara, the Abbess Werburgh (the street name in Irish is *Sráid Barbra*). The church was first mentioned in a letter to Pope Alexander III, dated 1179. The original church was destroyed by fire in 1301 and later rebuilt. It was re-designed by Thomas Burgh in 1715, although it is believed that the main west façade may have been designed by Alessandro Galilei during his visit to Ireland to design Castletown House in County Kildare. The façade is certainly more detailed than Burgh's usual treatment. Following a fire in 1754, further improvements were undertaken. It escaped the intrusion of Victorian stained-glass and the windows contain much of the original clear glass. Consequently, the church's Georgian interior is as interesting as it is attractive.[43]

In 1673 the parish was sued by the King's Bench for not having fire buckets for the protection of buildings in the parish. As was the case in The Liberties, the parish vestry was the local government authority of the area and had responsibility which included the collection of taxes, extinguishing fires and street lighting. The fire engines in the front porch date from as early as 1706. The eighteenth-century organ has unusual golden pipes and a royal crown, flanked by two bishops' mitres.

In the seventeenth century it became the burial place for many important Anglo-Irish families. There was a churchyard next to the church used for hundreds of years and beneath the building itself are twenty-seven vaults. Before the Castle Chapel was rebuilt St Werburgh's was, because it was for a time the Chapel Royal to Dublin Castle, 'one of the most fashionable churches in Dublin; it was regularly attended by the Lord Lieutenant and his suite, and was always densely thronged', according to the historian J.T. Gilbert.[44]

The church has a galleried interior and a fine example of a Gothic pulpit originally designed by Richard Johnston for the Chapel Royal in nearby Dublin Castle. Positioned in a relatively unfashionable area, the building escaped the attentions of the Victorian 'restorers'. The bell in the centre of the aisle bears the name James Napper Tandy, the popular patriot from

1798. By day he was church warden and by night he was one of the leaders of the 1798 Rebellion.

A son of the Viceroy, Viscount Townsend, born at Dublin Castle, was baptised in the church in December 1768 and the (Huguenot) La Touche family, founders and owners of Dublin's largest bank, lived in the parish, in Castle Street. Jonathan Swift, dean of St Patrick's was baptised here, as was John Field, composer and pianist, and Handel played here. Lord Edward Fitzgerald, commander-in-chief of the United Irishman who died in the 1798 Rebellion was buried in the vaults of the church in June 1798, after being waked at Cornmarket. He is buried in a vault allotted to the rectors of St Werburgh's and his coffin, which bore no name, had the initials 'E.F.' scratched onto it by an old man who recognised Lord Edward's aunt, Lady Louisa Connolly, as the sole mourner at his burial. The Guinness family is commemorated inside the church.[45]

St Werburgh's has a very interesting graveyard containing the family plots of prominent Dublin families and the man who captured Lord Edward Fitzgerald, the notorious Major Sirr, is buried here. The strange gravestone of John Edwin, an actor with the Crow Street Theatre, who died of grief after a bad review can also be found, with its inscription; 'Tis strange the mind, that very fine particle, Should let itself be snuffed out by an article.'[46]

Today, St Werburgh's is part of the Christ Church Group of Parishes. The fine building beside the church is the deanery of Christ Church Cathedral.

13

A TOUR OF THE LIBERTIES: BY THE SIGN OF THE LEATHER BOTTLE

A Liberties Sojourn

We will start our tour of The Liberties at Kevin Street, in the shadow of the cathedral and take a circuitous route around The Liberties. From Kevin Street on to Patrick Street/Nicholas Street/Bride Street, down St Michael's Hill (under Christ Church Cathedral arch), turn left along Cook Street to Bridgefoot Street, then back up via Watling Street to High Street, Cornmarket and Thomas Street, on to James's Street, back along Thomas Street to Meath Street, Francis Street, the Coombe, Cork Street, Marrowbone Lane, Newmarket and Weavers' Sqaure, the Tenters, and on to Fumbally Lane, bringing us back to New Street and within sight of St Patrick's Cathedral.

But first, the names. Dunghill Lane, Dirty Lane, Glib Lane, Faddle Alley and Cow Parlour are no more. Ardee Street was once known as Crooked Staff, Back Lane was Rochel Street, Bishop Street was Great Boater Lane, Dean Street was Cross Poddle, Christ Church Place was Skinners Row, Engine Alley was Indian Alley, Oliver Bond Street was Mullinhack (which comes from an Irish translation), Pimlico was Donour Street, Cathedral Lane was Cabbage Garden Lane, Brabazon Street was Cuckold's Row, St Michael's Lane was Macgillamocholmog's Street, Usher's Lane was Dog And Duck Yard, and the list goes on![1]

Other names are still in use and are reminiscent of a bygone era, names such as Brabazon Square, Earl Street, Meath Street, Ardee Street, Weavers' Sqaure, Hanover Lane, Chancery Lane, Lauderdale Terrace, Thomas Street, Marrowbone Lane, Francis Street, Augustine Street, Schoolhouse Lane, Cornmarket, Newmarket, Molyneux Yard, Swift's Alley, Engine Alley, Kevin Street, Bishop Street, Mill Lane, Patrick Street, John Dillon Street, Thomas Davis Court, Clarence Mangan Road, the Tenters, Spitalfields, Blackpitts, Fumbally Lane, Fishamble and Winetavern Streets survive from bye-gone times to give much insight into the history and activities of the area.[2]

One of the Earls of Meath, late nineteenth century. Owner of the lands of The Liberties. The family fortunes blossomed when Henry VIII dispatched the Machiavellian Sir William Brabazon to Ireland as Vice-Treasurer. He established the family at Kilruddery and his grandson was created 1st Earl of Meath in 1627.

The name 'Iveagh', one of the Guinness family titles, lives on in the Iveagh Trust developments which cover much of the area from Patrick Street to New Bride Street.

Streets with Saints' names are in plentiful supply across The Liberties but particularly around this locality where the number of parishes within a short walk of the Cathedral gives some idea of the density of the then population. The parishes of St Michael, John's Lane, St Werburgh, St Nicholas, St Catherine and St Audoen are all reflected in street names in the area as are the parishes of St Bride and St Kevin. Also, the cathedrals of St Patrick and Christ Church and the abbeys of St Thomas and St Francis are reflected in place names.[3]

The Iveagh League:
Kevin Street, Patrick's Street, Nicholas Street & Bride Street

This area includes the major housing initiatives, the Iveagh Buildings, the Iveagh Trust developments, and the adjacent streets.

Kevin Street

The name comes from St Kevin who is long associated with the area. In the twelfth century, when the parish system was first introduced, a parish of St Kevin was established south of the city walls. The ruins of the original St Kevin's church, which dates back to the twelfth century (around the corner from New Bride Street in Camden Row), are well worth a visit. The graveyard contains the remains of Irish martyrs and patriots, including Archbishop Dermot O'Hurley, the family of Thomas Moore and John Keogh, friend of Wolfe Tone, who once owned the land where Mount Jerome cemetery now stands. There are two St Kevin churches on the South Circular Road.[4]

Kevin Street Garda station stands today where Archbishop John Comyn built his palace, called the palace of St Sepuchhre's for the Liberty of the Archbishops of St Sepulchre. The palace of St Sepulchre was home to the Archbishops of Dublin from the end of the twelfth century to 1806 and the Court of the Liberty was held here.

John Comyn, Archbishop of Dublin began building St Patrick's Cathedral in 1011 and the church became a cathedral in 1213. While Narcissus Marsh was Archbishop of Dublin and living in the Palace of St Sepulchre he arranged for his niece, young Grace Marsh, to look after the housekeeping for him. It was from St Sepulchre's Palace in the winter of 1695 that Grace stole out and eloped with her lover. The Archbishop recorded the event in his diary and ended with the words: 'Lord consider my affliction.'[5]

The old Music Library in Kevin Street Public Library. LPs (vinyl records) and flares were in high fashion in the 1970s. (Courtesy of Dublin City Public Libraries)

The old buildings, some with castellated walls and buttresses, reminiscent of the old palace, are from a time when this was a significant centre of ecclesiastical power in Dublin. The site is very important both archaeologically and architecturally. The original palace, within a walled precinct, took the form of a quadrangle and a recent examination by archaeologist Danielle O'Donovan reveals that a large section of this medieval quadrangle still survives, incorporated within the existing buildings (the western wing is particularly intact; see for example the officer's mess, which was part of a large tower). Parts of towers, a chapel, barrel-vaulted cellars, a fine doorway, medieval walls, are being uncovered in excavations. The magnificent gate piers are about all that remains of the old Liberty Court, however.[6] The original 'police station' red lantern hangs over the front of the station itself, side-by-side with the more recent blue 'Garda' one. Across the road from the Garda station is Cathedral Lane, leading to the Cabbage Garden Park, formerly part of a Huguenot cemetery.[7]

The present-day St Patrick's Grammar School is the site of the old Deanery, where Dean Swift lived and wrote for many years. Deanery House is a handsome building, with a small courtyard in front. A nearly-hidden door at the back of the deanery opened on to St Patrick's Close and the entrance to the cathedral. A couple of doors along the street, at 35a, is a fine example of the 'Dutch Billy' dwellings favoured by the Huguenots who settled in the area in the seventeenth and eighteenth centuries.

The Moravian church opposite Kevin Street Public Library is an interesting building. On the front is a carving of the Lamb of God holding a flag, which is the symbol of the Moravians. The Moravians have a cemetery at Whitechurch, at the foothills of the Dublin Mountains. An unusual feature of the cemetery is that all the headstones are lying flat, the opposite to that found in most other cemeteries. The story about members of the Moravian church being buried standing up, so that they would have a head start on Judgment Day, is, sadly, a fiction. The story got around as a result of the Moravian practice, still observed, of marking each grave with a small, flat, square stone giving the simple details of the person buried there. In death as in life, simplicity and equality are part of the Moravian ethos.[8]

Kevin Street Library is another hidden gem in The Liberties: a simple building (1904) of orange-red coloured brick, the roof (partially glass) is surmounted by an iron cupola. Architectural features include an ornate entrance and cut-stone plaques. In early 2012, the cupola, suffering from corrosion, was temporarily removed for restoration.

An old horse trough is still in situ between Marsh's Library and the entrance to Kevin Street Garda station.

The Dublin Institute of Technology (DIT) is built on the site of the original technical school established in 1887.[9] Across the road from it are more of the

Old shop of P. Devereux, Kevin Street, 1960s. (Courtesy of Dublin City Public Libraries)

Iveagh Trust dwellings. The wide-open space at the junction is where the old market took place, and when you visualise the junction without the traffic lights, bollards etc., you would see just how big it must have been.

There is an underground toilet at the junction of Kevin Street and New Street. Closed since the 1960s, it was one of seven similar underground toilets in Dublin. It is an interesting cut stone structure with white tile cladding on the walls. There is also a number of striking circular air vents, now closed, around the edges.

Patrick Street

The name comes from St Patrick's association with the area in the fifth century. It was originally called St Patrick Street. The first university in Ireland was located here from 1320 to 1520. Most of the older buildings on Patrick Street, on the side facing the cathedral, were demolished in the latter half of the twentieth century and replaced by apartments blocks. Many will recall the Glen Abbey clothing factory, Birchall's and MacDonald's pubs and the famous pet shop. Birchall's was at 25 Patrick Street and was the former home of P.J. McCall, the composer of the famous 1798 ballad 'Boolavogue'.

The cathedral side of Patrick Street and Nicholas Street are, however, dominated by many fine red-brick buildings, which are the legacy of the Iveagh Trust and built (1901–1904) by Lord Iveagh of the brewing family, Guinness. They fell into disrepair over the years, but luckily the Dublin City Council made a huge effort at the end of the twentieth century to return them to their former glory.

Charles Dickens' Irish tour in 1858 included a visit to The Liberties. The record of his visit to Patrick Street is incisive:

> Leaving the quaint old Library (Marsh's) with regret, we take a look at the old Deanery House, now a barrack; and descending the hill, turn into the strange quarter Patrick Street, which is sometimes dignified with the title 'St. Patrick's Close'. In this squalid but picturesque ghetto (especially on Saturday nights) every conceivable article, from broken crockery to cast-off clothing, is for sale: the clothes indeed overflow; and the booths, which run along the hilly slope of the irregular street, not being sufficient to contain this collection of rags, the overplus is flung in a promiscuous heap on to a carpeting of sacks, spread out to save the merchandise from the mire of the street.[10]

This was not the first time Charles Dickens had visited Ireland (he had also sent a journalist, George Sala to write on the subject). One of his sketches on the Patrick Street market deals with the fancied autobiography, which he evolved out of a second-hand suit of clothes:

Patrick Street in the 1930s. (Courtesy of Dublin Forum.net)

He fits the coat and the hat with a wearer, and tells a piteous tale. His redun-
dant fancy could, however, hardly conjure a romance out of the heterogeneous
mass of cast-off apparel exposed to view in Patrick Street. The problem is, why
were they ever bought? And again, will they ever be resold–these sordid rags,
these questionable blankets, this infected bedding? The owners and purchas-
ers of such inodorous bundles are adepts in chaffering and cheapening, and to
a stranger their dialect, which belongs to the Coombe, is altogether incompre-
hensible. Buyers and sellers alike present an endless variety of pictures: boys,
like street Arabs, with hardly a shred of clothing, yet with faces Murillo would
have loved to paint; girls with all the grace of girlhood gone; old women, veritable hags, horrible to look at; disfigured as they are by drink; mothers with
babies; babies without mothers, sprawling on the pavement.[11]

The Iveagh Trust Buildings

Near St Patrick's Cathedral, embraced between Bull Alley Street, Patrick Street,
Nicholas Street, Werburgh Street and Bride Street, one can see blocks of very
striking five-storey red-brick buildings with green copper domes and fine
gables. These buildings are called the Iveagh Trust Buildings and the dates of
construction (1901 and 1904) are inscribed on the gable ends.

By the end of the nineteenth century the area between St Patrick's Cathedral
and Werburgh Street had become some of the worst slums in Dublin. Sir Edward
Guinness, a member of the famous brewing family who made Guinness stout
and was one of the richest people in Ireland, knew that many here lived in cold
and damp rooms without a fire or running water and often died prematurely as
a result. To help these people, he set up the Iveagh Trust in 1890 (Sir Edward
had been given the title 'Earl of Iveagh' and that is where the trust and the buildings got their name from). He donated a large sum of money, which in today's
terms would be worth almost €20 million, to build houses for the poorest people
in Dublin.

Land was bought near St Patrick's Cathedral and the area was cleared of the
old slum houses. Building started in 1901 and all houses were finished within a
few years. The buildings were very modern and much healthier to live in than the
old houses. Some of the blocks had shops on the ground floor while the people
lived upstairs.

He built the Iveagh Baths on Bride Road, designed by Joseph Smithem.
Building started in 1905 and the Baths opened in 1906. In 1951 the Iveagh
Trust gave the baths to Dublin Corporation due to increased running costs, and
in 1985 it closed to the public. A UNESCO delegation of architectural experts visiting Ireland in 1991 said the Baths are 'Ireland's most important building from
the Art Nouveau period'. The Quinn Group took over the baths in the mid-1990s
and transformed it into a fitness club.

He also built the Iveagh Markets on Francis Street, where you could buy vegetables, fish and second-hand clothes. The stall-holders from the market in the shadow of the cathedral moved over to the Iveagh Markets. He also designed St Patrick's Close beside the cathedral.

The rents for the flats were cheap and many more people could afford to live in them. The Iveagh Trust used the rents to do repairs and build more homes. In 1943 the Trust stated that they had 808 dwellings, 28 shops and the Iveagh Hostel with 508 beds. They also had a washhouse for the residents' use and to keep the dampness out of people's dwellings. By 1950 almost 3,000 Dubliners lived in dwellings built by the Iveagh Trust. Today the Iveagh buildings are still managed by the Trust.[12]

Bull Alley Street and the 'Bayno'

The street is dominated by The Liberties College, a hugely impressive late Victorian building that is often ignored because of the double screen of trees in front of it. It is without doubt one of Dublin's finest early twentieth-century buildings. The impressive hall and recreation complex known to generations of children as the Bayno was designed by McDonnell and Reid. In 1913 the first Earl of Iveagh opened a play centre for children, which was known locally as 'The Bayno'. The word 'bayno' is a derivation of 'beano' meaning a feast, as a bun and cocoa were given to the children.[13]

The Iveagh Play Centre was the centrepiece of the Iveagh Trust renewal scheme and was finally completed in 1913. The play centre provided enjoyment, education and nourishment to generations of Dubliners until it closed in 1975.

Liberties College began life as a post-primary school in the Myra Hall in Francis Street before moving in 1969 to shared premises with the play centre in Bull Alley Street.

In addition to the centre on Bull Alley Street, Liberties College occupies buildings on Mark's Alley West, which was the former Holy Faith Secondary School.

Famous Composer of 1798 Boolavogue

Patrick Joseph McCall (1861–1919) was a composer and musician from The Liberties, best remembered for his epic ballad of the Rebellion of 1798, 'Boolavogue'. He was also the composer of 'Kelly the Boy from Killanne', 'The Lowlands Low', 'The Boys of Wexford' and 'Follow Me Up to Carlow', songs that have become part of our national ballad repertoire. He was born and reared at 25 Patrick Street, the son of John McCall, a publican and grocer. McCall published five volumes of his poetry, ballads and humorous sketches together with two historical pamphlets relating to Dublin's main cathedrals, St Patrick's and Christ Church. Another publication dealt with the life and times of Zozimus – Michael Moran, the blind poet, who had lived at 15 Patrick Street.

He wrote 'Boolavogue', a song about Father John Murphy, one of the leaders of the Wexford rebels, for the centenary anniversary in 1898. Arthur Warren Darley put his Wexford ballads to music.

He spent his summer holidays in Rathangan, County Wexford, where he mixed with local musicians and ballad singers. He also collected many old Irish airs, but is probably best remembered for his patriotic ballads. He married Margaret Furlong, a sister of the poet Alice Furlong, in 1901.

Besides his famous Irish ballads he was part of the Irish literary and cultural revival at the turn of the twentieth century. 'In the shadow of St. Patrick's': was a paper he read before the Irish National Literary Society, in April 1893. The following year he wrote about Irish Noíníns (daisies). Over the next few years he wrote, *The Fenian Nights' Entertainments, Songs of Erinn, Pulse of the Bards (Cuisle na hÉigse): Songs and Ballads* and *Irish Fireside Songs.*[14]

Larry Dillon, the first chairman of The Liberties Festival, recalled that McCall passionately defended the necessity of protecting, preserving and promoting the community of The Liberties. The centuries-old roots of the people were embedded in the area since long before the time of St Patrick. It was from such a wealth of culture and tradition that society would develop, he had said.

Nicholas Street

Continuing up the hill from Patrick Street we have Nicholas Street. The name comes from the church of St Nicholas Within, built in the twelfth century. It was the location for the high market cross of the city, the symbolic focal point. In the seventeenth century it was a fashionable street on which to live. Unfortunately, by the nineteenth century it had become part of one of the worst slum areas in Dublin. The street is dominated by the ornate Victorian green-domed dwellings. A number of plaques on the walls facing onto Nicholas Street give a fascinating insight and snapshot into the lives of some of the residents over the years.

A fascinating public artwork consisting of twenty-one bronze plaques on the walls of the Iveagh Trust Buildings at Patrick Street, Nicholas Street, Ross Road, Bride Street and Bride Road, was unveiled in 2009. Artist Chris Reid created the permanent public artwork that was commissioned through Dublin City Council's Public Art Programme, arising from the refurbishment of these buildings. The texts on the plaques are based on recordings the artist made from 2004 to 2008 with residents and people associated with the area.

According to Chris Reid:

These flats, which were due for demolition in the early 1990s, were saved on the grounds that they were considered to be a part of Dublin City's architectural heritage. These flats are social housing and though many residents left after the refurbishment in the late 1990s some of those who remained are directly descended from the families that moved into the flats when they were originally built in 1905. Many other residents have families and connections living in The Liberties for many generations.[15]

However, he was of the view that the voices of these local people are generally not heard or included in the heritage of their area.

One plaque tells of a recovering drug addict who plans a new life for his family. In another, a man shares a joke through his first-floor window with curious bus tourists. Other plaques address hidden histories, and one speaks of the influence of the Catholic Church over family planning and its sometimes tragic repercussions. In another a woman recounts the changed behaviour and silence of returned British Army soldiers after the First and Second World Wars. Some plaques tell of everyday actions that have since been forgotten like the co-operation between women on each floor to keep the halls clean. Other plaques map social and physical aspects of the area that have since been transformed. One plaque lists venues where a woman in the 1940s danced and socialised – all of which have since disappeared. Altogether these plaques attempt to give historical significance to these local voices by making monuments to the ordinary.

On Nicholas Street, a plaque reads: 'The hill was steeper, the street narrower. The surface was all cobblestones. When winter weather made them freeze, horses struggled to climb. Sparks flew from their hooves.' And another on Ross Road:

> From the time I was born Moggy was there. I'd be swinging on the lamp post (or scutting the back of the coal lorry) and she'd be sitting there at the window her dog beside her, watching the kids and the people. She had six kids herself and she was left a young widow. She'd wash the dead or anything to earn a shilling to rear them and if she never had a shilling she was always in good form. She'd go around for a few glasses of stout at Corbett's and would come around singing.[16]

Werburgh Street

Across from Patrick Street/Nicholas Street we have another ancient street of The Liberties, Werburgh Street (Werburgh: *Sraid Barbra* in Irish), which is one that is often over-looked. For many years it was just associated with the Social Welfare Office – 'The Labour Exchange' or 'the scratcher' or 'signing on' or 'the labour', as it was widely known. It is also home to Dublin's oldest chipper, Burdock's (founded 1913).

Nowadays people tend to just pass through it on the way somewhere else, but it used to be of great importance due to its location within the immediate vicinity of Dublin Castle. The name derives from St Werburgh's church, called after the Abbess Werburgh, a daughter of a twelfth-century Norman king who built the church.

According to the historian, Gilbert:

> The buildings forming Hoey's Court were erected in the seventeenth century, apparently by Sir John Hoey, founder of the family of Hoey of Dunganstown, county of Wicklow. Jonathan Swift was born, on the 30th of November 1667, at the house of his uncle, Counsellor Godwin Swift, No. 9 in this court, which at that period was inhabited by some of the chief lawyers of Dublin. Robert Marshall, third Sergeant of the Exchequer, who resided here from 1738 to 1741, was the friend of Swift's 'Vanessa'. The Guild of Glovers and the Corporation of Brewers had their public halls till late in the last century in Hoey's-court, where William Ruxton, Surgeon-General, resided till his death in 1783, and on the north side of which stood Eade's tavern, closed about 1813.[17]

There is a wall plaque at the Dublin Castle gates at Ship Street Little commemorating Swift's birthplace. Across the road there are a number of wall panels illustrating one of the most famous sieges in Irish history – the 1534 attack on Dublin Castle by Silken Thomas.

The 'Goldsmiths Hall' (commemorated by Golden Lane) and office of the Dublin Assay Master were, until the late eighteenth century, in the house nearly opposite Hoey's Court. Round the corner, in a lane just off Werburgh Street, the Phoenix Tavern was one of the most fashionable and most frequented houses of its time in Dublin in the mid-eighteenth century.

In Cole's Alley, the passage from Hoey's Court to Castle Street, was the Royal Chop House, a tavern much frequented for billiards about 1768, according to Gilbert.

Gulliver's Medallions and Bride Street

Werburgh Street leads to Bride Street, mentioned in 1465 as Synt Bryd Street, a name derived from the parish church of St Brid (Brigid) rebuilt in 1684 and demolished in 1898. At the junction of Bride Street and Werburgh Street, just beyond the red-bricked Iveagh Trust Flats, there was a curious gateway with the inscription Derby Square. The gateway entered a covered passage which opened on to a small square at the rear. A school stood at one time in this square in which the poet James Clarence Mangan received his early education. Unfortunately, this historic site is now just a car park.

Just down the hill a few metres, a pub was named after the United Irishman, Napper Tandy, and was located at 100 Bride Street for many years until demolished by the developers at the end of the twentieth century. There was also a

Bride Street, with Iveagh Trust Buildings on the left, 1950. Behind the boys is St Patrick's Park. (Courtesy of Dublin.ie Forums/bridge)

popular huckster shop called Johnny Foxes where you could buy practically anything. These shops were a feature all over The Liberties.

Much of one side of the street consists of the red-bricked Iveagh Trust buildings. Across the road, the City Fathers in recent years have built new and very ornate red-brick dwellings using the very best of materials. The new Bride Street dwellings have some beautifully artistic depictions representing scenes from *Gulliver's Travels*. Cartan Ceramics, a company made up of graduates from the nearby National College of Art and Design in Thomas Street, produced them. About halfway up and stretching the length of the façade, they consist of fixed large rounded sculpted disks. While he wrote may works, mostly of a satirical nature, Jonathan Swift is probably best known for *Gulliver's Travels*. The original name he chose for the book was rather more long-winded: 'Travels into Several Remote Nations of the World, in Four Parts, by Lemuel Gulliver'![18]

Chancery Lane

Chancery Lane was so-named because of its nearness to Derby Square where there was the Examiner's Office of the Court of Chancery in the eighteenth century. Many important lawyers lived in the street during that century. Archaeologist Claire Walsh discovered an early-medieval stone-lined well and a remarkable pre-Viking roadway here, which may be related to the early monastic site of Duibhlinn, from which the city takes its name.

Golden Lane

Further along Bride Street we come to the junction with Golden Lane, so named because goldsmiths practised here in medieval times. It was originally known as Crosse or Cherry Lane. In the early 1800s the company of goldsmiths housed the assay office at No. 22 until it moved to the Custom House in 1838. In 1885, as part of a Royal Commission on the conditions of the working classes, the Prince of Wales and his son visited the area. The story is told that some of the disgruntled tenement dwellers in the area threw sewage in front of the prince as he was stepping out of his carriage. The unfortunate prince slipped and there were many red faces in the visiting party!

The Golden Lane/Bride Street junction has a stone monument with a plaque dedicated to John Field and opposite St Patrick's Park we have John Field Road. It was said that John Field was 'abandoned to his inspiration'.[19] He was undoubtedly Ireland's greatest contribution to the Romantic era, composer of the nocturne. He was born in Golden Lane, Dublin in 1782 and baptised in Werburgh Street church. He grew up to become an eminent pianist, composer, and teacher. His family was quite musical; his father, Robert Field, earned a living as a violinist in Dublin theatres and his grandfather, also named John Field, was a professional organist. With the latter, Field had his first piano lessons. Later he studied with Tommaso Giordani, who was in charge of music in St Nicholas of Myra church on Francis Street, the seat of Dublin's Catholic archbishops. In March 1792, he made his first appearance as a performer in Dublin, a performance which was well-received. By the end of the following year, Field's family had moved to London. In the English capital, young Field began his studies with Muzio Clementi, an apprenticeship probably secured through Giordani.

A plaque commemorating John Field at corner of Golden Lane. John Field (1782–1837) was an Irish pianist, composer, and teacher. He was born in Dublin's Golden Lane, in the shadow of St Patrick's Cathedral.

Under his tutelage, Field quickly became a famous and sought-after concert pianist; together, master and pupil visited Paris, Vienna, and St Petersburg. The Russian capital impressed Field so much that he eventually decided to stay behind when Clementi left, and from about 1804 was particularly active in Russia.

Field was very highly regarded by his contemporaries and his playing and compositions influenced many major composers, including Chopin, Brahms, Schumann, and Liszt. He is best known today for originating the piano nocturne, a form later made famous by Chopin, as well as for his substantial contribution, through concerts and teaching, to the development of the Russian piano school.

He gave his last concert in March 1836 and died in Moscow almost a year later, on 23 January 1837, from pneumonia. He was buried in the Vvedenskoye Cemetery. Once when asked what his religion was, Field replied with a characteristic pun: 'I am not a Calvinist, but a Claveciniste' (Claveciniste is the French for harpsichordist).

According to the great composer Franz Liszt:

None have quite attained to these vague eolian harmonies, these half-formed sighs floating through the air, softly lamenting and dissolved in delicious melancholy. Nobody has even attempted this peculiar style, and especially none of those who heard Field play himself, or rather who heard him dream his music in moments when he entirely abandoned himself to his inspiration.[20]

Molyneux House

Further along Bride Street we come to the unique building of Molyneux House, on part of the site of former home of Lord Thomas Molyneux, Physician General to the army in Ireland and younger brother of William Molyneux the philosopher and patriot who castigated Ireland for being bound by English Acts of Parliament. It was later owned by a circus promoter. It then became a home for the aged, and later still was occupied by the Salvation Army and Jacob's biscuit manufacturers. Behind its modern façade, one will also find the remnants of a long-forgotten church, St Bride's church. This area was once known as 'Lousey Acre'. The building was developed by leading (and controversial) architect Sam Stephenson, whose other landmark projects in Dublin included the Central Bank of Ireland in Dame Street, the Currency Centre in Sandyford and the Bord na Móna building in Baggot Street – and of course, the hugely controversial Wood Quay development.

Just around the corner from this building we have Peter Street and the front façade of the old Adelaide Hospital and across the road is the remainder of the wall of the Huguenot Cemetery that occupied a plot here for generations.

The Oldest Bird Market in the World

The Dublin Bird Market has been held on Bride Street/Peter Street for over 100 years and is said to be one of the oldest in the world. The renowned Irish artist, John Butler Yeats (father of W.B. and Jack B.) produced an oil painting in 1886 called 'The Bird Market'. The sympathetic scene shows a number of children ,including a barefoot girl, carrying bird cages and looking for buyers.[21] Bringing children to enjoy the bird market has been a long tradition in Dublin and the market is still flourishing, held every Sunday morning from 10.00–12.30 p.m. Here you will see bird fanciers gathering at the corner of Peter Street near the old Jacob's biscuit factory, where they hang their cages with canaries, budgies, parrots and pigeons, finches, love birds and other exotic species. The market probably originated with the Huguenots who had settled in the area (notice the plaque for the former Peter Street Huguenot Cemetery). They were renowned for their interest in bird-keeping and may well have brought the magnificent Lizard Canary to Dublin.

It is rumoured that years ago some local birds were often painted and sold as African and other exotic birds, but Noel Haughton, who has been actively involved in the bird market for over fifty years, discounts that. The sound of the sweet-singing birds on a Sunday morning against the backdrop of the cathedral bells of St Patrick's or Christ Church makes for a fascinating harmony.[22]

For many years, there was also a pub nearby called, appropriately enough, 'The Aviary'.

The National Archives in Time

The National Archives of Ireland is located on Bride Street and Bishop Street. The building stands on the site of the former Jacob's biscuit factory, a Dublin institution from the 1850s until it was destroyed by fire in 1987. The rebel forces occupied it during the Easter Rising in 1916. Jacob's factory is remembered on some of the old retained brickwork with the name 'W & R Jacob and Company Ltd' emblazoned on them. The documents held in the Archives help to provide an understanding of the social, economic and political history of Ireland. The National Archives was formed in 1988, when the Public Record Office (founded 1867, formerly at the Four Courts) and the State Paper Office (founded 1702, formerly at Dublin Castle) were merged to create a single institution.

Many of the archives accessioned by the Public Record Office of Ireland before 1922 were destroyed by fire and explosion at the beginning of the Irish Civil War in June 1922. Consequently, the archives that are now held by the

National Archives date mainly from the nineteenth and twentieth centuries, although some date back as far as the thirteenth century.[23]

On the external wall of the building, at the corner of Bishop Street and Bride Street there is a two-faced clock, made by Stokes in Cork, with a white face and aluminium encasing, that makes a striking statement as to the function of the building.

The Man in the Cloak and My Dark Rosaleen

Still on Bride Street we are near to where poet James Clarence Mangan (1803–49) was found sick in his rooms and brought up to the Meath Hospital to die. He was born at 3 Fishamble Street and lived in Hoey's Court, near Werburgh Street, for some time. He went to school at Derby Square off Werburgh Street and St Saul's Court behind St Catherine's church, Thomas Street. He lived his latter years in Chancery Lane, nearly opposite St Patrick's Park. He left school prematurely to help his impoverished family. While working in a scrivener's office, he began studies of European languages[21] and it was at this time that he adopted the name 'Clarence'. He had been baptised as James, but he used the adopted 'Clarence' constantly to sign his poems, quoting Shakespeare's Richard III: 'Clarence is come, false, fleeting, perjured Clarence'.

His poetry appeared in *The Comet*, the *Dublin Penny Journal*, and the *United Irishman* and in the first and subsequent editions of the Young Irelander's *The Nation* newspaper. In 1859, the Young Irelander, John Mitchel, edited Mangan's poetry, including his 'Dark Rosaleen' (his most famous poem with the starting lines: 'O my dark Rosaleen, do not sigh, to not weep...') and 'Woman of Three Cows' for a New York edition. He is Ireland's most prolific poet and wrote over 1,000 poems.

An eccentric in dress and habits, Mangan was frequently seen in the streets of The Liberties and the surrounding area dressed in a large pointed hat and a cloak, while a pair of dark green spectacles emphasised the paleness of his features. He was said to have carried two umbrellas, even in the warmest weather.

W.B. Yeats admitted that Mangan had been an important influence on him. James Joyce was also influenced by him and read a paper on Mangan to the Literary and Historical Society of UCD in 1902.

Mangan began drinking heavily early in life and also became addicted to opium. He often lay in the gutters of Bride Street and Peter Street totally debilitated. He fell victim to the cholera epidemic during the Famine (1845–9) and died in the Meath Hospital, yards from his home.[25]

There is a memorial to James Clarence Mangan in St Stephen's Green. It was the last work completed by James H. Pearse, the father of 1916 Rising leader, Patrick Pearse. It is an unusual piece of sculpture with two heads, one of the poet and the other, below his, of 'Roisin Dubh', his 'Dark Rosaleen'. There is also a road in the Tenters called Clarence Mangan Road, and Clarence Mangan Square is beside John Dillon Street.

The Street with One Address: Canon Street

Canon Street was for many years Dublin's shortest street. It was beside a pub off Bride Street and near St Patrick's Park. It was originally named Petty Canon Alley in the 1750s after the minor canons of St Patrick's Cathedral. A minor canon is a member of the clergy who 'assists in the daily services of a cathedral but is not a member of the chapter'. The street had just one address, the public house of Messrs Rutledge and Sons, and was described by the *Irish Press* in 1949 as the 'shortest street in the world' and in 1954 by *The Irish Times* as the 'shortest street in Europe'.[26] The pub was demolished and so the street disappeared in the late 1960s to make way for the widening of Bride Street.

St Patrick's Close

St Patrick's Close is a quaint curved road linking Patrick Street via the entrance to St Patrick's Cathedral to Kevin Street. It was built in 1864–69 as part of the cathedral's restoration and the main entrance to the cathedral is to be found here. The figure of Sir Benjamin Lee Guinness, the benefactor for the church's restoration, is on a plinth between the entrance and the cemetery. In his hands he is holding the plans for the restoration. Opposite the entrance is the Cathedral Choir school, founded in 1432. Further along the road is a graveyard containing a number of interesting gravestones and beyond that we come to the entrance gate leading up some steps to Marsh's Library, the oldest public library in Ireland.

In springtime, St Patrick's Close, with the blossoming trees along the tree-lined road, is particularly picturesque. To call the scene 'a jewel in The Liberties crown' is quite apt.

There is a black door in the wall behind the deanery with the words, 'The Vicarage', barely visible. This door leads to the vicarage, a smaller building next door to the deanery. There is an old granite horse trough together with granite bollards on the corner with Kevin Street. This was erected in 1882 in thanks to those who 'dedicated their lives to the protection of animals'.

Marsh's Library

Tucked away behind St Patrick's Cathedral in St Patrick's Close, and hidden behind a garden and entrance gate, is Marsh's Library. It was the first public library in Ireland and was built by Archbishop Narcissus Marsh (1638–1713) in 1701. Archbishop Marsh wanted to open a library for what he called 'publick use, where all might have free access seeing they cannot have it in the College'. The library was designed by Sir William Robinson (who also designed the Royal Hospital in Kilmainham). The interesting fact about Marsh's Library is that it has always been used as a library and is therefore one of the very few eighteenth-century buildings left in Dublin that is still being used for its original purpose. Jonathan Swift was governor of the library for many years.[27]

Marsh's Library contains many old and very valuable books, which were either bought by Archbishop Marsh or given to the library by other collectors. The library contains mostly books on religion, medicine, law, science, mathematics and music because these were the areas people were most interested in at that time. Many of the collections in the library are still kept on the shelves allocated to them by Marsh and by Elias Bouhereau, the first librarian, when the library opened. There are four main collections, consisting of 25,000 books relating to the sixteenth, seventeenth and the early part of the eighteenth century.

The inside of the library has changed very little since 1701. It has a scholarly atmosphere, heavy with the scent of leather and age. Walking in the door is like stepping back in time. Many of the books are still kept on the same shelves where they had been placed in the eighteenth century. It is a fine example of an early scholars' library with oak bookcases having carved and lettered gables topped by a mitre.

As books were very expensive then, the ones on the lower shelves were chained to a rod so that they could not be stolen. If you wanted to read one of the most valuable ones, you had to go to a small room at the side of the library where you would be locked in so that you could not steal the book. These rooms are called the 'cages' and are still there today.

Archbishop Marsh left strict instructions as to how the library should be run and he also gave the following rules for the use of the library:

> All Graduates and Gentlemen shall have free access to the said Library on the Dayes and Houres before determined, Provided They behave Themselves well, give place and pay due respect to their Betters, But in case any person shall carry Himself otherwise (which We hope will not happen) We order Him to be excluded, if after being admonished He does not mend His manners.[28]

There is also a ghost in the library and this is how it came about. One day, when Archbishop Marsh lived on his own in his bishop's palace, his niece Grace came to visit and stay with him for a while. She was only nineteen years of age, and she fell in love with a clergyman from Castleknock. She ran away with him and got married secretly. Archbishop Marsh was very upset and his niece felt guilty, so she wrote him a long letter explaining her actions. She left it in one of his books but the archbishop could not find it and so every evening his ghost revisits the library to search through the books for the letter ... but only when the library is closed.

Street Scene, Patrick Street, *c*. 1900. (Courtesy of NLI)

The Liberty Bell: St Patrick's Park and Well

St Patrick's Park beside the cathedral on Patrick Street now occupies the
ground where slum buildings once stood and was created at the time of the
building of the Iveagh Trust complex. It is a haven from the hustle and bustle
of the city. The well was rediscovered in renovation in 1901. It was believed
that St Patrick baptised people here and that is why the church was built and
named after him. In the park there is an interesting decorative brick-faced wall,
a veritable literary parade. The wall is set with various plaques inset into each
arched niche celebrating many of the most well-known Irish writers.[29]

Close to the literary parade is the Liberty Bell, a fine piece sculpted by Vivienne
Roche, that was erected in 1988 to commemorate Dublin's millennium. Outside
the park on the footpath is a piece of sculpture shaped like a bishop's mitre, commemorating St Patrick.

Overlooking the park we have one of Dublin's finest buildings that for the past
thirty years has been the home to The Liberties College. The tree-lined roadway
is called Bull Alley Street and was first mentioned in 1667 records as Bell Alley.
This name might seem appropriate, as the location is adjacent to the cathedral.
The name was recorded as Bull Alley in 1673, and later as Ball Alley. But in
Brooking's map of Dublin for 1728 and Rocque's subsequently, it reverts to Bull
Alley. It was also called Bull Lane.[30]

By the Sign of the Leather Bottle

Within and Without

At the top of the Nicholas Street hill opposite Christ Church Cathedral we have the remaining wall of the old St Nicholas Within church (as opposed to St Nicholas Without church on St Luke's Avenue, The Coombe). St Nicholas Within is a former Church of Ireland parish church. It was located at the corner of Nicholas Street and Christ Church Place, where part of its entrance may be seen next to the Peace Garden.

The original church was built in the eleventh century by Bishop Donat and was dedicated to St Nicholas of Myra, the patron saint of sailors. It received its name during the episcopate of Alexander de Bicknor (1317–1349), when the parish of St Nicholas was extended outside the city so as to include the Liberty of St Sepulchre and the Deanery of St Patrick. The parish was divided into two parts: St Nicholas Within the Walls and St Nicholas Without. It was the smallest parish in Dublin, measuring 5 acres.[31]

Around the corner past the little park on the left we have Christ Church Place, once called Skinners Row (i.e. the street of the skinners or those who traded in hides and leather. There was also a Shoemakers Lane nearby off Nicholas Street that ran parallel to Skinners Row). Until the 1820s it was a

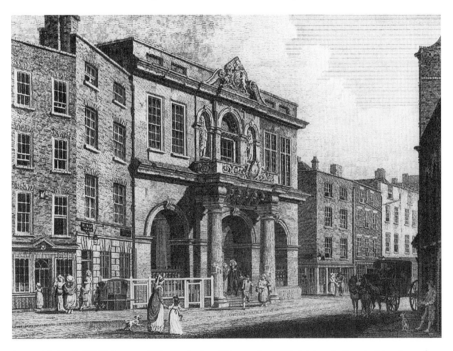

James Malton's 1798 image of The Tholsel at Skinners Row (Christchurch Place). (Courtesy of Dublin City Libraries/NLI)

fashionable street with booksellers, jewellers and goldsmiths having their businesses here. However, in 1821 Skinners Row was partly demolished to facilitate row widening and was re-named as Christ Church Place.

Archaeological excavations have revealed early evidence of tanning and leather works in this area and the tradition was maintained well into the twentieth century with Winstanley's Shoes across the road in Back Lane.

Skinners Row was also an important location for the Tholsel, which was taken down around 1806 because it had become unsafe. The Tholsel was the forerunner to the City Hall and it kept the 'Chain Book' of city laws and regulations. The Tholsel also held the town clock. According to Maurice Craig, in his book *James Malton's Views of Dublin*, it was built as the then equivalent of the City Hall in 1676, to a pattern familiar from the Middle Ages onwards in many English towns: an open arcade, surmounted by accommodation such as council-room, court-room and rudimentary offices. It was also deemed unsuitable because the Courts sat in the same building and 'attracted the most vicious of people' according to a contemporary report. Moreover, the kitchens below the offices emanated all sorts of distracting aromas in the course of preparing meals for ceremonies above. In 1765 Dublin Corporation was supplied with a plot of land adjacent at Cork Hill to build a new City Hall.[32]

Dublin's Best Coffee House

Music publishing began in Ireland around 1686 with one Robert Thornton at the Sign of the Leather Bottle on Skinners Row. Music publishing and indeed general publishing in Dublin benefited from the absence of any copyright laws, and pirated editions of works (including music) first published in London were commonplace. By 1730 Skinners Row, Dame Street and College Green had a considerable concentration of booksellers and publishers, possibly thirty-five or so, an extraordinary number for a city the size of Dublin at the time. Here in 1551 was printed the *Book of Common Prayer*, the first book to be printed in Ireland.

On the site of what is now Jury's Inn once stood Dick's Coffee-house, where auctions of books, land, and property were once held. The owner of the coffee-house, one Richard Pue, published a paper called *Occurrences*. The eighteenth-century newspaper claimed to contain 'the most authentick and freshest translations from all parts, carefully collected and impartially translated'. The first edition was published on 25 December 1703, in partnership with Edward Lloyd, and was predominant among Dublin newspapers during the eighteenth-century, ceasing publication in the 1790s.

Pue was certainly active in book auctions by this time and John Dunton described him thus: 'he is a witty and ingenious man, makes the best coffee in Dublin ... and has a peculiar knack at bantering, and will make rhymes to any thing'. Nothing is known for certain about his life before then. Pue was as much a printer, publisher and editor as a coffee-house proprietor. Dick's and other such establishments were central to political and journalistic discourse during this period, according to Henry Boylan of the *Dictionary of Irish Biography*. [33] Dick's Coffee House developed to become one of the main auction houses in Dublin, known especially for book auctions. However, in 1747, according to Edmund Burke, Pue was sitting in a shop under Dick's Coffee-house when the back-house fell in and buried Pue, the coffee-house keeper, and his wife in the ruins. [34]

The Lord Edward

On the corner of Christ Church Place and Werburgh Street, we have the landmark pub, the Lord Edward, which also contains Dublin's oldest seafood restaurant. This is an interesting old tavern on three levels. The ground floor is a 'locals' bar with interesting pub furniture and wall images including one advising on the 'Nine Pints of the Law'. The next floor, officially the lounge bar, has Tudor-style windows and is a veritable gallery to the 1798 Rebellion, with old posters and artifacts relating to Lord Edward Fitzgerald and Robert Emmet and the 1798 United Irishmen. Here you will find framed pictures from the mid-to-late nineteenth century with titles such as 'Illustrious Sons of Ireland' and 'The United Irish Patriots of 1798'. Images of Emmet, Tone and Lord Edward are celebrated and some swords remind one of the battles for Irish freedom that took place in The Liberties. Over the fireplace is a rare copy of the 1803 Proclamation read by Robert Emmet on 23 July 1803 in Thomas Street. This marked the commencement of the Rising of 1803 by the United Irishmen against British rule. The Proclamation was called 'The Provisional Government to the People of Ireland'.

Across from the Lord Edward we have the Bull and Castle Pub, owned by the long-established F.X. Buckley butchers. This was the site of No. 3 Fishamble Street where the famous poet James Clarence Mangan was bon in 1803. There is an interesting picture gallery inside the pub illustrating aspects of the butcher's trade in the mid-twentieth century.

Millennium Child

At Christ Church Place and beside the old ruined wall of St Nicholas' church, we have the miniature park and a sculpture of children playing. Called the 'Millennium Child', the sculpture is a celebration of children in the new Millennium. It was unveiled by the President of Ireland, Mary McAleese in November 2000. The artist was John Behan.

Fishamble Street and Copper Alley

Across the road from Christ Church Place and at the side of the cathedral, we have Fishamble Street (a shamble or stall from which fish was sold) and Dublin's oldest street, Copper Alley. Copper Alley today runs through the reception area of the Harding Hotel, and parallel with Lord Edward Street. It is still possible to follow this route today. It dates from the thirteenth century and follows the route of an earlier Viking street. The junction of Fishamble Street and Werburgh Street was a major crossroads inside the early Viking settlement. In the fifteenth century the lane was known as Preston's Lane but by the early seventeenth century it became known as Copper Alley, taking its name from the money minted there. The area was famous for taverns and eating houses, the most famous being the Unicorn Tavern. Handel's *Messiah* was performed in the music hall off Copper Alley at Fishamble Street in 1742.[35]

Copper Alley was also home to the infamous eighteenth-century brothel run by a woman called 'Darkey Kelly'. The building from where she carried on her business was originally called the Maiden Tower. In 1746 she was publicly executed for the alleged murder of her child.

For generations Darkey (real name Dorcas) Kelly was known in Liberties folk memory as the woman who was burned at the stake for witchcraft after she accused the Sheriff of Dublin, Simon Luttrell, of fathering her baby.[36] It is said that the notorious madam of the brothel called 'The Maiden Tower' (now home to Darkey Kelly's pub) became pregnant, she alleged, as a result of a liaison with Luttrell, a member of the notorious Hellfire Club, which held meetings on the isolated Montpelier Hill in the Dublin Mountains. When she demanded his financial support he refused to acknowledge the child and instead accused Kelly of witchcraft and the murder of her baby – though no body was produced. She was sentenced to death and burned alive in front of a jeering rabble.[37]

However, Eamon McLoughlin, the radio producer of a documentary *No Smoke Without Hellfire* questioned the authenticity of this story. He and fellow researcher Phil O'Grady had made new discoveries having read contemporary newspapers in the National Archives. He said their findings 'debunks the tale, passed on down the centuries, that Simon Luttrell, known as Lord Carhampton, was the principle cause of her execution.' Contemporary newspapers revealed, he argued, that Darkey Kelly was accused of killing John Dowling, a shoemaker. Investigators then found the bodies of five men hidden in the vaults of her brothel. After her execution prostitutes rioted on Copper Alley.[38]

Either way, she seems to have led an incredible life and the legend of the infamous Darkey Kelly lives on in the folklore of The Liberties. Some still say that Darkey has been seen here, wandering the streets of Medieval Dublin and making her way to the side gate of St Audoen's (C of I) church at the end of the forty steps, the place where unwanted babies were traditionally abandoned.

Walking down Fishamble Street brings us to the rear of the former SS Michael and John church, which was built on the site of the famous Smock Alley Theatre which originally opened its doors in 1662. It was the first custom-built theatre in the city and still remains in substantially the same form, making it one of the most important sites in European theatre history. While it was in operation as a theatre, it gave the world the plays of George Farquhar, Oliver Goldsmith and Richard Brinsley Sheridan, and the brilliant performances of Peg Woffington, Thomas Sheridan, Spranger Barry and Charles Macklin. The theatre closed in 1787. The building was then used as a whiskey store until Fr Michael Blake bought it for use as a church. When the bell tolled in 1811, eighteen years before Catholic Emancipation, this was the first Catholic bell ringing in Dublin in nearly 300 years.

In the early years of the twenty-first century, the church's role as a place of worship ceased and a new Smock Alley Theatre opened in its place. The building still boasts ornate stained-glass windows, the original ceiling plasterwork and the bell over the entrance. They remain in the Smock Alley as a witness of its time as a church. Scenes from the famous story of Dublin in 1913, based on the James Plunkett book, *Strumpet City*, were filmed here.

Winetavern Street

Crossing the road from Copper Alley at Christ Church Cathedral we come to Winetavern Street, which runs from St Michael's Hill to Wood Quay and until late in the twentieth century was cobble-stoned. The name derives from the number of taverns on the street. In 1185 the Abbey of Thomas Court was granted a tax from ale and mead sold in the local taverns. Originally the Guild Hall (later called The Tholsel) stood here before being transferred to Skinners Row on the opposite side of the cathedral. In the early nineteenth century tall and narrow red-brick houses were built here which survived until the late twentieth century. It was also the site for second-hand clothes merchants. One of Dublin's most famous pawnbrokers, known far and wide as 'the Bicycle Pawn Office' was located here. It advertised, 'one could pledge one's piano there if one had a mind to'. There were also pawnbrokers in Ardee Street and the Coombe.[39]

Although today you will see a modern office complex, this was the site of the original Viking city in Dublin. During recent excavations, before the council offices were built, archaeological digs revealed the layout, houses, walls, and quay of Dublin as they existed in the ninth and eleventh centuries. Adjacent to the footpath here, set in stones, is the outline of a Viking house marked out with red-coloured paving stones. On Wood Quay, a sculpture of a Viking longboat commemorates the Viking settlement.

The passageways between the office blocks are usually open to the public and nearby there is a park and a performance auditorium where concerts and mini operas are held during the summer months.

Another unusual feature is the graveyard of St John's that is to be found within the grounds of the Civic Offices.

Winetavern Street in the 1940s, with Christ Church Cathedral in the background. (Courtesy of Dublin.ie Forums/cosmo)

Synod Hall and St Michael's Tower

Going down the steep St Michael's Hill, we pass the Dublinia Heritage Centre and the old St Michael the Archangel church. The overhead bridge that connects the former Synod House and the cathedral was built in the late 1800s. It was presented to the General Synod of the Church of Ireland in 1875 by Henry Roe, by whose generosity Christ Church Cathedral had been restored. In 1983 the Church of Ireland ceased to own the hall and it was subsequently sold. It became a nightclub for a few years before becoming part of the Dublinia Heritage Centre. The archway linking the Synod Hall to the cathedral is still owned by the Church of Ireland.[40]

The Heritage Centre contains three exhibitions, an interpretative centre, where you will see the history of Dublin city from Viking and medieval times. Dublinia's late seventeenth-century viewing tower belonged to the church of St Michael the Archangel, which once stood at the site now occupied by

Debating whether to buy outside a clothes shop near Winetavern Street, 1953. (Courtesy of National Library of Ireland)

Dublinia, the Synod Hall. This medieval tower has ninety-six steps leading to a panoramic view of Dublin.

St Michael's Close was originally called Macgiolla Mocholmog Street after an Irish chieftain.[41]

Schoolhouse Lane

Just off Winetavern Street and parallel with the steep St Michael's Close we have Schoolhouse Lane, linking High Street to Cook Street. Known in later medieval times as Le Ram Lane, the first school was built here in the sixteenth century. The Court of the King's Bench was held here until 1745 in what was described as one of the narrowest lanes in the city (nearby Copper Alley is even narrower). All along Cook Street and Oliver Bond Street there are a number of narrow, steep alleyways descending from Thomas Street.

Cooks and Dunghills

Walls and Ovens

We then turn left into Cook Street which is referred to as early as 1270. The whole area around here is steeped in history. This street, at the base of the city wall, was first built in the thirteenth century and was so named because of the concentration of food vendors, whose ovens were placed outside the walls to reduce the risk of fire and particularly because Dublin was a city constructed largely of wood. The Guild of Cooks had their guild hall in this street. Other areas in The Liberties still have names which describe the ancient trades carried on there including Cornmarket, Winetavern Street, Weavers' Sqaure, Golden Lane, Copper Alley and Fishamble Street.[42] Cook Street was later famous as it was the hub of the printing industry. In 1571 the first book in Irish was printed here. There were several Catholic stationers and printers in the eighteenth century and the first copy of the *Freeman's Journal* came off the printing press here in 1763.[43]

Best Second-Hand Coffins

Cook Street was also a great street for coffin makers. From 1850 onwards, many coffin makers had their businesses here, opening shroud warehouses and displaying their wares in large open sheds that also housed the hearses. At one time there were twenty-five undertakers in Dublin and nineteen of them lived in this street. They used to say that it was the only place in Dublin where you could buy a second-hand coffin (that didn't mean that it was down and back up again – it meant it was shop soiled)![44]

The old walls of Dublin are still visible along here, as is a thirteenth-century gate, St Audoen's Arch, the only remaining gateway into the old medieval walled city. Standing in St Audoen's Park, view the doorway and belfry of the church, as it is the only surviving medieval church within the walls of the city. Standing in the park, you are now at the original height of the battlements, from which Dubliners would have defended the city from the likes of Silken Thomas and other disaffected Irish from beyond the Pale. If you walk through the arch and up the steps you will be able to see the old stones making up the wall which were part of the original seventh-century St Columcille's church which stood on this site. There is a real medieval atmosphere and sensation about this place at the back of St Audoen's church.

Walk down the narrow passageway and forty steps along the side of the church and view the impressive old city wall. On the way down there is another smaller archway at the base of St Audoen's church where once a medieval passage led down to the river Liffey. Remains of this passageway have been preserved and may be viewed inside the church. When you reach Cook Street from the forty steps, look back at the gate and the impressive stretch of city wall on either side of the gateway.

Interestingly enough there are two other forty steps in The Liberties area, one at the side of Dublin Castle connecting Castle Street to Ship Street, the other near St James's Hospital linking James's Street to Old Kilmainham Village.[45]

From Cook Street to Hangman's Lane

The present Carmelite community at Clarendon Street is directly linked to the first members of the Discalced Carmelite Order who came to Ireland, led by Fr Paul Browne; on arrival in 1625 they went to live with his mother in Cook Street! Several foundations were made from Cook Street, eventually resulting in the setting up of the Province of St Patrick, the Irish Province of the Discalced Carmelites.

With the succession in 1685 of a Catholic King (James II), the friars joyfully set up a chapel in Hangman's Lane, off Church Street. But following the defeat of the King by William of Orange at the Battle of the Boyne on 12 July 1689, the community was once again homeless.

The 1690s were a dark period for the little community. In 1692 the Carmelites set up a new chapel in Cornmarket but once again life was disrupted with a Proclamation of Banishment for all bishops and friars (1697). However, ten years later in 1707 a member of the ancient and powerful Hollywood family of Artane Castle gave them a residence at Wormwood Gate. They were to remain there for fifty years.[46]

Lower Bridge Street and the Happy Citizens

Lower Bridge Street separates Cook Street from Oliver Bond Street. It was here that the United Irishman, Oliver Bond, had his business and home, prior to his arrest. In the seventeenth century the street was a residential area for the gentry but by the early eighteenth century it had become the commercial centre for the textile and hardware trades. In the late nineteenth century a number of hotels had opened owned by a James Doherty.[47]

St Audoen's House and Oliver Bond House, two blocks of Dublin Corporation flats, were built in the late 1930s. St Audoen's was named after the nearby church, and Oliver Bond House (known as The Bond) after the famous United Irishman. The clock in the corner tower dates from 1868 and came from the building that formerly occupied the site – The Anchor Brewery – famous for its Darcy's Ale.

Above the St Audoen's House clock tower there is a fine gold-painted weather vane with the addition of part of the Dublin city emblem showing three castles. The Dublin City Coat of Arms is the emblem that identifies Dublin and has been in use for more than 400 years. The Coat of Arms shows the following features: an image of three burning castles or three gates into the ancient city, two female figures each holding an olive branch, and the city motto, '*Obedientia Civium Urbis Felicitas*'. The Latin motto of Dublin City translates as 'The obedience of the citizens produces a happy city'.[48]

The Brazen Head, located on Lower Bridge Street is reputed to be the oldest pub in the country, with references to it as far back as 1613 and it is likely that it was in existence for many decades before that. The first licensing laws in Ireland came into effect in 1635 but ale houses were known to exist in Dublin in 1185. The sign over the pub maintains that it was established in 1198. It would appear that the present building was erected in 1754 when new houses were built on the street.[49] The United Irishmen held some meetings there after the raid on Oliver Bond's house nearby, when the assembled delegates were arrested.[50] James Joyce mentions the pub in his writings and Brendan Behan and his fellow writers used to meet there.[51] A map dated 1781 shows that the tavern backed on to the old city wall. Across the road from the Brazen Head we have O'Shea's the Merchant pub, another landmark establishment for those interested in Irish traditional music.[52]

Mattresses and Water Rats: Jimmy O'Dea

It was at Lower Bridge Street that Ireland's most famous actor, singer, pantomime artist, and comedian, was born. The legendary James Augustine O'Dea, otherwise known as Jimmy O'Dea, was born on 24 April 1899 at Lower Bridge Street, not far from 'Biddy Mulligan´s' Coombe. In 1907 the family moved to 163 Capel Street, where Jimmy became a friend of future Taoiseach, Seán Lemass. He would later serve as best man at Lemass's wedding.[53]

On his father's advice O'Dea trained as an optician, but his true vocation was acting. In his early days during the 1920s and 1930s he was a serious actor. He acted in silent films from 1922–28 and also played at the Abbey Theatre, the Queens and the Empire (later called the Olympia). He met Harry O'Donovan, who became the writer of all Jimmy's sketches and other scripts. His most famous character, Mrs Mulligan, first appeared soon after he met Harry.

O'Dea played on radio and made forty-eight records between 1926 and 1948. He first married in 1925 and his second marriage was to Ursula Doyle, also an actress.

Jimmy toured all over Ireland and England in the 1930s and 1940s and played in pantomime in the Gaiety every Christmas.

Jimmy O'Dea was very proud that he was awarded the badge of the 'Grand Order of the Water Rat', the highest award for comedians, and always wore it. He and Maureen Potter had some great sketches together e.g. 'Dolores and Rose' and were a great duo.[54]

In the 1950s O'Dea turned to films again. One of his most famous was *Darby O'Gill and the Little People*, which was a Walt Disney film. He died in 1965 but even in the year 2000 the Chinese state TV played Darby O'Gill to an audience of one billion people.

Interestingly, some of the O'Dea family owned the famous Odearest mattress company. An *Irish Times* cartoon advertisement ran in 1951 with the caption: '... I can't write without Odearest – my cherished possession.'[55]

Mullinahack and Wormwood Gate

Between Cook Street and Oliver Bond Street, called after United Irishman leader Oliver Bond who lived in the area, we have Wormwood Gate/Mullinhack, a small enclave that bears no sign of its earlier importance when it was the site of one of the major gates into the old city of Dublin. Oliver Bond Street itself was once called Mullinahack. There was also a Crocker's Lane, now part of Oliver Bond Street.

The word Mullinahack comes from the Irish *Muileann an chaca*, mill of the dung hill. There was a pipe from the mill which discharged its foul-smelling contents here. On Rocque's map of 1756 the lane became Mullinahack or 'filthy mills', pointing to already dilapidated mills in the late eighteenth century, while Speed's earlier map of 1610 shows buildings at this location referred to as 'mills'. Excavations carried out in 1995 by Margaret Gowen, archaeologist, on Oliver Bond Street uncovered two of the Mullinahack mill walls.[56]

Old City Gate

Similarly, the Irish name *Geata Gormáin* (Gate of Gormáin/Gormund) gives a truer idea of the original name of Wormwood Gate, the location of a gate into the medieval city. And it was here that Richard Robert Madden (1798–1886), doctor, historian and public servant, was born at No. 9 Wormwood Gate, in 1798, the year of the United Irishmen rebellion. The great work of his life was *The United Irishmen, Their Lives and Times* (7 vols 1842–46), followed by *Literary Remains of the United Irishmen* (1846), which, though an adulatory rather than a scholarly monument to the leaders, established the nationalist tradition in relation to the Rebellion of 1798. He also wrote *The Life and Times of Robert Emmet*.

On discovering Anne Devlin (Robert Emmett's housekeeper who had helped to hide him under the name of Mr Ellis after the abortive 1803 Rising) living in extreme poverty in Dublin in 1843, Madden arranged for her support for the rest of her life. She died during one of his absences abroad, and was buried in a pauper's grave; upon his return he arranged for her re-interment in a plot beside the grave of Daniel O'Connell in Glasnevin Cemetery.

The great landscape artist Alexander Williams painted a watercolour around 1890 signed and inscribed: 'Old Wormwood Gate – A Vanished Dublin Slum'.

The artist's paintings of old Dublin and in particular The Liberties capture some of the atmosphere of Liberties life at the end of the nineteenth century.

Incursions by the Irish Clans: Gates to the Old City

Despite walls and fortifications raised around Dublin by the Ostmen and the Vikings, Dublin, along with the majority of the towns and cities in Ireland, remained subject to incursions by native Irish clans until well into the seventeenth century. It was even subjected to raids from the O'Byrnes and O'Tooles of Wicklow in the eighteenth century. The defences of Dublin eventually fell into disrepair but continued to serve a purpose as late as 1762 when the auction of the rights to collect tolls at each of the then seven city gates raised £4,000 for the city.[57]

The gates of Dublin were along the city's ancient boundaries: Castle Gate at Dublin Castle; Pole Gate near Werburgh Street; Nicholas' Gate in Nicholas Street; New Gate in Cornmarket; Gormund's Gate (Wormwood) at the corner of St Augustine Street; Bridge Gate or Ostman's Gate at the bridge across the Liffey at Ussher's Quay; Essex Gate in Essex Street; Dame's, Damas or Dam's Gate in Dame Street; the King's Gate or Winetavern Gate at the top of Winetavern Street; and lastly a gate at what is St Michael's Close but which originally was called Macgiolla Mocholmog Street after an Irish chieftain.

There was an older inner wall which ran from Brown's Castle along Cook Street and across Winetavern Street. The only surviving gateway is St Audoen's Arch. The archway is 12ft wide and 12ft high. The tower above the archway was previously demolished but much of the remaining masonry is original. Following protests from the public, the archway was restored by Dublin Corporation in 1880.[58]

Bridgefoot Street and the Mendicity

Continuing along Oliver Bond Street we come to the intersection with Bridgefoot Street. This was once called Dirty Lane and was a cobble-stoned street like many of the surrounding streets. To cycle or to bring a horse and dray down this hill with the wet cobblestones was risking life and limb. The Bridgefoot name came from its nearness to the old bridge that spanned the Liffey. Bridgefoot was the name of the residence of Sir William Usher (1610–71) located nearby. The street was the home of Thomson's Bakery for years and many of Dublin's poor gathered beside the warm external bakery wall for heat. It was also the favourite stand of Johnny Fortycoats.

Just off Bridgefoot Street, in Island Street, we have an old building with the dates 1818–1954 in bold letters over the front. This is the famous Mendicity Institution and it featured as a garrison for the 1916 Rising insurrectionists. It is one of Dublin's oldest charities and was founded at a time when there was very little public help for the thousands of poor forced to beg in the streets of

Dublin who, as a contemporary put it, 'crowded around the doors of shops, assailing customers'. The old entrance used to front on to the river Liffey at Usher's Island. It was a former grand house, called Moira House. It had romantic associations for republicans as Lord Edward Fitzgerald used to stay there before his arrest.[59]

Watling Street

Across the road from the Mendicity Institute is Bonham Street, from where we can see the old walls of the debtor's prison, the Marshalsea. This brings us to Watling Street, at the junction opposite the Guinness Brewery on Thomas Street and descending to the quays. The stench from the tanneries of Watling Street in the eighteenth century had to compete with the roasting of hops from the adjacent brewery. Today, the only evidence of tanning in the area is the inscription over the entrance to a former factory that reads 'The Central Hide & Skin Co. Ltd.' Today, one of the best views of St Patrick's Tower on Thomas Street is to be had from here. Likewise, from the bottom of the street, we have one of the best vistas of the four towering smoking chimneys of the brewery.

On a fateful day in the life of Dublin in 1905, James Joyce records in *Ulysses* that Mr Kernan turns off Thomas Street and walks down the slope of Watling Street. And, according to the famous ballad Finnegan's Wake, sung by the Dubliners, 'Tim Finnegan had lived at Watling Street...'[60] The annual Liffey Swim, continuing for over ninety years, starts at Rory O'Moore Bridge, beside Watling Street.

The Rupert Guinness Theatre is also located on Watling Street. One of the most sought-after events of the year in The Liberties was the annual Christmas Guinness concert, held in the lavish theatre which had seating room for 500. Each year, for six nights a week and for four weeks the popular variety show was put on. It had a mixture of both local talent and Irish celebrities such as Maureen Potter, Jimmy O'Dea and Noel Purcell adorning the stage.[61]

Heart of The Liberties

Watling Street brings us back up the hill to Guinness's Brewery and Thomas Street. For many people, locals and visitors alike, the heart of The Liberties is the area bound by Thomas Street, Meath Street, Francis Street and the Coombe.

High Street

High Street is an example of a street taking its name from a natural physical characteristic, as it is what it says, a street on a height. It was once one of the principal commercial streets of medieval Dublin. It was also the starting/finish-

Birthplace of Napper Tandy, one of the leaders of the 1798 Rebellion, High Street, 1959.
Notice the plaque on the wall over the shop. (Courtesy of Dublin City Public Libraries)

ing and crossing point for some of the most important routes connecting Dublin
to the rest of Ireland and was once the dividing line in the two parts of Ireland,
north and south, when two ancient kings decided to divide the country up
between them.

It was also where the United Irishmen leader Wolfe Tone was waked at No. 65,
prior to his burial in nearby Werburgh Street church and where fellow United
Irishman Napper Tandy lived at one time and a plaque commemorated this until
the developers bulldozed the street in the late twentieth century. Only the two St
Audoen churches survived the demolition. An alleyway leads off down to Cook
Street and it is where we will find the forty steps at the side of the church in the
picturesque St Audoen's Park.[62]

Cornmarket

Continuing on from St Audoen's church and to the right of Bridge Street
Upper we have Cornmarket where for generations, an annual fair lasted for
a fortnight each summer. Here merchants from all over Ireland and from

abroad would gather to buy and sell, to haggle and strike bargains, to quarrel and seek justice. By an interesting coincidence part of this plot was later occupied by the Iveagh Markets. This part of town has long had a tradition of markets and the retail of agricultural produce, a tradition that continues to this day.

The clusters of specialist streets such as Winetavern Street, Cook Street, Fishamble Street and Cornmarket identifies a long tradition centred on markets, trade, industry and innovation in the area.[63]

As the main western approach to the old medieval city of Dublin it was not surprising that Thomas Street, High Street and Cornmarket became a hub of agriculturally-based commerce. In turn the area reciprocated by becoming a centre

Advertisement for J.H. Webb & Co. Ltd, Clothing Manufacturers in *The Lady of the House* magazine, 1904. Webbs had a factory at Cornmarket in The Liberties. (Courtesy of Dublin City Public Libraries)

of production and distribution of tradeable goods such as leather, alcohol, tea and hardware.

Between St Audeon's church and Thomas Street, Cornmarket was the most important trading position in the old city of Dublin. From the thirteenth century large amounts of corn were traded and exported from here. Nothing remains of the original cornmarket except the name. The 'Corn Premium Office', a thirteen-bay structure was a building in which corn could be bought and sold and is illustrated on Brooking's map indicating its importance before it was demolished by the Wide Street Commissioners.[64]

From Corn to Paints and Paper
The Farrow and Ball building (a former AIB bank and now selling high quality paints) is a formidable and very impressive structure that adds dignity and grandeur to this stretch of Cornmarket. Next door we have MRCB Paints and Paper, a family business that started in Meath Street. What do the initials MRCB stand for? It depends on who you ask. Here are some of the answers: Mister Coghlan's Boys; Mother Riley's Currant Buns; Misers, Robbers, Crooks and Beggars, to give a few![65]

Established in 1936, the company MRCB Ltd was founded by two French gentlemen, Marcel Regent and Charles Bigoud – MR & CB – who decided to set up business on Lord Edward Street. The company built up the reputation as the store that stocked the most comprehensive range of specialist products and painting tools as well as the mainline brands of paints. This is still the same today, with over 8,600 items stocked. But in its early days it was a time when the vast majority of houses were decorated with wallpaper, unlike today when most houses are just painted on the inside. There was a time in the 1700s when Ireland was one of the biggest exporters of wallpaper.

Since the formation of the company it has changed hands several times. In 1989, Joe and Nora Coghlan purchased it. Joe and Nora were already in the paint retail business running Coghlan's Paints in Meath Street since 1980. In early 1990, the company relocated from Lord Edward Street to 12/13 Cornmarket. It is still a 100 per cent Irish-owned family business and it lends much colour to Cornmarket.[66]

Next door to MRCB is the Department of Health's Dental Clinic, also an impressive corner building, and that used to fill children with dread at the thought of having 'gas' during extractions!

The Dublin City Council has added ornamental paving and lighting in front of the buildings and the site hosts the annual Christmas tree for the area.

Up Off Our Knees!

Long-time trade unionist, Des Geraghty, hails from Cornmarket. He comes from a family which is steeped in the history, folklore and tradition of the city and has a special interest in traditional music and song. As a musician himself, he was a participant in the revival of interest in folk music in the 1950s and 1960s. He is a well-known trade unionist, who has represented workers in most major industrial sectors in Ireland. He was not, of course, the first prominent trade unionist to come out of The Liberties, as the 1916 Rising leader, James Connolly, started his party and union not too far away on Thomas Street.

Number 22 Cornmarket was another place of refuge used by Lord Edward FitzGerald, whose friends were most generous in running risks for his sake. At Moore's house in Cornmarket Lord Edward was disguised as a tutor to Miss Moore.

Old City Wall

As noted previously, the Anglo-Normans invaded Ireland in 1169 and by September 1170 the Hiberno-Norse or 'Ostmen' had been expelled from Dublin. The city was granted its first charter by 1172 and had rapidly expanded beyond the city walls into a large merchant port by the thirteenth century. The Anglo-Norman defences replaced or expanded the earlier walls and Dublin Castle was built in 1204, probably on the site of an earlier Hiberno-Norse fortification. The Anglo-Normans also brought a change in building techniques with the introduction of the sill-beamed structure and by the early thirteenth century stone buildings dominated. The excavations at Back Lane/Lamb Alley were particularly important in providing an overview of this change in building techniques from the Viking period right up to post-medieval stone structures.[67]

Maintenance of the walls caused endless headaches for the city fathers. The mayor often asked for permission to collect an additional tax called a 'murage' or wall tax, which had to be paid along with ordinary dues. People built their houses right up against the walls and even cut holes in the walls to use as back doors and the corporation had to regularly order that these gaps be blocked and fitted with iron gratings.[68]

This stand-alone section of the old city walls at Cornmarket/Lambs's Alley originally had a tower, which served as a prison in the late Middle Ages. Established as the city gaol by Richard I in 1285, it had four drum towers, one at each corner, with a gate and portcullis. During the Penal Times this jail was full of clerics jailed for their practice of Catholicism. One such prisoner was Bishop Donnelly of Dromore. While there he called three priests aside and consecrated them archbishops in late 1707 as he realised that he was the only remaining

This view looks east from Cornmarket in the early 1960s. The vacant edge in the foreground would have been the site of the two corner properties shown on Devin's 1909 map which defined the east edge of Cornmarket, with High Street to the left and Back Lane to the right. Tailors' Hall can be seen peeping up to the right of the billboard. (Courtesy of Archiseek)

bishop in Ireland and that when he died the line of continuity from St Patrick would be broken. Oliver Plunkett, Archbishop of Armagh was also imprisoned there for a year until 1680.

Newgate had been one of the entrance gates of the old city wall situated at the corner of the cornmarket. The prison was demolished in 1839.[69]

The Black Dog and the Black Pig

The Black Dog was a name later given to the prison because of a nearby tavern of the same name. There is a legend associated with the prison about a mysterious inmate known since as Dolocher, as described in the old *Dublin Penny Journal* of 1832 (a weekly newspaper that included James Clarence Mangan among its writers).[70] One day a notorious prisoner named Olocher was found to have committed suicide on the morning of his execution. Shortly afterwards several women were reportedly attacked by a demonic black pig which they christened the Dolocher, assuming it was the incarnation of Olocher. When one of the jail's sentries went missing and the attacks intensified, a band of men set out one night from a public house in nearby Cook Street, determined to slaughter every black pig they encountered. When morning came, not a pig, white or black, could be seen.' However, according to the *Dublin Penny Journal*:

> Next winter the Dolocher re-appeared! A young woman passing by Fisher's-alley on the Wood-quay, was pulled in, and a bundle of clothes which she had in her hand, beside her cloak, dragged from her. The alarm spread again; the Dolocher re-commenced his 'reign of terror'; women fled the streets, especially about Fisher's-alley, and Christ-Church-lane, and even the stouter hearts of men trembled within them at thought of encountering so direful a combatant. Yet strange, very strange to say, the demon-beast confined his assaults to that lovely portion of the creation whom we might have expected that even such an awful 'grizly king of swinish race', would have respected, if not adored.[71]

Months later a drunken blacksmith borrowed a cloak from a female acquaintance and set out for home. He was attacked by the Dolocher but fought back vociferously and delivered a fatal blow. The story goes:

> Just as the blacksmith reached HELL (the notorious and disreputable area between Cook Street and the back of Christ Church Cathedral), out rushed the Dolocher, pounced on its victim, and pinned him against the wall. The blacksmith was not a man to die easy at any time, and especially with a drop of the rale stuff in his noddle. He raised his muscular arm: 'Be ye Dolocher or Devil, or what ye may, take that!' letting fall a thumper that would have staggered Dan Donnelly.[72]

A crowd gathered and the demon was revealed to be the missing sentry:

> A crowd cautiously collected; the dying and groaning devil was lifted up, and out of a black pig's skin came the very man who had been carried off, body and soul, from his post at the BLACK DOG.

Before he died he confessed to aiding Olocher in his suicide and orchestrating the slaughter of the pigs for the purpose of attacking and robbing innocent citizens. And as fast as the pigs were killed they 'were removed to a cellar in Schoolhouse-lane, and that thus he had kept up the delusion for the purpose of robbery.'[73]

Back Lane 'Gurriers'

Back Lane, off High Street, is a narrow medieval lane originally called Rochelle Street. Back Lane stretches from Nicholas Street to Cornmarket behind Tailors' Hall and is so-called because of its position behind High Street.

Bertram's Court to the rear of nearby Lamb's Alley, lay outside the city wall, and was part of an industrial quarter in the medieval period. It was home to many factories involved in the leather and tanning industries. The gurrying house was a building situated off Back Lane where leather was beaten and softened ready for use. It is thought that this is where the expression 'gurriers' came from. Those who carried out the task of 'gurrying' needed to be hardy and tough individuals.[74]

Winstanleys Shoe Factory was also situated in Back Lane and was built in 1875. The site of the factory later became the Christ Church Festival Market and Mother Redcaps Tavern that opened in 1989. That year was the bicentenary of the French Revolution and the owner had a republican ethos; he named it after the fashion of the Sans-Culottes of Paris of wearing a red bonnet to denote their loyalty to the revolutionary cause.[75]

Tailors' Hall in Back Lane

The first mention of Dublin Tailors' Hall is in 1539 when it was in Winetavern Street and later in the century it was leased to the Corporation. The present building is one of the very few surviving buildings of the Queen Anne period and was built between 1703 and 1707. It is the only remaining guildhall in the city of Dublin. It must be entered through a huge gateway. Other guilds met in the hall besides the Tailors: the hosiers, tanners, saddlers and barber surgeons. That the Tailors' Hall was located in this part of The Liberties illustrates the huge importance the area had as the centre of commercial life in Dublin. The guild was exclusively Protestant until 1793, and was very powerful and influential in matters of trade and commerce.

From 1755 the Grand Lodge of Freemasons met regularly on the first Thursday of every month. It was also considered the most fashionable venue in Dublin for balls, musical evenings and public meetings. This continued until the mid-1700s, when the nearby Music Hall in Fishamble Street attracted society events, particularly after the visit of Mr Handel.[15]

The tailors themselves, however, while they had their meeting in the hall, had their famous dinners elsewhere, the dinner in 1767 taking place across the road in the Phoenix in Werburgh Street. The dinner on that occasion began at 4 p.m. to allow plenty of time for toasts and speeches. The toasts numbered twenty-eight and, as well as the usual ones to the King, the Queen and the Lord Lieutenant, some of the later toasts were rather curious; the twenty-first was 'May all badgers be hunted into their holes', and the twenty-sixth: 'May the Corporation of Tailors always be able to disrobe the borrowed plumes of copperplate, from the Faction, which would ever cajole them out of their Liberties'.[16]

Man on a bike in High Street, 1968. (Courtesy of Dublin City Public Libraries)

In 1792 a Catholic convention that met in Tailors' Hall was led by the United Irishmen leader Wolfe Tone (who was Protestant) and became known as the 'Back Lane Parliament'. This was undoubtedly the most important event in the long and varied history of the Tailors' Hall. The United Irishmen were initially a Protestant body, closely linked to the Freemasons, and it may have been through that organisation that the Tailors' Hall became the United Irishmen's Dublin meeting place. In the main the convention sought for Catholics' right to vote and to participate in jury trials and passed a resolution to petition the king with their grievances.

On 3 January 1793 the king did see them and this was seen as a moral victory for Catholics, although the petition in fact had minimum impact on the grievances of Irish Catholics.

Today, the building is seen as being very significant in terms of the social, political, religious, legal and economic history of Dublin and Ireland. It is now the headquarters of An Taisce – the National Trust for Ireland.

Thomas Street: Kings and Boundaries

In old Liberties language there was an expression, 'the sunny side and the money side' of Thomas Street. Did it refer to street traders on one side and bankers, brewers and distillers on the other? We can only guess! But it does illustrate the wit and wisdom of the community. Thomas Street was originally called St Thomas's Street, after the Abbey of St Thomas, located here in the Middle Ages. Part of Thomas Street, in front of John's Lane church (though at that point the Hospital of St John the Baptist) was once called Horsemarket.

Emmeline Henderson in her study, *Thomas Street* (An Taisce, 2001) noted:

> The Thomas St, Cornmarket and the High Street route has a unique and unmatched location flanked on one side by one of Dublin's great Cathedrals, Christ Church and at the other side by the world-famous Guinness Brewery, and just further along a little way, St James's Hospital. The street is rich in the history of Dublin and has many notable buildings on both sides of the street.[78]

Thomas Street is characterised by eighteenth and nineteenth-century mercantile architecture. However, the dominating feature must be the towering spire of SS Augustine and John church, known as John's Lane, which rises to be the focal point of the surrounding area from all directions. The area is known for the brewing and distilling industries that thrived here in the recent past, of which only the Guinness Brewery survives.[79]

Where It All Began

There is a wall plaque on Thomas Street, near the Guinness Brewery with the words Thomas Street and the date 1263 underneath. This may have been the first official mention of Thomas Street, but the route was in existence hundreds of years before that.

Running parallel to the river Liffey, Thomas Street is one of the city's oldest streets. It was the final part of the old Slí Mór, one of the four ancient highways of Ireland. It was the route by which farmers came to sell corn and buy other produce before returning home.[80]

Moreover, the junction of St Augustine Street, Thomas Street and Francis Street is possibly the most historic place in Dublin as it represents the beginning of the ancient road to the north of Ireland, known as Slighe Midluachra. To that end it had to cross the river Liffey, at the ford of the hurdles that itself gave rise to the evolving name of Áth Cliath. Francis Street represented the beginning of the Slighe Chualann leading to Leinster and the south-east of the country via the old Poddle Crossing at Dean Street. The earliest settlement probably grew up around this major crossroads on top of the ridge overlooking the ford.[81]

The importance of Thomas Street was further consolidated in the late twelfth century when King Henry II of England, came to Ireland and founded the Abbey of Thomas á Becket, named after the late murdered Archbishop of Canterbury (ostensibly to make atonement for his part in the murder of the archbishop).

According to a recent survey of the area by the Dublin City Council and the Dublin Civic Trust, 'The Priory of St. Thomas the Martyr served a profound role in the development of the street, and indeed, the wider area. As a royal foundation it was to be one of the most powerful ecclesiastical settlements and landowners in medieval Dublin.'[82]

Medieval Rights of Way

Thomas Street has many old lanes radiating off it: Swan Alley, Molyneux Yard, Vicar Street, Maddens Court and Marshalea Lane (recently closed off). The latter (between No. 143 and 144 Thomas Street) was where Robert Emmet had his principal depot. Molyneux Yard (opposite John's Lane church) has splendid views of the Dublin Mountains. Much of the activity still going on in this particular lane is reminiscent of medieval times as jarveys' horses from the Guinness Brewery visitor centre are housed here at night and locals often mention the 'rats as big as cats'. This lane was also an important meeting place during the War of Independence as it is where Michael Collins met and discussed his plans with local activists.

St Catherine's Lane West, at the side of St Catherine's church, Thomas Street is another example of an old cobbled lane from times gone by. It still has the old bollards along each side and leads to Hanbury Lane and the ancient cemetery at

Thomas Street in the 1950s. Opposite Chadwick's Builders. (Courtesy of Dublin.ie Forums/rashers5)

the back of the church. The cemetery is now called St Catherine's Park, with the entrance along by Thomas Court, and was officially opened as a park in 1986. Many of the old headstones are still visible. Sculptor Jim Flavin has an interesting piece of work there called 'Adult and Child Seat' which was erected as part of the Dublin Millennium celebrations in 1988.[83]

St Augustine Street

St Augustine Street, beside John's Lane church started as a new 'row' or street built just outside the section of the city walls which ran from Cornmarket/ Thomas Street down to the Liffey. Together with some lanes and alleyways, New Row was realigned in the nineteenth century to become St Augustine Street. Behind John's Lane church we have John's Lane itself, which gave its name to the church. We also have the steep little cobble-stoned alleyways behind the church that have not changed much in hundreds of years. John Street West is at the side of the church, with John's Lane at the back of the church.

Adorned with Fine Buildings

Because of its prime location, Thomas Street developed as a centre of commerce
in the medieval period and it gradually became the most important street in the
western part of Old Dublin, lined with timber cage-work houses and later brick
dwellings in the gabled 'Dutch Billy' style. The strong mercantile and industrial
tradition of the eighteenth and nineteenth centuries can still be seen today in the
impressive array of commercial buildings that line the street, interspersed with
modest townhouses and fine historic churches. However, much historic architecture, including some early eighteenth-century merchant houses, is hidden beneath
modern façades. It is when one lifts one eye above the shop fronts at street level that
one sees the evidence of a different era.[84] 'Established A.D. 1782' is proclaimed
boldly over No. 38 Thomas Street and gives some clue to the age and importance of
the building stock in the area.

According to the Dublin Civic Trust, the street suffered during the boom
years as it fell prey to 'site assembly' by developers, remained unused, and as
the so-called Celtic Tiger economy collapsed, became increasingly dilapidated.[85]

However, many fine landmark buildings remain. It has a remarkable wealth
of old buildings of various periods and is the one street in Dublin that needs to
have its older buildings preserved, such is the huge historical significance of the
area. There are many grand set-piece buildings offset by more modest structures.
However, while the imposing churches and industrial and commercial premises
such as the former Blanchardstown Mill, the IAWS headquarters and the NCAD
complex give the street its imposing air, it is the well-proportioned merchant
houses and shops that give the street its quality.

Coming from James's Street towards Christ Church we have: the Guinness
Brewery complex, St Catherine's church, the former Millar's Distillery (now part
of the Digital Hub where the name A.M. Miller may still be vaguely seen over
the entrance to the former premises of the distillers), the former Thomas Street
Public Library, the Vicar Street music venue, Chadwick's and the Tailor's Guild
Hall. Re-tracing our steps on the opposite side we have St John's Lane church,
the NCAD complex incorporating the old fire station and Power's Distillery, the
former Blanchardstown Mills building, now occupied by Lidl (an imprinted sign
on an adjacent glass door, 'Millers Hall' is a reminder of the building's former
function), the IAWS building and the adjacent Roe's Distillery windmill, just
before Watling Street. The very impressive and ornate IAWS building (where Lord
Edward Fitzgerald was arrested) is at No 151, the Social Welfare office, No 118,
the former Gilbeys' building is also along here. Massey's at No 141 dates from
c. 1740 and is one of the earliest built houses on Thomas Street still standing.
And between all these fine and historical buildings we have original buildings
dating from the eighteenth and nineteenth centuries, including the many old
pubs, shops, chemists, undertakers and more.[86]

Just next door to the Clock Pub we have the big gateway, aligned with two black steel bollards, that was a former entrance to Power's Distillery. And next door to it the words 'Private Residence' on the brass number plate of the front door of No. 109 and 'Letters' is inscribed on the brass letterbox. The door signifies the social standing of the former residents of this house on this prosperous street at the heart of Dublin's commercial life.

Thomas Street is consequently teeming with history – of patriots, of markets, of doctors and distillers, of butchers, brewers, and bankers, of publicans and churches, and of communities. The sounds and smells of Thomas Street are always evident, whether it is the brewery or the butchers' aromas wafting out, or the voices of the stallholders selling their wares.

Many will recall C. Seezer Pork Butchers who were in business here at 40 Thomas Street since 1900 until the end of the twentieth century. There was a sign in the shop saying that Charles Seezer, the pork butcher, was a 'humane killer'. Annie Craddock, a haberdasher, was renowned for her buttons, pins and zips. Other names include Millars, the Wholesale Tea, Wine and Whiskey Merchants; the Irish Thread Manufacturers, Gordon Thompsons; Duffy's; Findlater's; the Cherry Tree Salt Works, and many more. And between all the big businesses were the many shops such as The Maypole, Edward Cakes, Metropolitan Laundry, Sheppard's Dairy, Rogers, Pattisons, Baker Wardell, Brazils, Fortunes, Kearns, and Eastmans.[87]

Manning's Bakery, a small family business at 39–40 Thomas Street, began trading in the 1950s and is still going strong. This is a traditional bakery that started off baking home-made bread in a grocery shop. For many families, every celebration was marked with a cake from Mannings. The old Carpet Mills ('our products are being walked on every day') is no more; the only reminder is the neon sign frontage still there after forty-seven years of business. Morelli's chipper (established 1959) continues. Frawley's drapery shop, a popular shop for generations of locals, is no more (the name was kept, however, and is still remembered large and clear on the tiled floor at the entrance to the present business). Crowe Monumental Sculptors (the name of B. Crowe is on many of the headstones in Mount Jerome and other Dublin cemeteries) and other older businesses have not been forgotten, however. Nor has the old and ornate Thomas Street Public Library building, which became the Brewery Hostel. This beautiful building is being restored again back to its former glory and will once more add to the fine buildings on Thomas Street. Number 14 Thomas Street was for decades the home of the Pipers' Club and the Irish traditional music and cultural organisation and centre, Comhaltas Ceoltoiri Eireann, was founded here.

Further along, past St Catherine's church, a plaque on the wall reads: 'No. 1 Thomas Street. Dwelling House of Arthur Guinness 1725-1803. Master

The heart of The Liberties: view of a bustling Thomas Street in the 1970s. (Courtesy of Dublin City Public Libraries)

Brewer and founder in 1759 of the company that bears his name.' The grey stone Café Note building on the corner of Thomas Street and Francis Street, with the stone sculpted miniature harps over the entrance and side gives some indication of its past importance (it was a bank for many years). Nearby is the Vicar Street music venue, where the likes of the Dubliners, Bob Dylan and Neil Young have played. It has added to the fabric and colour of this outstanding street.

The Boundary Kings

The large, colourful and intricately sculpted pieces outside Vicar Street are the work of Patrick O'Reilly. Titled 'Boundary Kings', they are based on Celtic art.[88] The music venue opened in 1998 and is owned by Harry Crosbie. When Handel performed his *Messiah* in Fishamble Street in 1742, there was a musical society based at Vicar Street. It was also a watch house when Lord Kilwarden was murdered on Thomas Street in 1803 by the followers of Robert Emmet. His dying minutes were spent at Vicar Street.

Across the road we have the National College of Art and Design (NCAD) occupying the old fire station (now Harry Clarke House) and the old Powers Distillery.

Much of the architectural richness of Thomas Street today derives from a recent time when prominent banks were a feature of this street. When we see buildings such as NCAD, Lidl, Café Noto or Farrow & Ball we see the old heritage hidden under a modern guise.

St Patrick's Tower

The breathtakingly magnificent windmill of the former Roe's distillery is a twelve-storey 120ft high structure and was the tallest Smock Windmill in Europe at the time of its construction. St Patrick's Tower is the largest surviving windmill tower outside the Netherlands. It is a very famous landmark on Dublin's horizon. It was built years before 1757 (the year Peter Roe bought his original distillery) and belonged to a corn mill that had previously occupied the site. The sails of the windmill were in working order until 1860.[89]

The striking green copper-clad cupola is topped by a figure of St Patrick carrying a mitre and a crozier. Why St Patrick? The answer seems to lie in the fact that the water used in the Roe Distillery came from the Grand Canal and in particular the River Vartry. It was at the River Vantry near the foothills of the Wicklow Mountains that St Patrick and his followers first settled in Ireland, so it was no surprise when a figure of St Patrick was placed on top the tower when the sails were removed over a hundred ago and it became known locally as St Patrick's Tower.

Roe's Distillery used the building in the whiskey-making process. The windmill contained eight pairs of disk-shaped stones that could grind 1,500 barrels of grain a day. Guinness eventually bought Roe out.

At the base of the tower is a pear tree that dates from 1850. It's a sight to behold in the spring-time with masses of blossoms and it still grows pears in abundance. Guinness has never used St Patrick's Tower for brewing.[90]

This beautiful landmark is now part of the 4-acre Digital Hub multi-media complex and although accessible to view from the car park where it now stands, it is not open. What a shame – views of Dublin from the top would be outstanding and a keen eye could finally gauge how far the George Roe Distillery had extended in this city. But there is an interesting view of the tower from the Gravity Bar across the road in the Guinness Brewery visitor centre, where it is possible to look down on St Patrick!

At the back of the Digital Hub it is possible to see the old surviving walls of Marshalsea debtors' prison.

Marshalsea, Isaac Butt and Robert Emmet

Marshalsea Lane was off Thomas Street, between Bridgefoot Street and Watling Street. The lane, formerly beside Lynch's Pub (near Massey's at 141 Thomas Street), is now closed off. It took its name from a group of buildings known as the Marshalsea, built around 1770. The old word itself comes from a court held before the knight marshal of the king to administer justice between the king's servants.

Some of the imposing old walls are still visible from Bonham Street (off Watling Street) and behind the IAWS building on Thomas Street. The complex was built as a type of debtors' prison and had two courtyards, two chapels, several common halls and a ball court. Marshalsea's debtors from all parts of Ireland were confined with their wives and families. Despite the addition of extra accommodation in the nineteenth century the Marshalsea was described in 1821 as extremely overcrowded while the confined site impeded ventilation. The length of a prisoner's stay was determined largely by the whim of his creditors. It was run privately for profit; beds could be rented from the head warder for one shilling a night. Those who could not afford a bed were consigned to a damp airless dun-

Marshalsea Barracks, off Thomas Street, 1952. (Courtesy of Dublin.ie Forums/el gronk)

geon, about 12ft square and 8ft high, which had no light except that which was admitted through a sewer, which ran close by it and rendering the atmosphere almost unbearable. One section of the prison was called the 'nunnery' because it was used to hold prostitutes who had been captured by the parish watch.[91]

One of the most famous prisoners was the Home Rule party leader Isaac Butt (1813–1875) who was imprisoned here for months, pending the payment of debts owed to his creditors. The Home Rule party wanted a separate parliament in Dublin to legislate for Irish domestic affairs. Isaac Butt argued that Ireland suffered not so much from bad government but from scarcely any government at all.

The Marshalsea later became a military barracks. It was beside the site of Robert Emmet's armoury where he hid the guns and ammunition used in the 1803 rebellion. Here we are walking in his footsteps as in July of that year, Emmet and his men marched up this very laneway and into Thomas Street, and from there marched eastwards towards Dublin Castle.

After the 1916 Rising, British troops were quartered there, and later it accommodated tenants of Dublin Corporation, serving this role until 1970. It stood empty for some years before its demolition in 1975. Some of the stone went to repair the city wall at Cook Street. There are now City Council apartments here, called Marshal's Court, and the old prison wall is still visible behind them.[92]

The IAWS Building

A fine building architecturally and historically is the Irish Agricultural and Wholesale Society (IAWS) of 151 Thomas Street. For many years it has been the home of the co-operative movement in Ireland, founded by Sir Horace Curzon Plunkett (1854–1932) in the late 1880s. Following his long campaign persuading Irish farmers that pooling resources, thereby creating strength in numbers, was the only way for them to survive, the first dairy co-operative was formed at Dromcollagher, Co. Limerick in 1889. By 1900 there were eighty-seven co-operatives with forty-six independent agricultural societies throughout the country. The Irish Agricultural Society Limited ('Society') was established in 1897 by Plunkett to function as a wholesale commodity trading company on behalf of various farmer co-operatives. Horace Plunkett was regarded as the 'intellectual force' of the Irish co-operative movement. The location of the headquarters of the new movement on Thomas Street was of particular significance given the location as an entrance to the city from the west, as well as Thomas Street having a long history of agricultural markets.[93]

The IAWS building is famous for another reason: the unfortunate Lord Edward FitzGerald of the United Irishmen was arrested here, when it was the house of Murphy, a feather merchant. Another United Irishman was arrested at No 65 Thomas Street, now Tom Kennedy's pub. Thomas Ellis, a tape weaver by trade, lived there for many years, until he was also arrested for his part in the United Irishmen Rebellion of 1798. Nothing is known of him after being taken to Dublin Castle that year.

Crane Street and Sugar House Lane

Directly across from the IAWS building we have Crane Street (formerly Crane Lane), which dates from 1728 and is the entrance to the cluster of massive nineteenth-century brick buildings that form the Guinness Brewery. The historic Victorian industrial complex of the area is a maze of narrow cobble-stoned streets and alleys, and black wooden gates leading into the brewery complex. There are no houses along Crane Street, just the vast external walls of various Vat Houses, each one numbered. The cobbled street is like no other in The Liberties or for that matter in Dublin. Such is the height and closeness of the buildings that the sun has difficulty penetrating the area.

Sugar House Lane, built in 1765 at the junction with Crane Street and Rainsford Street, is the location of part of the Digital Exchange complex. Across the street from the entrance to this complex there are two old benches attached to the wall for the weary traveller. The streets and lanes of the Guinness complex are imbued with the smells from the various brewing processes. The sheer enormity of the various buildings, the ornate Guinness Storehouse (Market Street) with the glass-walled Gravity Bar on top, the vats, the chimneys and the clusters of huge silver-coloured aluminium maturation and fermentation flash-like vats make one ponder the area in awe.

Rainsford Street and the Theatrics of Brewing

Just off Crane Street is Rainsford Street, the starting point and first home to the Guinness brewery. The street dates from 1700. The old rail/tram tracks are still embedded in the cobblestones. On one of the walls, at least 20ft up, we see the faded yet powerful and emotional words:

> Stone Upon Stone
> Upon Fallen Stone.

And, beside it in Irish,

> Cloch Ós Cionn Cloiche
> Ós Cionn Clocha Leagtha.[94]

They were the brainchild of American sculptor and conceptual artist, Lawrence Weiner and would appear to have been there since the 1960s. They are appropriate words perhaps, as this area was originally the home of the Rainsford Brewery that was taken over by Arthur Guinness.

St James's Gate on James Street was the western entrance to the city during the Middle Ages. The St James's area has been associated with the brewing trade since the seventeenth century due its good supply of water. Many breweries were estab-

The heart of the Guinness empire in The Liberties in the early twentieth century. (Courtesy of Diageo/Guinness's Brewery)

lished in Dublin up to the mid-seventeenth century, competing with the burgeoning London beer trade. These included a brewery established by Alderman Giles Mee around 1670. Giles Mee was given a lease to the water rights at St James's Gate (called 'The Pipes') by Dublin Corporation. These rights passed to his son-in-law, Sir Mark Rainsford, a city alderman who was Mayor of Dublin between 1700 and 1701, who is credited as being the founder of the St James's Gate brewery.

Mark Rainsford's (grandson of the original founder) Ale Brewery had been on the market for ten years before it caught the attention of the young Arthur Guinness. There were about seventy breweries in the area at that time and what Mr Guinness had acquired was no more than just the average. Yet Arthur was in the venture to change all of that and make history. He was only thirty-four but he knew that the beer industry was highly unsatisfactory and he had a dream that changed the face of The Liberties and Ireland. His purchase of the brewery in 1759 was the birth of a new era in brewing. Since then Guinness has expanded well beyond the original 4-acre site on Rainsford Street.[95]

Rainsford Street was also the site of one of Dublin's three theatres in the early decades of the eighteenth century. In 1734 Dublin possessed three theatres, Smock Alley on Wood Quay, Aungier Street (Theatre Royal), and Rainsford Street but in 1737 Rainsford Street Theatre collapsed.

From Powers Distillery to Art College

Further down Thomas Street beside John's Lane church we have the birth-place of Dominic Corrigan (1802–1880), a prominent physician. His father had a shop here selling farm tools. Dr Corrigan was known for his original observations in heart disease. His work with many of Dublin's poorest inhabitants led to him specialising in diseases of the heart and lungs, and he lectured and published extensively on the subject. He was known as a very hard-working physician, especially during the potato Famine of the late 1840s.

In 1907, plans were announced to build a fire station on Thomas Street, to replace the makeshift station already at Winetavern Street, a proposal that had been on the table since 1898. In 1909, some city councillors moved to shelve the plans, proposing that the money be spent on paying off the Dublin Corporation's loans instead. However, after a lengthy debate, this motion failed to garner enough votes to pass and in November 1909 building of the station was finally given the go-ahead.

The fire station was designed and built by the renowned architect Charles J. McCarthy. It was constructed of Donegal sandstone and Portmarnock brick. At one stage both the firemen and their families lived overhead.

The fire station played a role in the War of Independence as the insurgents kidnapped the firemen and took the fire engine from this station. Consequently, it made the effort of quenching the deliberate burning of the Customs House that much more difficult. The burning of the Custom House was designed to attract international attention to the war and in this the Republicans succeeded. Not long afterwards, the British sought for peace negotiations to end the war.

It is now occupied by the National College of Art and Design (NCAD) and is called Harry Clarke House after the famous Irish stained-glass artist, whose work is to be seen is some of the churches in The Liberties, including next door in John's Lane church. We are still able to see the four original exit doors on the front of the building, from where we can imagine the fire engines hurtling out when on call. And behind, we can still see some of the glory of the old and world-famous John Powers (John's Lane) distillery.[96]

Dublin's Red Square

The college now occupies a unique position in art and design education in Ireland. Besides occupying the old distillery premises of John Powers, no matter where you are you will probably find that a graduate of the NCAD has contributed to the visual culture, which surrounds you. In the past many of the most important Irish artists, designers and art teachers studied in the college and it has long been the central and most important art and design educational institution in Ireland. Located in Thomas Street since 1980, it has only been since 1998 that all of the Faculties and Departments of the College have been located on this one campus.

This is a fascinating campus, full of history and architectural gems as well as the famous Red Square, a large open space at the centre of the complex, surrounded by most interesting structures. The square is between the old Granary Building and the new School of Design for Industry. When NCAD moved to Thomas Street, Irish Government Minister Ruairi Quinn of the Labour Party was the architect and the choice of colour for the paving stones was red (a mere coincidence). The paving accounts for the name 'Red Square'.

There is a wealth of buildings from different eras surrounding the square. On one side we have the six-storey Granary Building with '1817' atop the weather vane. Opposite this we have the modern School of Design building and next to that we have the back of the John's Lane Monastery and the towering back of the church itself.

The square has an extraordinary eclectic mix of weeping willow trees, stone benches, original stills from distillery times, a clock, the ruin of an old cottage, and students' art work – all vying for space and attention.

Joseph Fade and Banking

It was not only the Huguenots who had an influence on The Liberties. Protestants, Quakers, Jews and other religious groups had a profound and lasting influence. The vicinity of No 36 Thomas Street and the story of the 'The Glib Market' is a case in point.

Joseph Fade (a Quaker) started his merchant banking business at 36 Thomas Street in 1715. Fade's 'Bank at the Glib', later known as Frawley's store, became one of the most important of Dublin's bankers and remained so for many years. His name lives on with Fade Street, just off South Great George's Street.[97]

The City Saw Mills: Chadwick's

Chadwick's landmark building on Thomas Street was for many years called the City Saw Mills (Timber and Slate Stores) and before that it was Kelly's Timber Yard. It was built on the site of an old Priory Graveyard of St John's church outside Newgate jail. In 1909 William Thomas Chadwick established his first business called Chadwick's (Dublin) Ltd to supply builders' merchants and major building contractors with Irish and imported cement and plaster. Today Chadwick's is the second largest builders' and plumbers' merchants brand in Ireland, trading from thirty-one branches nationally.[98]

Another local businessman at the turn of the twentieth century was Albert Altman, better known as 'Altman the Saltman', whose business in The Liberties supplied salt and coal to the numerous public baths across Dublin for many years.

Street Traders

Street traders and markets have long been a feature of The Liberties. Meath Street has a number of markets, which entice shoppers and browsers, particularly at weekends. The famous Iveagh Markets in Francis Street replaced the outdoor markets on Patrick Street at the turn of the twentieth century. And long before that we had of course the famous corn market of the Middle Ages at Cornmarket and a market known as the Glib Market, shown on Rocque's map of 1756. 'The Glib' was that stretch of Thomas Street in front of the old Frawley's drapers. It was the name given to the early market that continues to this day.

As part of The Liberties Festival each year (going strong for over forty years), the street traders take on the local Gardaí in a football match. Apparently the Gardaí have a lot of catching up to do! The area really takes off in the Christmas run-up when the street traders 'all but paralyse the traffic along the street and you'd need a bulldozer to plough a way along the pavement' according to one shopper.

'Spud Murphy' and Tayto

Joseph 'Spud' Murphy (1923–2001), founder of Tayto crisps, was born beside The Liberties, one of five children of builder Thomas Murphy and his wife Molly (*née* Sweeney), who owned a wallpaper and paint shop on Thomas Street. The brand name Tayto came about because Joe Murphy's son Joseph, as a very young child, was unable to pronounce 'potato' and called it 'tato'! So, by adding the letter 'y', Tayto was born in the early 1950s in The Liberties.[99]

Children and shoppers at a second-hand clothes sale, outside St Catherine's Church, Thomas Street, 1969. (Courtesy of NLI)

O'Connell and Cosgrave: From James's Street to Pimlico

Continuing back along Thomas Street we come to St James's Street which was originally part of the early medieval route, Slige Mhor, from Dublin to Galway.

40 Steps to Cromwell's Quarters

Just off James's Street we have a very unusual place name, Cromwell's Quarters, linking the street to Bow Street West in Old Kilmainham Village. In fact the steep steps linking the two are also known as the Forty Steps. This means there are three areas of The Liberties that have forty steps connecting different streets and are all called Forty Steps! The question is, of course, which is the real one? Most locals say that the Forty Steps besides St Audoen's church are the original.

A view of James's Street and Thomas Street in the late 1970s. Some of the landmarks of The Liberties are visible including the smoke billowing from the brewery and St Patrick's Tower onion-dome top in the centre background. (Courtesy of Dublin City Public Libraries)

St Patrick's Hospital

The entrance to Jonathan Swift's St Patrick's Hospital is near the fountain on James's Street. Over the entrance, the words 'St Patrick's Hospital Founded by Jonathan Swift D.D. Dean of St Patrick's AD 1745' are carved in stone.[101]

Ireland's first President of the Executive Council of the Irish Free State was William T. Cosgrave, who was born at 174 James Street (now Kenny's Pub and just across from the hospital), Dublin on 5 June 1880. His father was a publican and grocer at this address. He was educated at nearby Francis Street Christian Brothers School but left school at the age of sixteen to join his father's business. During the 1916 Rising he served at the South Dublin Union (a workhouse later called St James's Hospital) under Eamonn Ceannt. Cosgrave founded Cumann na nGaedhael (later Fine Gael) in 1923 and was elected President of the Executive Council until 1932.

He played a prominent role in building the new state, helping to establish a new police and court system and local government. Cosgrave was also credited with ensuring the smooth transition of power to Fianna Fáil in 1932. He died in 1965.[102]

CBS James's Street

Blessed Edmund Rice founded the Christian Brothers School (CBS), James's Street ('Jambo') in 1820. The schoolhouse was originally located at the back of 69 James's Street. The school moved to its present location on Basin Lane behind James's Street in 1869. The current school building was built in the 1970s. The school is located between Guinness's Brewery and St James Hospital. Among

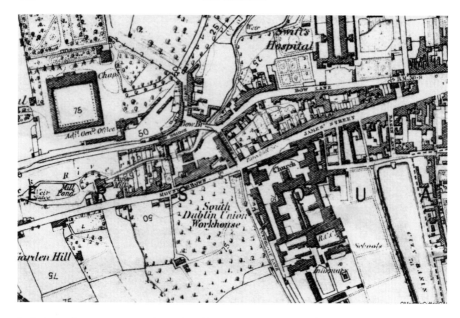

Early map of James's Street with South Dublin Union (James's Street Hospital) and St Patrick's Hospital. (Courtesy of Old Dublin Society/Dublin City Libraries/NLI)

the many famous past pupils of the school was Brian Kerr who became the Irish soccer team manager.[103]

The Workhouse: South Dublin Union and the Hybrid Love Seat

In the old days prisoners in Newgate Jail at Cornmarket were not fed and used to have to beg for alms through the prison bars. That led in 1667 to Dublin Corporation spending £300 in laying foundations for a poorhouse, the South Dublin Union, on the site now occupied by St James's Hospital. However, the wars between King William and King James culminating with the Battle of the Boyne in 1689 intervened and the work was abandoned until 1703 when Mary, Duchess of Ormonde, laid the foundation stone for the new development.

In 1727 a foundling hospital was opened on the site and many famous people, including Jonathan Swift and the original Arthur Guinness, served on the board of governors over the years. The foundling hospital was closed in the early years of the nineteenth century and the buildings were then used as a workhouse for the poor and it became known as the South Dublin Union.

In 1916 rebel forces occupied the South Dublin Union and during the subsequent fighting a member of the nursing staff was accidentally killed. The hospital continued to develop as a municipal hospital with the formation of the new state and the name was changed to St Kevin's Hospital (particularly because of the stigma attached to the South Dublin Union workhouse). In fact the stigma still attached to the St Kevin's name and it was not until it was again re-named as St James's Hospital, that the stigma and memories of the workhouse ('Poor House') abated.

Later in the century plans were made to amalgamate some of the smaller voluntary hospitals in the city and to build a new hospital at the St James's site. The board of St James's Hospital met in 1971 and the planning of the new hospital began. In the mid-1980s the government's need to cut back on public spending brought about by the closure of Sir Patrick Dun's Hospital, Dr Steven's Hospital and the Royal City of Dublin Hospital in Baggot Street. Mercer's Hospital had already closed in 1983. Most of the services provided by these historic hospitals were incorporated into the rapidly developing St James's Hospital.[104]

At the entrance to the hospital, just facing the Luas stop, there is 'The Hybrid Love Seat' along by the railings. This is a public art project featuring small individual sculptures that have the appearance of prehistoric animals and figures perched one by one atop the railings. They were created mainly by young people of The Liberties from the Presentation Secondary School, Warrenmount and Basin Lane CBS, as well as students from Crumlin Secondary School.

Just beside the hospital there is a development of fine solid and attractively built houses, called Ceannt Fort, the name deriving from the 1916 Rising leader Eamonn Ceannt who was so active in the South Dublin Union during the rebellion.

Echlin and Pim Streets – Coopers and Casks
Just off James's Street, we have some more interesting old streets, including Bond Street, Pim Street and Echlin Street. In the latter street a terrace of four-storey houses dating from the late nineteenth century is striking in its uniformity and

Cask-filling department in Guinness's Brewery. (Courtesy of Diageo/Guinness's Brewery)

solidity. The Old Harbour pub on the corner, in the shadow of the brewery, is a reminder of the time when it was adjacent to the Grand Canal Basin, where barges were laden with casks of Guinness for transportation to the length and breadth of Ireland via the Grand Canal. The basin is now no more, but the pub is a lasting legacy of the time when there was a harbour here. Other reminders of the basin include the curved terrace of houses beside the pub with names such as Grand Canal Place and Harbour View.

Just around the corner in Pim Street we see another reminder of former activities. The Liffey Cooperage Company, for many years involved in the manufacture of wooden casks, has ceased trading, but the name over the entrance gates indicates the hugely important trade. Those who made and repaired the casks or barrels were known as 'coopers'. Some coopers were specially appointed as 'smellers' to weed out any foul-smelling casks for treatment in the cask repair shop. The wooden casks were frequently referred to as 'barrels', but in fact 'barrel' actually refers to a specific size of cask. In the 1920s about 300 coopers (half the city's total) worked in Guinness's Brewery, with the rest working in companies such as the Liffey Cooperage Company. The old sign is a monument to a hugely-important trade that employed many locals from The Liberties.

Pimlico

Coming back along James's Street to Thomas Street, we come to St Catherine's church and just beside it we have Thomas Court/Thirlestance Terrace and the road into Pimlico. The area itself is located between Thomas Court, Marrowbone Lane, the Coombe and Ardee Street. The Pimlico Parliament referred to courts that were held along by Thomas Court for many years until 1820. Pimlico was in the Liberty of Thomas Court and Donore.

Pimlico was named after a street in south-west London. The name was brought by woollen merchants who settled here at the start of the eighteenth century. The Earl of Meath leased part of the medieval street known as Donore Street (originally called Donour Street) to them.[105]

For many years Braithwaite Street appears to have been a poor street inhabited by artisans working locally in the weaving industry. The Revd James Whitelaw from nearby St Catherine's church in Thomas Street visited the street in 1798 to do a census. He found that in the thirty-one houses on the street there were 367 residents. Another survey carried out in 1816 showed little change and that an average of two to four families crowded together in a large room of each house. No. 6 had 103 people living in the house while in the thirty adjoining houses there were 917 inhabitants.[106]

At the Thomas Court end of Pimlico are fine red-brick and very ornate residences, similar to the Iveagh Trust buildings on Patrick Street, and built over a hundred years ago. Across the road, just off Marrowbone Lane, is a quiet enclave of artisan cottages called Pimlico Cottages. One estate agent called them 'charming and character-filled' and a local wit asked 'How many characters can you get into a cottage?'[107]

Because of Pimlico's location beside the Guinness Brewery, the smell of hops and roasting barley suffuses the air. Many of the Guinness employees lived close to the brewery because of the twenty-four-hour work shifts. The brewing process was no 9 to 5 activity!

'Dublin in the Rare Aul Times' is a popular song often sung by the Dublin City Ramblers, The Dubliners, and Flogging Molly. Composed by that great songwriter, Pete St John, some of the memorable lines are:

> My name it is Sean Dempsey as Dublin as could be
> Born hard and late in Pimlico in a house that ceased to be
> My trade I was a cooper, lost out to redundancy
> Like my house that fell to progress my trade's a memory
> I remember Dublin City in the rare old times.[108]

One of the 1916 Rising leaders, James Connolly, lived here with his family (his wife, Lillie and daughters Mona and Nora) for a number of years in an end of terrace house at No 54 Pimlico. And before their move to the United States, they lived in a cottage in nearby Weavers' Sqaure off Cork Street.

Thirty years ago, you might have seen a person leaving the original St Catherine's Bakery at Thomas Court with a white sack over their shoulder,

Acting the goat at Taylors' Lane, off Thomas Street, 1940s. (Courtesy of Dublin.ie Forums/el gronk)

T & M Pacelli's, Meath Street Area, 1958. (Courtesy of Dublin City Public Libraries)

looking very suspicious but closer inspection would reveal that it was a pillow case used by some customers to keep the Batch Loaves or Turnovers warm on the way home. Another famous bakery was the Myra Bakery in nearby Francis Street.[109]

A former Liberties resident, Mairín Johnston highlighted her happy memories of growing up in the area in her enjoyable read, *Around the Banks of Pimlico*.[110] In an interview with the *Irish Independent* she said, 'It has a closeness and community spirit'.[111] Her father's family were weavers who came over from Yorkshire in 1680 to settle in Pimlico. Her mother's people moved there from Gort around the time of the Famine in the 1840s/1850s.

James Stephens, author of *The Charwoman's Daughter* (1912), which has been required reading in Irish schools for those preparing for the Leaving Certificate for many years, lived on Thomas Court. Born in a Liberties slum, Stephens knew all about poverty, and this awareness makes *The Charwoman's Daughter* the more convincing. He also wrote *The Crock of Gold*, which became a best-seller.[112]

In the open green area in the centre of Pimlico there is spiral pathway with words carved into the stonework. The spiral represents the journey of life, growth, change, and the journey of the soul to eternal life. A large metal sculpture consisting of coloured boxes with jagged edges called 'Parable Island' was erected in the central open area of Pimlico in 1988. Unfortunately, for safety reasons it was subsequently removed and replaced with a tree, but the message about the journey of the soul to eternal life, written on the paving, remains.

Brabazon and the Saint: Meath and Francis Streets

Returning to Thomas Street, we have Meath Street and Francis Street linking the main thoroughfare with Dean Street and the Coombe. Take a right turn on Thomas Street (if you're heading towards Christ Church) and you'll take a big step back to the past. As with Thomas Street these two street are of particular historical significance in Dublin, with their origins rooted in the expansion

Halton's Grocers, Francis Street in the 1960s. (Courtesy of Dublin City Public Libraries)

of the medieval western suburb of the old city. Their building stock has seen much change in recent years, with many of the old tenements demolished, but many historic buildings remain, some of which are among the oldest in Dublin. Today the streets play an important role in the social and commercial life of The Liberties, with a distinctive character that is worth protecting.

These streets retain some of their medieval origins with laneways and streets linking them to each other and to Thomas Street. Carman's Hall, Earl Street, Brabazon Square, Swift's Alley and Thomas Davis Street evoke historical figures whilst giving access to smaller residential streets and adjoining enclaves.

Meath Street and Francis Street were the homes to many shoemakers and saddlers, whose supplies came from the numerous tanneries in the area.

From Barons to Bones: Meath Street

This old and historic street was named after William Brabazon, second Baron of Ardee, who was created Earl of Meath in 1627. This is a busy trading street.

Meath Street in the early 1970s. (Courtesy of Dublin City Public Libraries)

Towards the end of the eighteenth century it was the centre of a brewing industry. The old archway at No 26 was the entrance to the meeting house of the Quakers and a soup kitchen operated from here during the Famine years.

Meath Street emerged in a planned fashion in the late seventeenth century, according to Graham Hickey in his study on Francis Street and Meath Street. It was to be a spacious speculative development devised by the Earl of Meath to be a fashionable residential enclave in the western suburb of what were still relatively rural environs outside the walled city. By the early eighteenth century the area had become a fully urbanised quarter, with streets and lanes knitted together and densely populated. The expansion was fuelled in no small way with the arrival of Huguenot refugees fleeing religious persecution on the Continent. The combination of manufacturing, trade and development reached its pinnacle during the eighteenth century.[113]

The earlier prosperity of the area, however, did not last and the mid-eighteenth century ushered in a period of decline. There are a number of reasons

Meath Street in the 1960s. (Courtesy of Dublin City Public Libraries)

for this: other parts of the city became more fashionable, with people and businesses moving; the break-up of the guild system in the 1760s that was once so central to the prosperity of the trades, threw industry into disarray; competition from Britain and a tax on exports further weakened The Liberties industries and livelihoods in the area. Poverty and overcrowding soon crept in. By the 1800s and the passing of the Act of Union, The Liberties was in irreversible decline. While the northern end of Francis and Meath Streets continued to prosper to some extent, squalid houses and tenements soon made their mark nearer the Coombe.

Harry Sive's rag-a-bone and clothing merchant, who had his business in Meath Street for many years, was an early twentieth century example of recycling old clothing for re-sale, but it also reflected the poverty-stricken times and circumstances many of the residents lived in. However, despite the decline, some industries such as brewing and tanning continued to prosper.[114]

Meath Street today is a bustling commercial thoroughfare and with its shops and markets it is a hive of activity and an absolute delight to the senses. Here you will see long-established business such as Larkin Brothers, Dunne's and Tony Martin's Butchers, O'Neill's Fish and Poultry, and St Catherine's Bakery – all thriving. You will see butchers hauling carcasses to and fro and enjoy the aroma of freshly baked batch loaves wafting down the street. The original famous bakery was in Pimlico, just off Thomas Street. It now continues in Meath Street. It was the only place in Ireland where one could get a sliced Turnover Loaf. You can still buy batch loaves, Tipsy Cakes/Russian Slices and Gur Cakes here. Other businesses are still going strong: Fusco's, the Bull Ring, the Liberty and Molly Malone Markets and Bazaars, as well as the many pubs, hairdressers, chemists, various other exotic shops, and street hawkers with their tried and trusted calls for us to buy – jostling for our attention and all pointing to a vibrant business and local community. It is always teeming with shoppers.

'Our local business has always been family run, we have had generations of customer loyalty. We could consider ourselves not so much a shop, more a way of life', opined Jack Roche of Roche's Grocers on Meath Street. People of The Liberties still remember when Taoiseach Bertie Ahern brought Russia's Mikhael Gorbachev to The Liberties during the course of a visit to Dublin. Apparently he was opening a Russian shop. When he arrived he walked the length of Meath Street. Miriam Lord, writing at the time (early 2002) in the *Irish Independent*, noted that he 'popped in to a butcher's shop and one local woman exclaimed about the chops in the window – "They'll have to call them Gorbychops now!".' Jack Roche still recalls the visit of the Russian president. He handed him a bowl of fruit with the two landmark words '*glasnost*' and '*perestroika*' emblazoned on top and with a handwritten note thanking him for

Meath Street in the late 1960s. Larkin Brothers butchers are still going strong! (Courtesy of Dublin City Public Libraries)

his work in Russia. It was something he just did on the spur of the moment, he recalled. And as he approached the president, he could sense the heightened alert in the attitude and the body language of the security guards in case there was a bomb hidden amongst the fruit!

President Gorbachev then visited the Bull Ring where he met owner, Clare Mooney, the mother of a former Fianna Fáil TD, Mary Mooney.[115]

The Liberty 'Screech'

A number of important buildings include the church of St Catherine of Alexandria and the Liberty Crèche. Situated at the Thomas Street end of Meath Street, the Liberty Crèche is a very attractive building in the area and deserves closer attention. In 1893, a committee of mostly Quaker women opened the strictly non-sectarian crèche for children of women 'dependent on their own exertions away from their home for means of support'. This became the 'Liberty Crèche' in 1897, expanding slowly from the two front rooms to occupy the whole building and the next-door premises. It earned the nickname 'Screech' not from its screaming children but because the word 'crèche' was a tongue twister for adults.[116]

Cast iron bollards flank the entrance to the Liberty Crèche and these are amongst the last surviving elements of historic street furniture on Meath Street.

At the time of its closure in 2008 it was the longest-existing crèche in Dublin, if not Ireland. Happily, the crèche re-opened after a short closure, and is now run according to the ideals of Rudolf Steiner. It is still owned by the Quaker Trust with the same philosophy of providing inexpensive child-care.

President Mary McAleese (in her second term as President of Ireland) toured the Liberty Crèche - the second time an Irish President has visited in its long history. 'I had thought it [the nickname] might have more to do with the slight noise coming from the place', said the President as she met the crèche's thirty-eight children, all less than four years old. 'It was among the first crèches of its kind and was a new phenomenon in those days ... The people who started it were very radical and quite revolutionary in their ways, but 100 years later their work is taken for granted', she said.[117]

Janet Guy, Liberty Crèche Manager, said the original emphasis was on helping 'respectable mothers earn their daily bread' knowing their children were kept safe, fed and clean. So successful is the crèche that some local families have been associated with it for six generations. However, she said that despite its long and colourful heritage, the crèche is evolving with a changing Dublin. 'Today we are seeing a positive change in the crèche. As more and more families from diverse cultural backgrounds come to live in Dublin, their children are joining us. This encourages friendships to be forged and integrates families into the growing Liberties community'.[118]

There was once a Quaker chapel beside the crèche. There was also a Savings Bank in the middle of the Liberty Crèche building where Indian meal was distributed to the poor of Dublin during the Famine.

The Meath Mart
A short terrace of houses on the left side of Meath Street, with Flemings Londis Supermarket in the centre has unusual numeration. While they are numbered 1, 2, 3, 4/5 Meath Mart they also go by the numbers 25, 24, 23 etc Meath Street!

The Family Brabazon: Brabazon Square
Well worth a visit, Brabazon Square is one of a few hidden-away tree-lined attractive small squares with cottages in the area. (See also Meath Square, Gray Square, Park Terrace and Reginald Square all located between Meath Street and Ardee Street and Pimlico.) It is hard to believe that this very attractive square is located near the hustle and bustle of Meath Street. The Earl of Meath owned lands around the square, and the Dublin Artisans' Dwelling Association built the housing in the late nineteenth century. The Dublin Artisans' Dwellings Company was established in 1876 by members of the Dublin Sanitary Association. Lady Brabazon was on the committee. Her ancestor, one Reginald Brabazon, was of a family line which had held the titles of

'Baron of Ardee' and 'Earl of Meath' since the sixteenth and seventeenth centuries. And before Reginald (note: Reginald Street), we had William Brabazon, who started the whole process.[119]

In the Coombe area between Pimlico and Meath Street, 216 red-brick one-storey cottages and two-storey houses were built on sites that had been cleared under the Public Health Act and Labourers' Act of 1875. Two references were required before a tenant could occupy a dwelling. They also had to have a steady job. In 1885 the Prince of Wales visited the area to see progress on the initiative. Other streets in the area were named after the Earls of Meath, including Meath Street, Grey Square, Reginald Square, Brabazon Street, Earl Street and Ardee Street.

Gray Street and Napoleon

Just off Meath Street we have Gray Street, named after Edmund Dwyer Gray (1845–1888), MP for the area. These houses were also built by the Dublin Artisans' Dwellings Company. Gray had a very illustrious career. He was an Irish newspaper proprietor, politician and MP in the House of Commons. He was also Lord Mayor and later High Sheriff of the City of Dublin and became a strong supporter of Charles Stewart Parnell.

In 1868 Gray saved five people from drowning in a wrecked schooner at Killiney Bay, an action for which he received the Tayleur Fund Gold Medal for bravery from the Royal Humane Society. By coincidence, the rescue was witnessed by his future wife, Caroline Agnes, who he would meet shortly afterwards. Agnes was the daughter of Caroline Chisholm (an English humanitarian renowned for her work in female immigrant welfare in Australia), and although Gray was descended from a Protestant family, he converted to Catholicism to marry her in 1869. From 1875 to 1883, Gray served as a member of the Dublin Corporation, and in 1880 served a term as Lord Mayor. Unusually for an Irish nationalist politician, Gray was very much focused on urban rather than rural affairs, and like his father was heavily involved in public health and water provision for Dublin. He also promoted reform in the municipal health system. Thanks to his efforts, improvements were made in the housing and sanitation conditions in The Liberties.

He was the proprietor of the Dublin nationalist daily *Freeman's Journal*, of which his father Sir John Gray, an associate of Daniel O'Connell, had previously been proprietor. In an obituary, a Mr MacWeeney, the doyen of the Freeman's Journal staff, described Gray as the 'Napoleon of Irish Journalism.'[120]

At the junction of Gray Street and Reginald Street stands a cast-iron monument that was built as a water fountain in 1898. The dome was surmounted with an eagle until the Black and Tans shot it off during the War of Independence. The fountain was replaced with a statue of Christ by the local parishioners of St Catherine's in commemoration of the centenary of Catholic Emancipation in 1929. It was restored to mark the visit of Pope John Paul II to The Liberties on 29 September 1979. Mass is celebrated annually by the local parishioners at the memorial.

Swift's Alley

Linking Meath and Francis Streets, this alley is not named after Dean Swift but after a seventeenth-century merchant, Goodwin Swift. However, this may be debatable (or irrelevant) as the great Dean had a brother called Godwin. There is a Godwin Swift buried in Mount Jerome cemetery.

Swift's Alley, from Engine Alley to Francis Street. This photograph is one of those taken by W.J. Joyce in 1913 to illustrate the dreadful living conditions in Dublin. Swift's Alley was located between Engine Alley and Francis Street. This photograph was taken facing towards Francis Street. Over 100 people lived in Swift's Alley in 1911. (Courtesy of Dublin City Public Libraries)

Francis Street

Francis Street was an important ancient route linking Thomas Street to the Coombe and beyond that via New Street to Wicklow and southeast Leinster. The Thomas Street, Augustine Street and Francis Street junction was a major point for travellers going north, south or west from Dublin to other parts of Ireland.

To call Francis Street 'Dublin's Antique Quarter' may be appropriate, as it has always attracted traders of second-hand goods. This title, however, has been a relatively recent addition. It was a Franciscan foundation – the Friary of St Francis – in the twelfth century that gave its name to this street. Ralph de Porter granted the grounds to the Franciscans in the Middle Ages.

According to Graham Hickey, in his study on Meath Street and Francis Street, the friary was suppressed during the Reformation in 1537. Following the Restoration of King Charles II in 1660, the Franciscans returned to the friary site and built a new chapel, which later became the Pro-Cathedral for Dublin under Archbishop Patrick Russell in the 1680s, and remained so under nine successive archbishops. The chapel survived until the early nineteenth century, when the current church replaced it dedicated to St Nicholas of Myra.[121]

It may have mostly antique shops now but not so long ago this was a tenement-filled street with hundreds of families, huckster shops, nine pubs, and all sorts of businesses. The tenements are gone, replaced with modern apartment blocks. Luckily, some of the older buildings still survive, often behind new exteriors, but they do lend dignity and character to a street with much heritage and history. Its businesses are still remembered fondly by many Liberties residents: the Myra Bakery with its penny cakes loved by the locals sold in thousands; Johnny Ray's ice-cream parlour, renowned throughout Dublin; the popular Joyce's Bakery which used to have great queues for pancakes on Shrove (Pancake) Tuesday for years; and not forgetting the Mushatt family of chemists at No 3 who became an institution in The Liberties for over forty years.

Some of the old pubs such as Swift's and the Liberty Belle are still there (the Barley Mow has only recently closed), whereas many of the old shops and businesses are long gone, but not forgotten. Alas, that great institution, the Old Dublin Restaurant is no more; it used to advertise: 'Taste the unique flavour of Russian and Scandinavian cuisine in elegant surroundings.' The restaurant was a famous dining spot for many in the latter years of the twentieth century.

Dublin City Spares, operating at different times on different locations on Francis Street was beloved by generations of motor-bike enthusiasts. It was for many years the place to go to for that important spare part for your bike.

Past pupils will have memories of the Francis Street CBS School ('Franner'), the entrance to which will not be found on Francis Street but alongside the back of St Nicholas of Myra church on John Dillon Street.

Francis Street, 1959. (Courtesy of Dublin City Public Libraries)

Both sides of Francis Street are now lined with antique shops and art galleries, giving the street an antique fair feel. This beautiful old street is not only a heaven for antique collectors with money in the pocket but for everyone with a taste for fine art and furniture.

Here you'll find the long-established and one of the most famous in Ireland, O'Reilly's Auction Rooms. O'Reilly's has been in business since 1948. Although it has been located on Francis Street for many years it was originally at nearby Winetavern Street where the words 'Auction Rooms' were emblazoned across the front of the building just below the roof. The name John O'Reilly was written over the entrance. The Wednesday auction of fine jewellery and silver is well worth a visit and is an education in itself.

Johnston Antiques, Sean McGahan & Sons, Martin Fennelly, Michael Connell, Lantern Antiques, Esther Sexton antiques, Niall Mullen and O'Sullivan Antiques (with the workmen and the dangling piano on the upper outside wall!) are just a few treasure shops, many of which are family-run businesses. Art lovers will enjoy the Bad Art Gallery and Monster Truck, Portfolio and Gallery Zozimus. And just across the road from the Zozimus we have the popular and innovative Constant Knitter shop that is a reminder of the long history of the textile industry in The Liberties.

The Iveagh Markets

At the turn of the twentieth century the Guinness family built the Iveagh Markets in 1906. This came about as a result of an act of parliament in 1901, which extinguished the rights of street traders to operate a market on nearby Patrick Street. The purpose of the Act was to clear the area around St Patrick's Cathedral for social and sanitary reasons, thereby laying out St Patrick's Park and the Iveagh Trust housing complex. Lord Iveagh gave a commitment to make provision for these traders at an alternative location in the area within five years, fulfilling this promise with the enclosed Iveagh Markets. The markets acted as a significant regenerating boost to the area. However, it also marked the end of the ancient street markets, which had been held in Patrick Street, in the shadow of the cathedral, for generations.

Dublin Corporation Disinfecting Department, Francis Street, 1960s. (Courtesy of Dublin City Public Libraries)

The Iveagh Markets stand on a site that had once been taken up by an important brewery, Sweetman's. The markets building is a fine piece of architecture, with its brick and stone façade in the Queen Anne style hiding a large functional cast-iron galleried market hall. The keystones of the several arches at the front of the building are ornamented with carved heads, which represent the various trading nations of the world. These extraordinary-looking heads are well worth a closer look considering the facial expressions on some of them! The large bearded grinning face is reputed to represent Lord Iveagh. There used to be a washhouse at the back of the Iveagh Markets used by local people who brought their washing there.

The famous markets were in use right up to the 1990s when they closed their doors. A food market akin to the English Market in Cork is now planned for the site.[122]

Myra House and Monto

Myra House at No 100 Francis Street was where the worldwide lay religious organisation, the Legion of Mary, was founded in 1921. A local woman, Mrs Elizabeth Kirwan, who was involved in the Society of St Vincent de Paul, was the person who founded the Legion of Mary, and not, as is widely believed, the Department of Finance civil servant, Frank Duff. She was particularly aware of the poverty in the area and decided to take action. Frank Duff, who succeeded Kirwan as president of the Legion, was told by Dr Edward Byrne, the Archbishop of Dublin in the 1920s, to keep away from social reform and to stick to religion and in that way the problems of the day would soon be solved! He followed this order, although with some reluctance, initially.

The Legion was also associated with the demise of Monto, Dublin's infamous red-light district. The area called Monto (in and around Montgomery Street/ Gloucester Street, off Sackville Street (now O'Connell Street) became infamous also as the British Empire's biggest red light district, its financial viability aided by the number of British Army barracks and hence soldiers in the city, notably the Royal Barracks (later Collins Barracks and now one of the locations of Ireland's National Museum). Monto finally closed in the mid-1920s, following a campaign against prostitution by the Legion of Mary, its financial viability having already been seriously undermined by the withdrawal of soldiers from the city following the Anglo-Irish Treaty of 1921 and the establishment of the Irish Free State. Despite the demise of Monto, prostitution still featured in The Liberties with some dwelling houses serving as brothels.[123]

The Tivoli

A significant cultural development in the early twentieth century in The Liberties was the construction of the Tivoli Cinema, which opened its doors in 1934 with the screening of *Cockeyed Cavaliers*. For local historian Eamon MacThomais, the

'Tivo' was more than a picture-house; 'it was a University where we learned all about the Blue Nile and the White Nile, about Stanley and Livingstone and things we never learned in school!'

The official opening of the 1,7000-seater Tivoli cinema was on 21 December 1934. It was opened by local councillor Patrick Medlar, a former local undertaker with Medlar & Claffey of Thomas Street. If you were heard to have a serious cough, you'd be assailed by the phrase 'Medlar's got you!' On a slightly macabre note, Medlar had a glass panel inserted in his coffin so that his face could be seen when the coffin was closed. In his speech at the opening of the cinema he recalled that he had attended school in the area forty years previously and said he was very proud to be there to open the third largest cinema in the city of Dublin. Also present in the audience that night was a fellow Alderman, Alfie Byrne, TD and nine times Lord Mayor of Dublin. The cinema closed in September 1964. It was subsequently used briefly as a Bingo Hall and for concerts, until it burned down and lay derelict for many years. Following two brief temporary openings as a theatre in 1986 and 1987, it opened as a permanent double theatre, seating 1,560, in 1988.[124]

Leigh & Sons Ltd, Car Repair Service, Francis Street, 1969. Notice the television aerials on houses and the Gold Flake sign above the The Liberties Lounge. (Courtesy of Dublin City Public Libraries)

It was bought and re-developed by a successful local businessman who grew up in the area, Tony Byrne. In his younger days, he loved going to the 'Tivo' in its heyday. It is still in operation today, but now as a theatre.

'Go to Mushatts for Cures'

Foley's Chemist on Thomas Street has a virtual museum called 'Mushatt's Natural Medicines' in their front windows to celebrate a local institution that was a feature of The Liberties for over forty years. It is dedicated to Harold Mushatt, 'Kill or Cure' chemist who operated the family business, Mushatts' Chemists originally at No 3 Francis Street before moving to where Foley's is now on Thomas Street.

If you were sick or needed a cure Mushatts was the best (and in most cases the only) place to go in the first half of the twentieth century. Daddy Nagle in Meath Street was another popular chemist. He was known as the 'Lucky Man' because of similar healing renown. With their mixtures and preparations, they seemed to cure all the ills of the poor of the area. They were part of a Jewish community that had started to come to Dublin from Eastern Europe from the 1830s to

Inside Halton's Grocers, Francis Street, 1960s. (Courtesy of Dublin City Public Libraries)

1880. Many settled in the nearby Portobello area (called 'Little Jerusalem') and some, including the Mushatts, settled in The Liberties. The Mushatts were from Lithuania. Louis Mushatt was trained as a chemist in the Mistear's Medical Hall or Pharmacy at Leonard's Corner, Clanbrassil Street (later Hayes, Conyingham & Robinson). The Mistear's made a lot of their own preparations and it was this hands-on approach to compounding and putting together of medicines that was to make the Mushatt brothers locally famous. When Louis qualified as a chemist the family opened their business in Francis Street in 1922, in a building that was a tenement house. The younger brother, Harry, then trained there as a chemist.

Over the years they developed a keen interest in conditions such as eczema, psoriasis and dermatitis, and soon became famous for producing formulations which helped with a variety of skin conditions. The shelves of their shop were lined with brown bottles full of ready-made remedies for sale, the formulae for which were all penned in a black notebook, carefully kept under lock and key. The front window displayed dozens of Mushatt's skin soaps with a big painted foot on a card for Mushatt's foot paste showing the sole of the foot.

Most of their customers were from the tenements in Dublin, particularly those in The Liberties. The people of the tenements who lived in abject poverty went to the Mushatt brothers because they really couldn't afford a doctor. They sold all their preparations over the counter and, because of the local peoples' poverty, they often brought with them their own Baby Power bottle (a small Irish whiskey bottle) for maybe a penny or tuppence worth of the various mixtures - camphorated oil for a child's cough or iodine if they had a cut.[125]

They sold their own brand of remedies labelled KK – KK Foot Paste for example was for 'corns, welts, callousses and bunions – no need to use dangerous razors, knife blades or burning acids'. It was claimed that KK really stood for 'Kill or Kure'. The chemist closed down in 1967. The following is an excerpt from a poem called 'Shop of Cures', written by Gerard Smyth who grew up in Francis Street:

They came with their shivers, crowds of the sick
crowding into the cramped space between glass jars
of glucose sticks, iron for the blood,
into the presence of those high priests who knew by heart

where to reach for wart-cures, cough mixtures,
preparations that tasted sweet,
ointments that had to be rubbed on, rubbed in,
that radiated the balm of healing.[126]

Though Mushatts is long gone, their notebook has been handed down to another generation of pharmacists today, Séan Foley and so KK medicines are still available in Foley's Pharmacy on Thomas Street. Interestingly the Mushatt family is still in business today in the USA where they run a successful business in skin care products. The company trades as Mushatts No. 9 (since 1922).

John Dillon Street

The link between Francis Street and John Dillon Street (formerly Plunkett Street) via the side of St Nicholas of Myra church was long known as Chapel Lane. The Christian Brothers' School, Francis Street (known as 'Franner') was established there in 1818 and a new school building was built in 1959 to replace the old structure.

House of Mirrors and the Chatting Houses

Like nearby Thomas Davis Street, Dillon Street derives its name from the leaders of the Young Ireland movement of the 1840s. John Blake Dillon (1814 -1866) was a nationalist and co-founder with Thomas Davis and Gavan Duffy of *The Nation* newspaper. There are over 120 red-brick houses on and around this street, built around 1886.

Just beside the back wall of St Nicholas of Myra church there is a very interesting architect-designed house with a rooftop garden and an open courtyard. It is known locally as the 'house of mirrors' and the 'double house'. It was built in a former graveyard of the church and because planning regulations stipulating that it must not be higher than the churchyard wall, the lower floor of the house was built deep down underground and a courtyard was used to good effect to facilitate natural light penetrating the depths. On the outside we have two entrance doorways and two mirrors.

According to Emmet Scanlon of Tom De Paor Architects:

> Dublin has two mirrors on John Dillon Street. As you approach this pair of houses, a neighbour's plastic neo-Georgian window unexpectedly becomes a framed object of contemplation. As the taut mirror passively reflects the life of the street, the house actively begins to chat with it, working its way into the traditional, red-brick neighbourhood. This witty device makes visible the spirit of the double house. It seems delighted to have moved in, but respects the lie of the land and the rules of the road.[127]

Jonathan Swift and James Clarence Mangan are remembered in adjacent roads off John Dillon Street where red-bricked one-and two-storey dwellings from the late nineteenth and early twentieth century are a feature.

Hanover Lane/Square

Continuing from John Dillon Street we have another very attractive enclave of red-brick houses and new apartments around Hanover Square, and linking Francis Street via a tunnel to Patrick Street. The red-brick houses were built in 1873 for artisans.

Carman's Hall and Spitalfields

On the opposite side of Francis Street, facing St Nicholas of Myra church, we have Carman's Hall, Spitalfields (printed as Cammon-hall in Rocque's Map of 1756). It was briefly called Wall Lane before reverting back to its present name. An unusual name for a street, it links Meath and Francis Streets and houses a local primary school and local community centre, which is well worth a visit to see the exterior and the interior. It got its name from being a car man's (driver) coach terminus for the Wexford coach. Now it is used as a centre of community activity and as a vibrant heritage centre, which is a hive of activity seven days a week. There are striking statues of St Patrick and Our Lady over the school. There is also a very good view of the front of St Nicholas of Myra church from this street. The Dubliners' rendition of 'The Ragman's Ball' ballad refers to Carman's Hall.[128]

Linking Carman's Hall to Mark's Alley West is a short neat terrace of two-storey houses built in 1918 called Spitalfields. The name derives from the area with the same name in the East End of London and is a contraction of 'hospital fields', in reference to the open land that lay behind a nearby hospital. Huguenot weavers inhabited the area for many years and when some of them settled in The Liberties, they brought the name with them. Also, Irish weavers went to work in Spitalfields in London, particularly at times of a lull in the silk trade at home.

Opposite the terrace of houses stands a new apartment block called Tandy Court, after the 1798 leader Napper Tandy, who lived locally.

Fallons's The Capstan Bar

At the southern end of Francis Street we come on to Dean Street. The name comes from its close proximity to the deanery of St Patrick's Cathedral. It was originally named Crosspoddle Street where at the junction with Patrick Street women washed their clothes in the River Poddle. After a bad flood in 1860 when the cathedral was flooded the river was culverted, but to this day it floods at various stages along its route.

Fallons (The Capstan Bar) is a long-established (since 1620) and landmark pub on the corner of Dean Street, New Row South and the Coombe. The name 'Capstan' comes from a brand of unfiltered cigarettes that were popular at the turn of the twentieth century ('capstan' also has a nautical meaning referring to a rotating machine used to control or apply force to something else. Therefore the term might well have been applied to trying to cross the River Poddle which

Resting up at Chamber Street on a sunny day in the 1940s. Chamber Street links Weaver and Newmarket Squares. (Courtesy of Dublin.ie Forums/el gronk)

flows under New Row South and was (and remains) the cause of much flooding in the area). Like so many of the pubs in The Liberties it is a cosy little gem of a street-corner pub that has remained essentially unchanged over the years. It is a pub with lots of character, solid pitch and yellow pine all over and local Dolphin's Barn brick, all original. The collection of artifacts scattered around the shelves includes a well-preserved hydrometer from whiskey bonding days, a mirror from the days of D.W.D Irish whiskey, the front window with Powers (John's Lane Distillery) imprinted on the glass, and two old gas heaters, all evoking the essence and activities of The Liberties in bygone times. 'Celebration Ale' and the Guinness Toucan with two pints finely balanced on her beak are further reminders of those times. It was here, in the 1840s, that the pub echoed to the sounds of blind ballad singer Michael 'Zozimus' Moran, or a few years earlier, to the voice of Dan Donnelly, Ireland's prize-fighting champion, as he pulled pints for his customers. This was Dan's second foray into the licensed trade.[129]

Donnelly was born in the docks of Dublin in March 1788, the ninth of his mother's seventeen children. He had worked as a carpenter earlier in his adult life. He fought at a time when boxing was of the bare-knuckle variety and bouts had no time limits. He took part in only three major fights, winning each of them. His first triumph was over Tom Hall at the Curragh of Kildare on 14 September 1814 in front of 20,000 spectators. His second victory on 13 December 1815, at the same location and with a similarly-sized crowd, was his most celebrated and a source of Irish pride because his opponent, George Cooper, was from England. Donnelly broke Cooper's jaw in the eleventh round of the twenty-two-minute match, and collected the prize of £60. A squat, weather-beaten, grey obelisk surrounded by a short iron fence marks the exact site, which has been called Donnelly's Hollow since the bout. The inscription on the monument: DAN DONNELLY BEAT COOPER ON THIS SPOT 13TH DEC. 1815.

In his third and final fight on 21 July 1819, he defeated Tom Oliver in thirty-four rounds on English turf, at Crawley Down in Sussex.

He had a reputation for enjoying the good things in life. After his victory over Cooper, Donnelly was the proprietor of a succession of four Dublin pubs, all of them unprofitable. Fallons Capstan Bar is the only one still in existence.[130]

He died at Donnelly's Public House, Greek Street, the last tavern he owned, on 18 February 1820 at the age of 32 and was buried in an unmarked vault at Bully's Acre Cemetery, in the grounds of the Royal Hospital, Kilmainham.

Almost two centuries after his death Donnelly remains the subject of urban legend. One contends that he had the longest arms in boxing history, with the ability to touch his knees without bending down. Another claims that he was knighted by the Prince Regent.

Bully's Acre itself, encompassing 3.7 acres, was also known as the 'Hospital Fields' such was its proximity to the Royal Hospital for old soldiers. It is one of Dublin's oldest cemeteries and features a large tenth-century decorated granite cross shaft, possibly the remains of the boundary cross associated with St Maigneann's Monastery founded here in AD 606. According to tradition, Brian Boro camped here before the Battle of Clontarf in 1014 and Robert Emmet's remains lay overnight here, pending removal to an unknown resting place.

The burial ground was in use from the time of St Maigneann up to the year of the great cholera epidemic in 1832 when it was closed to the general public. It also contains the remains of many monks, knights, princes and Dublin citizens. It was popular with the poor as it was the common ground where burial could be performed without charge. Traders, merchants and wealthier citizens were also buried here, attached to the holy ground associated with the monastery. The majority of those buried, however, were poor and their graves left unmarked.

At times unusual events took place at Bully's Acre. During the eighteenth and nineteenth centuries it was known to be the haunt of body snatchers or sack-em-up men who sold the stolen bodies to doctors and surgeons for experimental purposes. From early times, at mid-Summer each year, large and unruly crowds gathered to celebrate the feast of St John (24 June). This caused havoc in the cemetery, much to the annoyance of the nearby hospital authorities who tried to have the celebrations suppressed. Matters came to a head in the early 1760s when a General Dilks attempted to turn the cemetery into a botanic garden for the Royal Hospital and he caused the graves to be levelled, spread a thick covering of lime over the entire surface, and enclosed the place with a high wall. The local men of The Liberties, led by the notorious Liberty Boys, however, fought a pitched battle against the soldiers of the Royal Hospital. Following the rioting and legal proceedings, the public right to access was vindicated. Eventually the wall was levelled and the place was restored to its original purpose. Only about seventy tombstones now remain, ranging in date from 1764 to 1832.[131]

Highway to Dublin: The Coombe and Cork Street

Continuing on from Dean Street we have the Coombe. This name 'combe or coombe', originally from the Gaelic word 'com', refers to a hollow or river valley and was originally the path along where the Coombe Stream, a tributary of the River Poddle ran to the sea. The Poddle, coming from the Dublin Mountains via Kimmage and Harold's Cross, flowed underneath New Row, the Coombe, St Patrick's Cathedral and other parts of The Liberties and brought water to the mills that were once so numerous in the area. The valley feature is still in evidence today, particularly when one notes the pattern of side streets like tributaries descending from both sides to the Coombe.

According to William Frazer in his study of Newmarket and Weavers' Square, off Cork Street:

A medieval traveller coming to the old city would have travelled along the ancient Slí Dhála ('highway of the assemblies', now Cork Street). Following the route flanked by agricultural fields and abbey millstreams, he would have proceeded in the direction of Waxamay's Gate (near the west end of the Coombe at Ardee Street) along the Upper Coombe and across the Commons Water (near Ash Street). He would have walked through Coombe Gate (at what is now the junction with Hanover Street) and then passed St Francis' Gate on his left where Francis Street now joins Dean Street. From there he would have turned left and continued up St Patrick's Street into the city, passing first through St Patrick's Gate and then through the city wall at St Nicholas' Gate.[132]

Huguenots and Weavers

By the late 1680s many French Huguenots, fleeing the religious persecutions of Louis XIV, had settled in the Coombe. Fiercely Protestant, they brought with them their love of tanning, milling and weaving, and using the open waters of the Poddle, developed the Irish silk and woollen industry. They left a lasting impression on The Liberties.

Thousands of weavers toiled at their looms in the Coombe and its side streets. Streets such as Chamber Street, Poole Street and Weaver Square, all near the western end of the Coombe are often called 'Huguenot streets' in reference to the establishment of the weaving industry by the refugees.

In the late seventeenth century much building had started in order to house the weavers moving into the area, many constructed in the Huguenots' traditional style of house, Dutch Billies, with gables that faced the street. There is an excellent example of this at No. 32 the Coombe.

A weavers' hall was built by the Weavers' Guild in the Lower Coombe in 1682 and by 1745, when the building of a new hall was required, it was a Huguenot, David Digges La Touche, who advanced the £200 needed. There was a statue of King George II over the entrance.

The statue was sculpted by John Van Nost. He was the son of J. Van Nost, a native of Mechlin, Belgium a town famous for its lacemaking. Young John Van Nost learned his art from his father. In or shortly before 1750 he came to Dublin, where he immediately found plenty of employment. In that year he executed the first of the many important works that he undertook in Ireland, the statue of King George II for the Guild of Weavers. It was placed in an arched niche over the door of the Weavers' Hall in the Coombe, where it was until the 1960s, and was exposed to public view on the first anniversary of the Battle of the Boyne, 'when the covering was taken off,' said *Faulkner's Journal*, 'in the sight of many spectators, who all expressed their satisfaction thereat by the loudest acclamations and demonstrations of joy.'[133]

Van Nost executed other important works in The Liberties. In Christ Church Cathedral are his monuments to John Lord Bowes and to Thomas Prior, the latter put up by the Dublin Society in 1756. In St Patrick's Cathedral is the monument to Archbishop Arthur Smyth, designed and begun by Van Nost, but finished in 1775 by Henry Darley, which cost £15,000 and was described by the *Hibernian Magazine* as 'the most magnificent ever seen in this Kingdom'. In the City Hall there was a bronze statue of George III on a marble pedestal. William Makepeace Thackeray, in his *Irish Sketch Book*, refers to this work as 'a pert statue of George III in a Roman toga simpering and turning out his toes.'[134]

Charles Dickens and the Coombe

The great writer Charles Dickens wrote of his travels in The Liberties in the 1850s and 1860s. He found the area 'an almost indescribable aspect of dirt and confusion, semi-continental picturesqueness, shabbiness – less the shabbiness of dirt than that of untidiness – over-population, and frowsiness generally, perfectly original and peculiarly its own.'[135]

He also noted:

The Coombe, now a poverty-stricken and most desolate quarter, was at one time most prosperous and thriving, for here was the home of the weaving trade, which, like the woollen trade (of which more later), was actively carried on in Ireland. The weavers of Dublin owed their high reputation for the manufacture of brocades and delicate paduasoys to the Huguenot refugees, who, driven out of France by the bigotry of Louis XIV and his ministers, sought refuge in other countries. It was a short-sighted policy on the part of the French monarch to send forth men of talent and skilled artisans to teach other nations the arts formerly only known on the Continent.

He continued:

Success followed this undertaking. The fame of the wondrous fabrics wrought by these foreign weavers spread rapidly. Soon a Huguenot settlement sprang up in the very heart of the Coombe, traces of which still remain in a few houses with gabled roofs and high doorways which are to be found in Weavers' Square and the adjoining street, also the Weavers' Hall and Almshouse in the centre of the Coombe. The Almshouse has fallen into decay, but the Weavers' Hall is in good preservation. Over the door there is a fine statue of George II, full length, in a Court suit, and full-bottomed wig. Across his arm are slung the different implements of the weaving trade – shuttles and the like.[136]

The Weaver and the Lamplighter

There is a very ornate pub that is one of the last original buildings in the Coombe, the three-story building on the corner of the Coombe and Brabazon Street, called the Lamplighter pub. This was formerly known as The Weavers'. And next door is the long-established Liberty Florist. Shanahan's is another interesting pub on the corner of the Coombe and Hanover Street. At the junction of Brabazon Street and Cork Street you will find the see-through red-bricked building with windows and doors deliberately missing.

Further Developments and Notable Buildings

The Coombe area centres on the main road passing through it – the historic street linking Dean Street, Ash Street, St Luke's Avenue, Cork Street and Ardee Street. In the year 1708, an act of parliament was passed setting up a new Church of Ireland parish, St Luke's, for the area. In conformity with the act, a Glebe House was erected on the Coombe for the vicar and the church of St Luke was built just off the Coombe. Over the next few years new parish buildings including a school, an almshouse and a widows' house, were built along the Coombe to provide for the increasing population. The original Meath Hospital was also located here but was later relocated to Long Lane/Heytesbury Street, while retaining the old name.

Sweets in a Coombe shop in the 1950s. Notice the Cough-no-more and Royal and Blind Mice sweets. (Courtesy of Dublin.ie Forums/el gronk)

The Coombe bypass was driven across the former tree-lined avenue between the St Luke's church and the Widows' Alms House at the entrance, destroying its historical setting. The Widows' Alms House has been restored and integrated within that new development on the corner.

The old red-brick Victorian building with the cross on top reminds us of the Holy Faith Convent schools where thousands of local children were educated since Sister Margaret Aylward founded her convent there in 1865. She was asked to take charge of a poor school in a 'very tumbledown school building' in West Park Street, which became the first St Brigid's.[137] Conditions were difficult in these buildings and there was great excitement when the second St Brigid's opened in 1887. By 1915 there were 1,110 pupils and eighteen sisters in the school – meaning some sixty pupils per class! This building served thousands of students for 121 years until the opening of the third home for St Brigid's School, across the road on St Luke's Avenue, a road that seems to slice through the very heart of The Liberties. Facing the old convent there is a newer, similar convent, with a cross on top directly facing the one across the road; renamed the Holy Faith Secondary School, it closed down in 1989.

Combe Lying-In Hospital

Passing westwards through the Coombe, along to where Margaret Boyle's old Coombe Hospital once stood, we see the remains of the original entrance. She founded it in 1826 for the poor of Dublin. The story began on 10 October 1770 when Lord Brabazon laid the foundation stone of the new Meath Hospital in the Coombe. In 1774 it became the County Dublin Infirmary and in 1822 the patients were transferred to the new Meath Hospital at Long Lane. A few years later Mrs Margaret Boyle founded the Coombe Lying-In Hospital in the vacated building. The Guinness family became benefactors and built a dispensary block. In 1967 the hospital was relocated to new premises in Cork Street. The old building was demolished to make way for a Dublin Corporation housing development, but the portico was retained and is still there.

A plaque reads:

> Towards the end of the year 1825, two women whilst making a vain attempt to reach the Rotunda Hospital, perished, together with their newborn babies, in the snow. When this became known, a number of benevolent and well-disposed persons founded 'The Coombe Lying-in Hospital' in the year 1826, for the relief of poor lying-in women. Leading the charitable Committee was a Mrs. Margaret Boyle, of Upper Baggot Street, Dublin. The portico surrounding this plaque formed the entrance until the year 1967 when the Hospital moved to a new location in Dolphin's Barn. It has been retained and restored by Dublin Corporation as a memorial to the many thousands of mothers who gave birth to future citizens of Ireland in the Coombe Lying-in Hospital and also to the generosity of the staff and friends of the Hospital. The Housing Scheme which was subsequently created on the site was officially opened in November 1980.[138]

The Pride of the Coombe

'Biddy Mulligan, the Pride of the Coombe' (sometimes just called Biddy Mulligan) is a song written by Seamus Kavanagh in the 1930s, and made famous by the performances of the great music-hall singer, comedian and star of the Gaiety Theatre pantomimes for generations of Dublin children, Jimmy O'Dea (a Liberties lad from Lower Bridge Street where his mother kept a small toy-shop), who also took on the persona of the charismatic stall-holder.

Kavanagh collaborated with the scriptwriter Harry O'Donovan, who in turn had formed a partnership with Jimmy O'Dea. Kavanagh based this piece on the song 'The Queen of the Royal Coombe', which he had found in a nineteenth-century Theatre Royal programme. Other similarly themed songs performed by O'Dea were 'The Charladies' Ball' and 'Daffy the Belle of the Coombe', concerning Biddy Mulligan's daughter.[139]

He made a number of recordings of sketches starring the 'buxom' widow Mrs Mulligan.[140] The role drew on Jimmy's previous manifestations as 'Dames' in variety performances and pantomimes. Biddy Mulligan was the representation

Chatting outside a shop in The Coombe, 1952. (Courtesy of Dublin.ie Forums/el gronk)

(caricature, parody and stereotype) of a Dublin street-seller, with all the work-ing-class repartee, wisdom and failings implicit.

According to the song, Biddy Mulligan sells goods such as apples, oranges, nuts, sweet peas, bananas and sugar-sticks from her stall on the corner of the Coombe and Patrick Street. On Fridays, she sells fish on a board - for 'dinner and tea', and is especially proud of her Dublin Bay herrings. On Saturday nights she sells second-hand clothes from the 'floor of her stall'. She's proud also, of her son Mick, who plays flute in the Longford Street Band, and she watches them march out for Dollymount Strand (north-east of Dublin City) each Sunday. On a Sunday, too, she goes to 'the Park' (probably St Patrick's Park, next to the cathedral), wearing her 'Aberdeen Shawle', and basks in the admiration of her neighbours.[141]

The song is a rare musical documentation of the Dublin street-seller – Molly Malone being the only other and most famous example. Street-stalls have long since disappeared from the corner of Patrick Street and the Coombe but a vari-ety of markets, including the Bull Ring, Molly Malone's Market and the Liberty Market continue to thrive on nearby Meath Street.

According to a former Liberties resident Isobel Smyth, 'Jimmy's favourite role' was created by an encounter on Henry Street when a woman came out of a pub in nearby Moore Street, shouting at a man behind her 'Go along outa that, you bowsie'. The story goes that O'Donovan and O'Dea exchanged glances and

Biddy was born in the heart of Moore Street, and was transferred to become a lady of The Liberties, who lived in the Coombe and sold her wares at St Patrick Street corner!'[142] Singer and comedian, Brendan Grace, was born at No. 9.

Other names associated with the Coombe include the company John C. Parkes, who specialised as button-makers, engineers, coffin-makers etc., and Jemmy Hope. He was a weaver who became prominent in the United Irishmen. His tombstone reads: 'One of nature's noblest works, an honest man'.[143]

And not forgetting the old sweet shop on the Coombe where local children were able to get their bon bons and bulls eyes!

Ardee Street

Linking Pimlico, the Coombe, the Tenters and Cork Street, Ardee Street derives its name from the Earl of Meath's family. Unfortunately the road-widening and the new St Luke's Avenue have dissected the street and the community. Excavation along the street, prior to the building of St Luke's Avenue and apartment blocks, revealed the old Commons River, a tributary of the Poddle. There was a millpond here, probably linked to the Abbey of St Thomas. It is likely that the area, like the adjacent Coombe, was intensely developed from the 1660s to the 1670s. The excavations also revealed that the area was used as a site for seventeenth-century defences of the city against invaders.[144]

The original entrance doorway and some buildings of the old Watkins Brewery are still standing at 10 Ardee Street. Granite bollards guarding the entrance and cobblestones just through the gates are also reminders of a different era, as is the blackened, faded nameplate on the door with the names 'Watkins, Jameson, Pim & Co. Ltd' barely visible. These are major names in the history of brewing and distilling, not only in The Liberties but the whole of Ireland and point to the importance of the area for the industry.[145]

W & J Bolger, also of Ardee Street, is one of the last of the old businesses on the street to survive. This furniture restorer has been in business here since 1890.

There is an impressive listed Georgian building at No. 4 Ardee Street. Watkins Buildings and Watkins Cottages are adjacent dwellings built in the nineteenth century to house the brewery workers. The old refurbished grey-bricked building opposite the cottages is another reminder of earlier enterprises in the area.

The Highway of Cork Street

Continuing on from Ardee Street we come to another important street in The Liberties: Cork Street. The name Cork Street dates from before 1728 and comes from the Boyle family, Earls of Cork who built a mansion at Cork Hill, continuous from Lord Edward Street.[146] Cork Street runs from St Luke's Avenue/Ardee Street junction to Dolphin's Barn Street at the junction with Emerald Square. On old maps it is described as 'The Highway to Dolfynesberne' and it is part of the old *Slighe Dála*, one of the main routes into the medieval city. In the South Gate apartment complex on Cork Street the ancient origins of the road are celebrated on the side of the seven-storey block. A large number of flat silver/aluminium-coloured panels and projecting pieces are strategically placed on the side of the building and the work is called 'Dance of *slí dála*'. It was sculpted by Felim Egan in 2005.

In 2010 archaeologist Claire Walsh identified a sequence of post and wattle structures here of probable early twelfth century date. These small buildings were well preserved beneath the basement floors of later eighteenth-century buildings and seemed to represent a line of Viking houses which fronted onto Cork Street. The buildings were located at quite a remove from the walled town of old Dublin and indicate that during the eleventh and twelfth centuries Dublin was an ever-expanding city whose early suburbs extended well beyond the city walls.[147]

Cork Street was an important industrial centre with a vibrant community. Perhaps one of its most important firms was the Cork Street Foundry and Engineering Works of William Spence. The famous Dye Works, Plunkett's grain and malting works were also located here and Donnelly's Bacon and

Unloading a Hanlon's fish truck in the 1960's. Hanlon Ltd was founded in 1845 in Howth. Founded by brothers Paddy and Michael Hanlon, the business has had a series of moves around Dublin before finally settling on Cork Street. The growth of Hanlon's did not go unnoticed. Indeed, James Joyce referred to the Hanlon brothers in *Ulysses*. (Courtesy of Hanlon Ltd, 75-78 Cork Street)

Sausage Factory was a major employer in the area for generations. On 13 July 1979, after 150 years of trading in The Liberties, Donnelly's closed its doors for the last time. This closure brought to an end an era of bacon-curing and sausage-making that dated back to the beginning of the nineteenth century. The Donnelly Centre now is a reminder of the old factory. Paddy Whelan Cycles on Cork Street was another important stop-off for locals, who would also be able to purchase their television sets and prams from the same shop. The Plant Life Company now occupies the old malting site and the tall chimney and the remains of the old buildings here are a reminder of former industrial activities in the area.[148]

Cork Street has a considerable number of cul-de-sacs branching out from it, resulting from private developments constructed in the back gardens of larger residences. With the exception of Marrowbone Lane, all the roads or lanes on the northwest side of Cork Street were very short because of the adjacent old city boundary, which ran along the back of Cork Street and can be seen at Pyro Villas, Marian Villas, Spence Terrace and Ivy Terrace. Cork Street also contained a number of important buildings, most of which were demolished by developers at the turn of the twenty-first century, but Nos 112 and 116 survive and are a reminder of these fine dwellings from a different era.

Emerald Square

Emerald Square, just off Cork Street (adjacent to Maryland and opposite the new Coombe Hospital) is fondly remembered in Lar Redmond's reminiscences of the same name. Against a background of poverty and political upheaval, life in The Liberties in the 1920s and the subsequent decades bubbled on with a determination that was brimming full of vitality and humour, he said. *Emerald Square* is his story of growing up in this part of The Liberties – a story of want and hardship, but teeming with wit and sarcasm that is the Dubliner's most deadly weapon. Redmond brings to life the street traders, pawnbrokers, money-lenders, drunks, and the haunted-looking children with the 'pink glow' of the early stages of consumption.[149]

The Quakers and the Fever Hospital

The old Cork Street 'Fever Hospital and House of Recovery', consisting of three large buildings, is today Brú Chaoimhín, a senior citizens home run by the Health Services Executive (HSE). The Quakers originally opened it in May 1804 and the objectives of the hospital were to care for the diseased in the neighbourhood and prevent the spread of infection in the homes of the poor. In the year 1812 over 2,200 patients were admitted. The hospital did succeed in checking the spread of disease, but the worsening unemployment in The Liberties following the Act of Union and occasional epidemics, such as Scarlet Fever, pushed up the mortality rate for the first few years of its existence. However, by 1815 the mortality rate in the hospital had declined to 1 in 20 (from 1 in 11 in 1804). An 1817 report noted that ventilation is so good that 'no bad odours persist'. All articles of dress and furniture in the hospital were white 'so any dirt can be spotted quickly and fumigation applied if necessary' and, 'after the removal of a dead patient the ward is fumigated and sometimes whitewashed before the admission of another'.[150]

Dublin had six typhus epidemics in the eighteenth century (it was not at the time known that a louse-born organism, which flourished in unhygienic conditions, caused typhus) and the hospital was extended in 1817–1819 to help cope with the problem. Three thousand cases were admitted to the hospital in one month in 1818. Another typhus epidemic hit Dublin in 1826 and 10,000 people were treated at the hospital for the infection. It was so overcrowded that tents were erected in the grounds and these provided 400 extra beds. Typhus struck again at the time of the Great Famine of the 1840s, with the huge influx of people into The Liberties trying to escape the worst ravages of the famine. In 1847 there were nearly 12,000 during a period of about ten months, although many could not be accommodated in the hospital. Typhus returned in the 1880s.

In 1832 Dublin was also ravaged by a cholera epidemic. Despite the best efforts of all concerned, thousands died and were hastily buried in nearby Bully's Acre.

Even in the late nineteenth and early twentieth centuries, parts of Dublin including The Liberties were ravaged by diphtheria and anxious parents used to check the newspapers (each sick child had a number) to see how their sick children were getting on (or if they had died) in the Cork Street Fever Hospital as they were not allowed to visit. In 1953 the hospital was moved to Cherry Orchard, Ballyfermot. The old Cork Street hospital was renamed Brú Chaoimhín and used as a nursing home.[151] An unusual feature of one of the three impressive buildings in the complex is that the double doorway entrance has two door knockers as opposed to the usual one. An old ornate clock still chimes over the main building.

This important clock is a very fine posted-frame clock, built by the renowned Dublin clock makers James Waugh, and dates from 1810. Waugh was one of Dublin's earliest clock makers. The clock is important also because it is an example of his emphasis on quality, craftsmanship, and attention to detail. It is fitted with an Ashbourne cast bell. Waugh clock makers operated from nearby 24 James's Street.

Across the road from Brú Chaoimhín is a fine dark red-bricked Victorian building, the James Weir Home for Nurses, built in 1903. This was built specifically for the nurses in the Fever Hospital. The site was a Quaker burial ground and several gravestones are still visible in the grounds.

Maryland and Mary's Abbey

In 1954 the Maryland housing development off Cork Street/Marrowbone Lane was constructed by Dublin Corporation. 1954 was a Marian year, hence the name Maryland. One road is called Ave Maria Road.

Father Spratt (Carmelite) was born in Cork Street on 5 January 1796. It was he who found the ancient wooden statue of Our Lady of Dublin, which originally stood in St Mary's Abbey and is now on display in Whitefriars Street church. He also saved the ancient 'lucky stone' which belonged to St Audoen's church and was responsible for getting the site in Whitefriars Street for the Carmelite church.[152]

In 2007, the Sisters of Mercy, who had occupied the red-bricked convent at the junction of Cork Street and Weavers' Sqaure for over 100 years, opened the impressive Sophia Housing Project with fifty housing units provided. The nuns themselves are still based in the convent.[153]

Cork Street also featured in a Richard Burton film, *The Spy who came in from the Cold*, and some of the scenes have Cork Street houses in the background.[154]

Marrowbone Lane and the 'Back of the Pipes'

Marrowbone Lane is a street off Cork Street and continues on to Thomas Street via Pimlico. The name is a corruption of St Mary Le Bone and it was known as Marrowbone Lane as far back as 1743. The Marrowbone Lane Distillery (Jameson's Whiskey) featured in some of the fighting during the 1916 Rising as it was an outpost of the South Dublin Union on James's Street.

In 1942 Dr Robert Collis wrote the play *Marrowbone Lane* based on his experiences of the terrible conditions of the tenements there. All the old tenements were demolished in the second half of the twentieth century and there is little evidence of the appalling living conditions of those who had lived there for generations.[155] Names given to apartment blocks and housing developments give some indication of the former activities in the area, such as The Malthouse.

The Dublin City Council waterworks headquarters is based here at Marrowbone Lane, whose water pipes, linked to the City Basin at nearby St James's Street, played a crucial part in the supply of water to the city for generations. Water from the River Poddle, flowing from the Dublin Mountains via Tallaght, Kimmage, Harold's Cross, Dolphin's Barn and James's Street, advanced on to James's Walk and the summit of an elevated rampart of earth and stone which became known as the 'Back of the Pipes' or the 'Ridges' and from there to a cistern near the present Waterworks Headquarters at Marrowbone Lane. In Dublin slang 'at the back of the pipes' was famous as a haven for courting couples and the term became a response to an enquiry regarding the unknown whereabouts of an object or person.[156]

Older residents recall with fondness the old Coombe Dairy and Burdock's that were located here.

Weavers' Squares and Fumbally

Weavers' Square and Newmarket

On the opposite side of Cork Street we have the Newmarket and Weavers' Squares that border Cork Street, the Coombe and the Tenters. The squares are intersected by Ardee Street and linked by Chamber Street.

Excavations in the squares in recent years show that the area was mainly rural until the late 1600s but that much development took place after that. In 1674 the Earl of Meath applied for permission to hold markets and a fair on the land here. Two years later the area was rapidly developing. The Earls of Meath also had control and rights ('liberties') over water which they maintained until the mid-nineteenth century. For generations this was a major bone of contention and disputes arose between the city authorities and the Earl of Meath, who controlled the Liberty of St Thomas, so that by the eighteenth century it was the joint property of the city and the Earls of Meath. The area in the Meath Liberties appealed to seventeenth-century entrepreneurs because of the availability of water, lots of land, and the nearness to Dublin city but freedom from the control of the city Corporation. These were all crucial factors offering opportunity.[157]

As a result the area attracted tanners, clothiers and brewers. Initially, artisans both lived and worked in the same houses. Newmarket and Weavers' Squares were ideal as open spaces and were also needed for many other industries. Trades such as knackeries and renderers' yards were carried out adjacent to skinners, glovers, cloth workers and brewers and maltsters. And of great benefit to the weaving/textile activities were the adjacent tenter fields just off the squares. Soon then both of these squares were of vital importance in the weaving/spinning/bleaching/dyeing and textile industries.

However, as sure as bust follows boom, and with the combination of restrictive English laws against Irish weaving/textile exports and greater industrialisation, the area gradually dwindled and the fine houses evolved into tenements. Despite this, in one form or another, the tanyards, breweries, malt houses, and weavers continued their activities well into the early years of the twentieth century and some of the old buildings in Ardee Street, Newmarket Square and Fumbally Lane are a reminder of a rich industrial past in The Liberties.

The last weaver of The Liberties was a man called Padraig Breathnach who worked in Elliot's of South Brown Street, off Weavers' Square, up until the 1970s, before it closed down.[158]

Most of the old buildings on Newmarket Square have been demolished, leaving little evidence of the huge importance it played in the life and prosperity of Dublin. In one corner there is a turreted gateway leading into the back of the old St Luke's church. On another corner with Brabazon Place, we have Gray's Newmarket Inn, formerly the Red Lion Inn often associated with legendary local character, Bang Bang and Lord Dudley's favourite pub. This is one of the very few historical buildings remaining and deserves attention, despite the fact that its real history is hidden behind modern cladding.

The Guinness Maltings faced onto Newmarket Square for many years. Minch Norton grain works was also located here. Newmarket used to have a fruit market here and today hosts a Farmers' Market.

The squares have been taken over by developers in recent years and blocks of apartments nestle side-by-side with some older dwellings. Part of Weavers' Square has been given over to allotments, and adjacent wide-open spaces call out for activity. As with Newmarket, only the name of the square gives a clue to its former importance.

The imposing late nineteenth-century red-brick Sisters of Mercy Convent (formerly the Tenter House used in the local linen industry) is still there overlooking Weavers' Square, but it is no longer the hive of activity it once was. The nuns, however, have done much to re-generate and bring life back to their site.[159]

Number 48 Newmarket Square was a tenement house where Lily O'Neill, a young woman known as Honor Bright, lived; she was murdered in 1925, her body found on a quiet mountain road to the south of the city. Following a sensational murder trial in 1926 the two co-accused, a medical doctor, Patrick Purcell, from Blessington, and Leopold J. Dillon, an ex-superintendent of the Civic Guards, from Dunlavin, Co. Wicklow, walked free. Lily O'Neill was soon forgotten.

Chamber Street

Linking Newmarket and Weavers' Square is Chamber Street, named after the Chambré family of Stormanstown near Ardee, Co. Meath. Mary Chambré married Edward Brabazon, 2nd Earl of Meath. Many of the former three-storied houses here had triangular gables, occupied by master weavers. The street was known as a centre for silk weaving. Unfortunately by the end of the eighteenth century the street had degenerated. Subsequently, the houses were mostly occupied by small weavers and artisans. Despite efforts of concerned conservationists in the 1950s to preserve some of the old buildings, they were eventually demolished in 1964.

Late nineteenth-century image of 'Dutch Billies' at the junction of Ward's Hill-New Row. The junction of New Row South, Ward's Hill, Mill Street and Blackpits, is in The Liberties. The pair of houses known as 'The Seven Gables' is shown still largely intact but after the loss of the original twin, pediment topped, curvilinear gable profiles. (Courtesy of Dublin.ie Forums/Gatsby)

Mill Street and New Row South

Just off Newmarket Square, down Wards Hill, we see some grey-brick buildings that were former mills and distilleries. These mills were originally built on one branch of the River Poddle, which flowed into the River Liffey from here and all along here and in nearby Mill Street there is still evidence that the area was a hive of mill activity. There were calico, cotton, rope, and many more textile activities. New Row South now contains a mixture of buildings from different eras all making for an eclectic mix. The edifice of the old Bush's Mills, off New Row South, is still standing. Some still recall a major fire in a distillery here with the flaming whiskey flowing down towards Dean Street!

Lauderdale Terrace contains a fine selection of red-brick houses facing a new apartment complex, which has ruins of St Luke's church on a hill forming an interesting backdrop.

Home to the Brabazons and the Warrens

Mill Street itself derives its name from a millpond to the south of the street, which was fed by the Poddle River and is a reference to the number of mills in the area. Around 1700 there were seven Huguenot families living in Mill Street, including a family called Disney who were the ancestors of the cartoonist Walt Disney. The old red-brick ruins of the former Earl of Meath's house, faces towards Newmarket Square (junction of Mill Street and Mill Lane). This ruined but listed imposing building is a monument to the end of the Brabazon era in the area – an involvement that lasted for centuries from the time of the Reformation. At the front of that house, 'A & J 1903' is carved on the blank wall in an ornate fashion. It could well have been A & J Clothing, a textile business that subsequently moved elsewhere.

Nearby, through a black-gated wrought-iron arch with a cross on top, is the entrance to the former home of a Lord Mayor of Dublin, Nathaniel Warren. This fine house that subsequently became part of the Presentation Convent has been renovated back to its former glory and the doorway and the ornate windows are a particularly unusual and attractive feature of the house, as is the garden with mirrors in front of the house. The house is now used as an adult education centre for The Liberties.

O'Keefe's the Knackers

Newmarket Square/Mill Street isn't the same since the smell of Edward O'Keefe ('O'Keefe's the Knackers') Renderers has gone. They specialised in buying dead animals, particularly horses, crushing the bones to make manure. The animal carcases were placed in a huge boiling vat which would strip the flesh from the bones. The bones would then be ground down to a finer material. The rendering plant worked like a giant kitchen with the boiling process going on morning, noon and night and with the smells wafting through the air. The ground outside O'Keefe's would be littered with dead animals, entrails, skulls, etc. Many times a local lad playing Gaelic or soccer in Newmarket Square would have to wade through this to retrieve a ball!

To locals it was only a smell (regarded by some as useful for keeping down disease, though it in fact attracted scores of rats to the area), but O'Keefe's were celebrated for their manures by Irish manufacturers, as they were the best and the cheapest. Former pupils of the nearby Donore Avenue School recall the windows of their classrooms open on a warm day and the smell of putrid flesh and the rendering of the animal bones from O'Keefe's wafting in! Residents in the area, and around the wider Liberties, say that 'a blind man could make his way around Dublin because of the smell' at the time. A local resident recalls: 'It was the smell off O'Keefe's the Knackers that kept us Dubs so strong. Nobody got sick as the smell kept the germs away. I miss the smell'.[160]

It was not just the smells emanating from O'Keefe's they had to endure. Washing and boiling the hops in the Guinness Brewery was an important task in the making of the famous stout. Some claim that the smell from this process (the opposite to the roasting of the barley which gives a pleasant coffee-like aroma) was not for the faint-hearted and even surpassed that of O'Keefe's! Not only that, but the cigarette-processing smell coming from the Player Wills factory on the not-too-far away South Circular Road, was another one added to the mix. And not forgetting the smells emanating from the numerous pubs, smaller breweries, malting houses and distilleries that dotted the area for many years.

When O'Keefe's ceased trading in the 1970s the premises was occupied by Eircom for a number of years. Latterly it is the headquarters of the famous Viking Splash World tours of Dublin. This novel and successful enterprise is run by a businessman with roots in Meath Street where his mother ran Clarke's Grocery shop.

Ward's Hill

From Newmarket Square to New Row South we have the cobble-stoned Ward's Hill. The name comes from the Ward family who had a brewery on the corner with New Row South. In 1703 four acres of land were leased for a market garden to a man called Rowe. It was he who introduced the growing of pineapples into Ireland. The local Huguenots meanwhile had introduced the art of topiary to the area, cutting box hedges into interesting shapes.

The Tenters

Mill Street leads us to The Tenters. On Clarence Mangan Road in the Tenters there is a monument called 'The Tenters' and it has the inscription: 'This area is known as The Tenters, because linen cloth was stretched out on tenterhooks to bleach in the sun. When the linen trade failed, the fields were used for market gardening. In 1924 this fine housing scheme was built.' There may be a question mark over this date as a number of the fine terraced houses in the area have '1922' imprinted on their front gables, giving, presumably, the date of their construction.[161]

The Huguenot weavers lived around Chamber Street and Ardee Street and came out into the open fields in the area to do their weaving of poplins, silks, satins etc. They taught the people of the area how to weave silk and poplin.

At first, everything seemed to prosper and many more people came to live in the area. However, difficulties arose because of the Irish weather. The cloth needed to be stretched and dried on tenterhooks in the fields between what is now O'Curry Avenue and Clarence Mangan Road. Many times the weavers had either to suspend work in rainy weather or use the alehouse fire.

In 1814 Thomas Pleasants built a Tenter House on the land between Cork Street, Brickfield Lane, Brown Street and Ormond Street (the old stove Tenter House was in the grounds of what later became the Sisters of Mercy Convent, Cork Street). It was a brick building 275ft long, three stories high, and with a central cupola.[162v]It had a form of central heating powered by four furnaces, and provided a place for weavers to stretch their material in bad weather. He gave orders for Irish craftsmen and Irish material to be used and the building was to be fire proof.

The decline of the weaving trade meant that the old Tenter House became vacant. In 1861 a Carmelite priest bought the house and opened it as a refuge for the homeless. He ran the hostel for ten years until 1871, when Margaret Alyward of the Sisters of Mercy came to the area and converted the premises to a convent.

This part of The Liberties is a veritable rabbit warren of streets, side streets, cul-de-sacs, lanes and avenues. Many of the street names have literary associations, e.g. Oscar Square (after Oscar Wilde), Clarence Mangan (after James Clarence Mangan, the poet), Ingram Road (after Sir John Kells Ingram, the poet), and O'Curry Road and Avenue after Eugene O'Curry, an expert on early Irish manuscripts. Interestingly, Cow Parlour, the site of the former abattoir, which is no more, became part of O'Curry Road/Avenue. There is also O'Donovan Road, called after the great Fenian leader O'Donovan Rossa and there is a plaque on one of the houses here to the 1916 volunteer Joe Clarke who fought with the Mount Street Bridge garrison. A lifelong Republican he was also very active with the National Graves Association. In recent years the new owners of Clarke's former home, in the course of renovating the house, discovered some old documents underneath the floorboards. These are of particular historical significance as some relate to Countess Markievicz and the shelling of the Four Courts during the Civil War.

St Thomas's Road is called after the martyr St Thomas à Becket, who also gave his name to Thomas Street. The houses in Rutledge Terrace were built between 1898 and 1910 by Robert and Andrew Rutledge, the same builder who built houses in Francis Street and Golden Lane. Oscar Square has a very picturesque park in the centre with excellent views of the Dublin Mountains. A short street links it to Weavers' Square.

Blackpitts

According to Karl Whitney, a former resident of the area, 'Blackpitts is the gateway to a dense warren of streets packed with terraced houses and small factories, under all of which a complex network of man-made rivers runs.'[163]

Viewed from Fumbally Lane, we see 'Blackpitts Ironworks' and the old, now closed-down, Tenters Pub. Some people maintain that Blackpitts was named

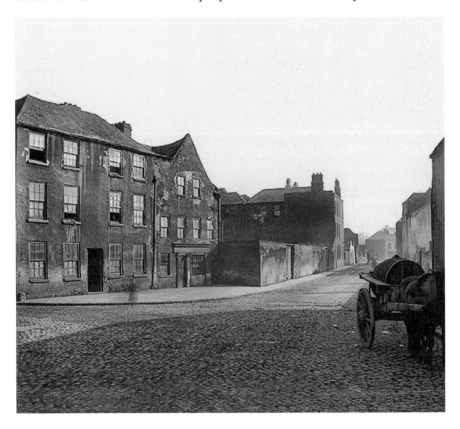

Blackpitts, c. 1890. (Courtesy of National Library of Ireland)

from the mass graves of a medieval plague. It was more likely named after the dark-stained vats the tanners used when curing hides. The Poddle runs under part of Warrenmount Convent. It has been claimed that one can hear the river flowing under the basement from time to time.

Home of Dublin's Lord Mayor: Warrenmount

The present site of Warrenmount Convent and School may have been used as a tenter field or as pure agricultural land prior to its occupancy by Nathaniel Warren in the eighteenth century. This house, with its spacious grounds, was built by Nathaniel Warren who became High Sheriff of Dublin 1773–1774 and later Lord Mayor 1782–1783. His choice for the location was because of its proximity to the River Poddle. He named his residence 'Warrenmount'. By 1813, the Georgian house had become a Carmelite convent started by Catherine Lyons (Sister Clare). In 1892 the Carmelites said good-bye to their monastery of St Teresa at Warrenmount. Subsequently, the Sisters from the Presentation Convent in Clondalkin came to Warrenmount.[164]

View of Warrenmount Convent, early twentieth century. (Courtesy of Dublin.ie Forums)

Fumbally Lane

Fumbally Lane is a narrow and historic street on the edge of The Liberties and in name and character it is perhaps the most evocative of all The Liberties streets. It connects Blackpitts and the Tenters to New Street and is well worth a visit as many of the old buildings, instead of being demolished, enjoy a new life as modern businesses in Fumbally Square and Fumbally Court.

The lane itself was set out by local brewer and Quaker Jacob Poole in 1721 to connect Blackpitts (where he had property) to New Street. The lane has long had mixed industrial and residential use. Historically, tanning, brewing and associated industries flourished in this part of Dublin, partly because the River Poddle is close by. The industrial heritage of the area even dates back to the mid-seventeenth century and is linked to and influenced by both Quakers and Huguenots. In 2006 archaeologists found evidence of medieval leather tanning off Fumbally Lane and nearby New Street with wood-lined soaking pits and elaborate ditch systems. They also identified that one of the existing former brewery buildings on Fumbally dates from the 1740s suggesting the possibility that the first Dublin porter was brewed here. The Poole and Taylor families, who were related, had brewing interests here from at least that time and probably before. Both families are remembered in street-names in The Liberties.[165]

From 1779 Samuel Madder operated the Blackpitts Porter Company on the north of the lane after having acquired a brewery from a James Farrell. In 1830 John Busby a distiller, acquired a brewery property in Fumbally and erected a new distillery here. This stone-faced building, now refurbished, is part of the Fumbally Studio development and now home to both apartments and offices. 'J.B. 1836' is still visible on a steel girder over Fumbally Square.

The City of Dublin Brewery was situated on the corner of Fumbally and Backpitts and between 1867 and 1883 they took over the Busby buildings including a still house spirit store and a brew house. Later the complex was put to other industrial uses, including use as a textile factory in the late nineteenth century; many of the buildings on the brewing complex and along the lane subsequently fell into disuse or dereliction. A significant detached three-storey house possibly dating from the 1720s existed in the street until the late 1980s. This rare example of an early Irish house may have been built by the relations of Jacob Poole as offices for the brewery owner; a deed from 1789 connects it to the brewery. This house was later used as a textile factory, housed 'Blair's Fancy Linens' and was subsequently burnt down and demolished around 1990. Now only the large curved entrance walls and a cobbled forecourt remain.[166]

In 2006, the then Taoiseach, Bertie Ahern TD, noted at the opening of some new offices:

Fumbally Court is now shared by a number of organisations ranging from design companies, international architects such as Murray O'Laoire and national organisations like the Disability Federation of Ireland and GLEN. This type of development reflects the ongoing rejuvenation of The Liberties. The Liberties are at the heart of our thousand-year-old city. Today, these historic streets are again on their way to becoming one of the most successful, vibrant, diverse and livable communities in Dublin.[167]

Fumbally Fame – But Which First Came

The name Fumbally is a peculiar one and provokes a wide range of theories as to its origin. It has not always been called Fumbally Lane and has had many name variations since the 1720s.

The lane first appears in Charles Brooking's map of 1728, without a name, and with variations in subsequent maps including John Rocque's map of 1756 as 'Bumbailiff's Lane' and in Wilson's map of 1798 as 'Fumbailie's Lane'. Revd McCready in *Dublin Street Names: Dated and Explained* (late nineteenth century) called it Fumbally's Lane and said it was referred to in *Thom's Directory* as a 'corruption of Bumbailiff's-lane'. Fumbally's Lane is also the name James Joyce uses in chapter 3 of his novel *Ulysses*, when he refers to 'the tanyard smells' of the lane.[168]

However, there is some evidence that the name derives from a local Huguenot family named Fontvielle, Fomboilie, Fombily, Fombela, Fonveille or Fombally (the name appears differently in a wide variety of sources). Architectural historian, Christine Casey, refers to the street's association with a Huguenot family called Fombily and confirming this, historian Peter Pearson provides two names: David Fombily and Anthony Fombily who were described as 'skinners' (working in tanning/leather). Pearson, in reference to a study on the houses of The Liberties by Peter Walsh, refers to a 1741 lease given on two houses on 'Fombily's Lane'. There is further evidence from a Registry of Deeds entry of an assignment dated 7 October, 1762, mentioned in a RSAI Journal in 1893 and from a reference to the RDS, written in 1915, that refers to a Royal Dublin Society prize for life drawing in March 1746 which was won by a 'Mr. Fombally'. These all suggest that a Fombally or Fombely family resided in Dublin and was associated with this lane in the mid-eighteenth century.[169]

The Blind Bard of The Liberties

Zozimus, or Michael Moran as he was originally known, was a blind storyteller who lived in Fumbally Lane during the nineteenth century. He was also known as the 'Blind Bard of The Liberties' and the 'Last of the Gleemen'. He was born about 1794 off Blackpitts/Fumbally Lane, in Faddle Alley. A fortnight after his birth he became blind from illness, and consequently became a blessing to his parents (such were the times), who were soon able to send him to beg at street corners and at the bridges over the River Liffey. He developed an astounding memory for verse and made his living reciting poems, many of which he had composed himself, in his own lively manner. By the time he had grown to manhood he was the admitted king of all the ballad-mongers of The Liberties. and was described by the celebrated songwriter P.J. McCall (from Patrick Street) as 'the last gleeman of the Pale' (gleeman meaning an itinerant minstrel or musician).[170]

Moran's nickname derived from a poem written by Bishop Anthony Coyle of Raphoe about St Mary of Egypt. According to the legend, she had followed pilgrims to Jerusalem with the intent of seducing them, then, turning penitent on finding herself prevented from entering the church of the Holy Sepulchre by a supernatural force, she fled to the desert and spent the remainder of her life in solitary penance. When she was at the point of death, God sent Zozimus of Palestine to hear her confession and give her Holy Communion, and a lion to dig her grave. The poem was so popular, when recited by the blind balladeer, and so often called for, that Moran was soon nicknamed 'Zozimus', by which name he is remembered.[171]

Many of his rhymes had religious themes, though others were political or recounted recent events. He is said to have worn 'a long, coarse, dark, frieze coat with a cape, the lower parts of the skirts being scalloped, an old soft, greasy, brown beaver hat, corduroy trousers and Francis Street brogues, and he carried a long blackthorn stick secured to his wrist with a strap.' He began each oration with the verse:

> Ye sons and daughters of Erin,
> Gather round poor Zozimus, yer friend;
> Listen boys, until yez hear
> My charming song so dear.[172]

Liberties resident, poet and author Liam O'Meara, wrote a study on Zozimus, and revealed in an interview:

He would sit on Capel Street Bridge and sound off about the Government. He would be in court and the judge would be about to give him a fine and he would say hear my poem first. He would then recite the poem and it would generally be very humorous. The papers used to pick up on this and they made him famous. In one particular year he appeared in court several times and some of the accounts are hilarious. He was fined five shillings at one stage and he asked the judge could he pay it in installments. When the judge said he couldn't Zozimus emptied his pockets that were full of halfpennies and the court was in uproar laughing at that.

Liam said that although Zozimus could never be called a great poet, he was one of the city's best-loved street entertainers.[173]

In his last few years, his voice grew weak and cost him his only means of livelihood. He ended up feeble and bedridden and he died on 3 April 1846 at his lodgings in 15 Patrick Street, aged around sixty-one, and was buried in Glasnevin Cemetery. He had feared grave-robbers who were rife in Dublin at the time and in one of his narrative songs, he begged his long-established companion, 'Stony Pockets' to save him from the 'Sack-em-ups' (grave robbers):

> Oh Stony, Stony
> Don't let the Sack-'em-Ups get me
> Send round the hat
> And buy me a grave.[174]

Glasnevin's Prospect Cemetery was guarded day and night (the guard towers still align the walls of the cemetery) to deter grave robbers. His grave remained unmarked until the late 1960s when the famous traditional Irish ballad group, the Dublin City Ramblers, erected a tombstone in his memory. The grave is still intact in the 'Poor Ground' of the cemetery and can be located not far from Daniel O'Connell's burial site.

His epitaph reads:

> My burying place is of no concern to me,
> In the O'Connell circle let it be,
> As to my funeral, all pomp is vain,
> Illustrious people does prefer it plain.
> – Zozimus.[175]

Zozimus was remembered in a satirical weekly magazine published in Dublin from May 1870 to August 1872 by A.M. Sullivan. Its chief artist, who drew most of the cartoons and covers, was John Fergus O'Hea. His first cover depicted Zozimus chasing the emblem characters of the English magazines *Punch*, *Judy*, *The Tomahawk* and *Fun* out of Ireland. Harry Furniss and Wallis Mackay also contributed cartoons and illustrations. Subsequently, O'Hea, Dowling and Edwin Hamilton founded another famous magazine, *Ireland's Eye*, which is still available.

Zozimus's name is remembered today by an art gallery in Francis Street – Gallery Zozimus.

Poplin and Cabbages

New Street: The Cabbage Garden

Fumbally Lane brings us out onto New Street. Despite its name, New Street is one the oldest streets of Dublin, first mentioned in 1218, and was one of the most important routes from the old city to Wicklow and Leinster. Its antiquity is marked on the right as one exits Fumbally Lane by four standing stones and ten flat wall stones, some of which have Celtic swirls on them.

As a result of major road-widening at the end of the twentieth century there is a swathe of new houses in the area between New Street, Kevin Street and New Bride Street. There is also the not so new complex of Iveagh Trust red-brick flats development on New Bride Street and Kevin Street.

The Cabbage Garden is a hidden-away neighbourhood park nestled at the rear of the houses between the Iveagh Trust on Bride Street, Kevin Street Upper and New Street. The park, however, has a long history which dates back to the 1600s. In 1649 Cromwellian soldiers rented land from a local landowner Philip Fernley (whose name is remembered with the Fernley Court houses overlooking the park) south of St Patrick's Cathedral. The land was used to grow cabbages which were not grown in Ireland before this time and hence the name 'The Cabbage Garden' was derived.[176]

1649 was one of the most important years in Irish history as in August of that year the landmark Battle of Rathmines occurred, which greatly facilitated the landing of Oliver Cromwell's troops in Dublin. This culminated in the defeat of the Irish forces and the subsequent march and laying siege by Oliver Cromwell's soldiers of many Irish towns and cities and the notorious 'to Hell or to Connaught' war-cry which saw thousand of Irish dispossessed of their land and property and forced to flee to the poor lands of Connaught.[177]

In 1666 the Cabbage Garden land was granted to the parish of St Nicholas Without by the Dean of St Patrick's Cathedral for the purposes of a new cemetery as the small one attached to the cathedral had become overcrowded. Later part of this new plot was reserved for the burial of Huguenots, who worshipped in the Lady Chapel of the cathedral. The entrance to the graveyard (and the park today) is directly across from St Patrick's Close and the cathedral).

One of the most important of Dublin's Huguenots is buried there. David Digues de Rompieres La Touche (David La Touche) established a silk, poplin and cambric business when he arrived in Dublin towards the end of the seventeenth century. Huguenots passing through Dublin and involved in weaving and other trades and businesses entrusted him with money and valuables and eventually he set up a bank with fellow weaver Nathaniel Kane in 1722. This famous La Touche Bank was the precursor of the Bank of Ireland. He died on 17 October 1745 while attending a service in the

Viceroy's Chapel. He was buried in the Huguenot section of the Cabbage Garden cemetery.[178]

The graveyard continued to be used until 1858 and then fell into neglect. In 1897 Lord Iveagh signalled his intent to convert the old cemetery into a 'pleasure ground' but this never materialised. In 1938 Dublin Corporation recorded the layout of the burial plots and the oldest burial stone recorded was that of John Paine, dated 1703. The City Council opened the old burial ground as a public park in 1982. The gravestones today (still in the park) contain messages like this father's tribute to his daughter:

> The voyage of life's end,
> The mortal affliction is passed,
> The age that in heaven she'll spend.
> Forever and ever shall last.[179]

Part of the cemetery was used as a park and the rest for public housing constructed by Dublin Corporation at the junction of Cathedral Lane and Upper Kevin Street, which opened in 1982. The park can be reached by way of Cathedral Lane which, until 1792, was called Cabbage Garden Lane.

The Queen's Favourite and Atkinson's House

Atkinson House is the only old building surviving on New Street and is the last remaining intact Georgian building in the area. The house was originally owned by Richard Atkinson, the silk merchant, industrialist, philanthropist and twice Lord Mayor of Dublin. He was recognised as a generous philanthropist and funded a refuge for widows: Atkinson House. The words 'Asylum for aged widows founded by Richard Atkinson, Lord Mayor of Dublin, 1837' are carved in stone over the entrance.[180]

Richard Atkinson was the pioneer in the development of Irish poplin. In 1820 he converted a cottage industry into a factory base. This secured employment and much improved living and working conditions for the inhabitants of The Liberties. Selling through his shop in College Green, Dublin he built a following for Atkinsons at home and abroad.

He became the leading Dublin silk poplin manufacturer and by 1837 Atkinson's Irish poplin fabric was so popular Queen Victoria granted him a Royal Warrant. He was Lord Mayor of Dublin in 1857 and again in 1861.

The tradition of silk and poplin weaving in The Liberties continued throughout the nineteenth century and even up to the twentieth century, with firms such as Frys, Pims, Elliots, Atkinsons and Mitchells. Elliots, the last factory in production, closed around 1965. In the late twentieth century weaving was revived in Fumbally Lane.[181]

The New Inn

On the opposite side of New Street near the major junction we had a pub called the New Inn (adjacent to a huge turf depot), the major rock band venue in the early to mid-1980s. All the names of the time played there, including a group called Engine Alley, named after a local street in The Liberties. The DJ, promoter, journalist and sometime publisher of *Gun* magazine in the early 1970s did much to promote the New Inn as a rock venue.

Among the pub's previous names was the Gulliver's Inn and prior to that it was Biddy Mulligan's, names derived from the area. For many years it was one of the major cabaret venues in the city with top comedians such as Hal Roach performing there. Of course he was entertaining on home territory as although he was from Waterford, in 1951 he married Mary, daughter of May Burdock of The Liberties fish and chip family. He was a comedian whose career spanned six decades and he starred for twenty-six consecutive seasons in Jury's Cabaret in Dublin. The pub was demolished in the late 1980s to make way for the Patrick Street dual carriageway.

The Four Corners of Hell

Lowes/Kenny's, TJ's/Nash's, O'Beirne's and Quinn's/Dunne's were the four pubs (although the pub names changed over the years) on what was known as the 'Four Corners of Hell', the corners of the junction of Patrick Street, Kevin Street, New Street and Dean Street. In the 1960s Peggy Dell used to play the piano at sing-songs in Quinn's. Apparently when priests were giving Church missions and retreats in the first half of the twentieth century they used to rail against these pubs and the toll they inflicted on families and the community in the area. It was a time when some men would spend their wages in the pubs and there would be fights outside at closing time. Local women used to say that the junction was like the four corners of Hell, as you could not cross without passing a pub![182]

Red Biddy was the name of a popular cheap but strong wine that sold widely at the time. It was the forerunner to the cheap flagons of cider favoured by later generations.

14

CELEBRATING
THE LIBERTIES

Celebrated in Music and Song

There is much to celebrate in The Liberties. The Liberties Festival is still going strong more than forty years after it first started. Some of the older residents still recall hearing the sounds of the great tenors Enrico Caruso and Count John McCormack, and the arias from the great operettas, wafting out of the tenement windows on Francis Street, Meath Street or the Coombe. Others recall the singer and accordion player Paddy Aldrith – fondly known as 'Paddy All Right' – and the great Irish composer of the nocturne, John Field, born in Golden Lane.

The St James' Brass and Reed Band is the oldest brass and reed band in Dublin, and one of the oldest in Europe. One memorable event in the band's history occurred during the War of Independence. On 15 May 1921 the band was practising in rooms in Bridgefoot Street when they were interrupted by the arrival of the Crown forces and the band was arrested en masse. The forty-seven members were loaded into army lorries and brought to Arbour Hill prison just across the Liffey. No charges were pressed and they were released after a short time. The music continues to this day!

Vicar Street is a hugely popular music venue. Interestingly when Handel came to Dublin in 1742, there was an important musical society based in Vicar Street. Today, the place is packed with rock memorabilia and in the front window there is a Harley Davidson 1200cc Sportser that was presented by U2 to broadcaster Gay Byrne on his last *Late Late Show* on 21 May 1999. High up on the exterior walls some of the words of the U2 song, 'Wake Up Dead Man' are written in a long unbroken line.[1]

Speaking ahead of their eleventh appearance at the Vicar Street music venue, Eddie, the oldest of the Furey brothers, was keen to point out to local publication, *The Liberty*, that the band had ties with The Liberties going back to childhood. The family is originally from Oliver Bond House on Oliver Bond Street. 'We [the Furey family] came out from The Liberties to Ballyfermot originally in the very early '50s so to us it's like coming home [to play in Vicar Street],' he explained. 'And there's always a great atmosphere there.'

Despite moving away from The Liberties at a young age, Eddie still felt a great affinity with the area:

My wife is from The Liberties, from Oliver Bond Flats ... we'd know all the families around there ... All the businesses on the street, they always give us a wave when we're going by. I love going around there and looking in at the shops and all. [I remember] the Limelight up in Thomas Street when that was going on ... I'd have only been going along for a listen, listening to other people playing after I came back from America and other parts of the world. There was an awful amount of folk [music] going on in those days.

And across the road from the Vicar Street venue is the church where Eddie and his wife got married. 'Every time I look across to John's Lane church from Vicar Street I start crying,' he joked. The wit of The Liberties, that is such an intrinsic and vital part of The Liberties personality to this day, remains undiminished![5]

Soprano Sandra Oman was the 2004 recipient of the Margaret Burke Sheridan Memorial Award for her contribution to opera in Ireland. She was born in the heart of The Liberties. Imelda May, another hugely popular singer, is also a child of The Liberties and Liberties singer-songwriter Fiach Moriarty, known as Fiach, released his debut album *So, I* in March 2010 to great acclaim.

The Liberties is also much celebrated in song. 'Dublin in the Rare Old Times', composed by Dublin Pete St John (who also composed 'The Fields of Athenry'), is regarded as a classic ballad about the changes wrought on the city since the 1960s. The song refers to Pimlico and the 'rebel Liberties'. He composed it originally for the Dublin City Ramblers. His songs often express regret for the loss of old certainties and this one is no exception – the song regrets the loss

A quarter of a million wooden barrels once stood in the cooperage yard at St. James's Gate. And every one was hand-made by a cooper. How many man-hours per barrel; how many man-years for a quarter of a million?

As familiar a sound then as the thud of barrels was the plodding clop of patient draught horses — now, like wooden casks and their makers, almost vanished from Dublin.

Guinness wooden barrels, c. 1940s. (Courtesy of Diageo/Guinness's Brewery; Dublin.ie Forums/Archangel)

of Nelson's Pillar and the Metropole Ballroom, two symbols of old Dublin, as progress makes a 'city of my town'. The song is sung by fans of Dublin GAA teams.[2]

Another is 'Lamentation on the Coombe Tragedy' about a murder case in which a local man murdered his wife. And who can forget Ronnie Drew of the Dubliners' rendition of 'Finnegan's Wake' which James Joyce immortalised in *Ulysses* and is commemorated with a plaque on the corner of Thomas Street and Watling Street.[3]

Jimmy O'Dea, legendary pantomime artist, actor and comedian, and formerly from Lower Bridge Street, portrayed and sang 'Biddy Mulligan, the Pride of the Coombe' for countless generations of children in the Gaiety and Olympia

Jimmy O'Dea dressed as Biddy Mulligan the Pride of the Coombe. Born in Lower Bridge Street in the heart of old Dublin (not far from 'Biddy Mulligan's' Coombe) on 28 April 1899, Jimmy O'Dea was one of eleven children, four of whom went on the stage. (Courtesy of Dublin Opinion)

theatres. P.J. McCall of Patrick Street gave us some of the greatest ballads celebrating the 1798 Rebellion, including Boolavogue. Zozimus, as Michael Moran was known, was the blind ballad singer born in Faddle Alley in 1794 and who died in 1846 at 14 Patrick Street. His famous piece, 'Ye Men of Sweet Liberties Hall', was always a particular favourite. He was also known as The Blind Bard of The Liberties and The Last of the Gleemen. He died in his home at 15 Patrick Street and is buried in Glasnevin Cemetery. In his memory, the folk group, the Dublin City Ramblers erected a headstone over his grave.

In the area of folk music, The Dubliners, Floggin Molly and the Dublin City Ramblers folk groups have long celebrated The Liberties in song. Besides 'Dublin in the Rare Old Times', others with a strong Liberties theme include 'Spanish Lady' and 'The Dublin Jack-of-All-Trades'. The Dubliners also made famous the ballad, 'The Ragman's Ball', with the lines '... I'll sing you a verse or two, about a famous ball. Now the ball was given by some friends, who lived down Ash Street, in a certain house in The Liberties, where the ragmen used to meet.'[4]

The Chieftains, besides having roots in The Liberties (No. 6 the Coombe), are celebrated with a plaque on St Catherine's church, Thomas Street, where they played their first public concert. Other famous musicians and bands such as The Script and Engine Alley, also hail from The Liberties.

The Wolfe Tones are an Irish rebel music band that incorporates elements of Irish traditional music in their songs. They are named after the Irish rebel and patriot Theobald Wolfe Tone, one of the leaders of the Irish Rebellion of 1798, with the double entendre that a wolf tone is a spurious sound that can affect instruments of the violin family. Tommy Byrne of the folk group was born and raised in The Liberties in the 1940s and 1950s. He was the eldest of eleven children. He used to work in the nearby Guinness Brewery before he joined the Wolfe Tones band full time 'and thank God I have never looked back', he said. Other members include Brian Warfield and Noel Nagle. But the Trio's story wasn't one of overnight success. Brian and Derek Warfield (one of the original members) of the Wolfe Tones had taken tin whistle lessons at the Pipers' Club in Thomas Street. Essentially, the Wolfe Tones learned to play there.[6]

And not forgetting The Dubliners. Barney McKenna, although known as 'Banjo Barney of Donnycarney' was originally from the Coombe, having been born there before the family moved to Donnycarney. He was unerringly drawn back to The Liberties and served part of his musical apprenticeship at the Pipers' Club and it was here that he and future fellow-member of the group, John Sheahan, met as teenagers in the 1950s. Barney became one of the founding members of The Dubliners.[7]

Sean McGuiness of the Dublin City Ramblers was born in James's Street and in 1972 he resigned his employment with the Post & Telegraphs (the P&T as it was known and later became Eircom) having formed The Ramblers in 1970. Sean started his music career in 1963 by forming a band called The Jolly Tinkers. It changed the name some years later to The Quare Fellas, being influenced by that great author and character, Brendan Behan.[8]

Another stalwart of the Pipers' Club was John Potts, the famous traditional Irish musician who hailed from the Coombe where his house, No. 6, was a great meeting place for practitioners of their music. He was also the grandfather of Seán Potts of The Chieftains.

Chieftains music legend Seán Potts himself, in keeping with the family tradition, has proven that age is no barrier to productivity by releasing his first solo recording of music on the tin whistle entitled, *Number Six* (a reference to his grandfather's house), months before his eightieth birthday in March 2010. He also received the TG4 Gradam Ceoil lifetime achievement award at a ceremony in Wexford. The founder member of The Chieftains and Ceoltoiri Chualann launched the record, which he hoped would generate much-needed funds to help promote the manufacture of the uilleann pipes and the further development of the piping headquarters in historic Henrietta Street (originally in Thomas Street). Since retiring from touring as a professional musician, he has dedicated over thirty years of his life to the promotion of the uilleann pipes in his role as chairman and honorary president of NPU. However, it is Seán Potts' whistle playing, described by his former Chieftains colleague Paddy Moloney as 'the greatest he as ever heard', that made him famous all over the world and *Number Six* was a celebration of his rich musical legacy.[9]

The Pipers' Club

There is a plaque on the wall of this now derelict building at 14 Thomas Street that commemorates the Dublin Pipers' Club that occupied the premises and also the founding of Comhaltas Ceoltóirí Éireann in 1951. In 1946 the Pipers' Club moved from 134 Thomas Street to Arus Ceannt, at No. 14 (known as The Power House of Traditional Music), which had previously been the headquarters of the 4th Battalion Old IRA of which 1916 Rising leader Eamonn Ceannt was the commandant. During the War of Independence it was raided by the Black and Tans.

Eamonn Ceannt had been one of the founders of the Dublin Pipers' Club in around 1906. He was a member of the Gaelic League and had extensive knowledge of Irish and its literature. He was also a skilled piper. He attended the Jubilee Celebrations held in Rome in 1908, in honour of Pope Pius X, and led the Irish athletes as they marched into the Roman arena to compete in the celebrations.

Ceannt, who looked quite regal playing his pipes and dressed in an eleventh-century Irish costume with kilt, was 6ft tall and so presented quite a dramatic image. He played to a cheering crowd, making such a sensation that the Pope heard of his performance and summoned him for a papal appearance. When Ceannt appeared before the pope, the pope was surrounded by a group of elderly Irish priests who had been long exiled from their native land and Ceannt marched up to the group playing 'Wearing of the Green'. According to Mick O'Connor, the historian of the club, the Pope was surprised that the 'wild music of the pipes moved the old Irish priests to such a state of emotion that many of them burst into tears.'[10]

Some of the great names in Irish music are associated with the Thomas Street club, including Leo and William Rowsome, John Potts, John Brogan, James Ennis, Jack Wade, Tommy Rock, Jim Seery, John Keenan, Paddy McElvaney, Sean Seery, Jim Dowling, Sean Kane, the Quinn family and many more committed to Irish traditional music and culture.

According to Mick O'Connor, 'the development of Irish music in Dublin can be traced mainly through the fortunes of the Dublin Pipers' Club from the period 1900 to the present day'. He also noted that some of the members of the 4th Battalion sent their children to the Club to learn traditional music. Many of the great Irish céilí bands were connected to the club.

Of particular interest is that O'Connor himself is originally from The Liberties where many of the Dublin piping families lived. He was a member of the Pipers' Club in the 1950s through to the 1970s when he trained the Pipers' Club Céilí Band. He is a well-known flute player, archivist, researcher and music historian. As a musician, he has broadcast and recorded with Seán Keane of the Chieftains fame and Charlie Lennon in former years. In the 1960s, he was leader of the famed Castle Céilí Band. A former Assistant Secretary and current President of the Association of Irish Traditional Musicians, he is a popular lecturer and teacher at the Willie Clancy Summer School and Scoil Éigse at Fleadh Cheoil na hÉireann. He has also saved for posterity one of the largest collections of archival photographs of older traditional musicians.

In the 1950s and 1960s the club was a huge attraction for budding and visiting musicians. Barney McKenna (later a member of the Dubliners) caused a stir when, after a stint working in England, he turned up at the door of the Pipers' Club, banjo case in hand, wearing a red shirt, black lace tie and winkle pickers (fashionable shoes of the era). During this time, he played the banjo at concerts, cabarets, and a stint in a quartet with Martin Fay and Paddy Moloney, who were forming The Chieftains. He once remarked, 'I should have been a Chieftain but instead I grew a beard and became a Dubliner'. He met Ronnie Drew following a Gate Theatre show with John Molloy and shortly after The Dubliners was formed in 1962. The world-famous folk group celebrated their 50th anniversary in The Liberties – in Christ Church Cathedral in early 2012. In March of the same year Barney died at the age of seventy-two. He was the last of the founding members.

At Barney McKenna's funeral in April 2012, fellow Dubliner John Sheahan reminisced how he first met Barney when they both frequented the Pipers' Club. He likened these sessions to 'serving an apprenticeship for a career that would unite us for 50 years'.[11]

Celebrated in Film

The Liberties is celebrated in a series of twelve well-crafted short films, each with a focus on a different character within The Liberties community. Directed and produced by Tom Burke and Shane Hogan of Areaman Productions, *The Liberties* celebrates ordinary people living in The Liberties – such as tailor Eugene Fagan, Meath Street butcher Declan Larkin, and flower ladies Phyllis Kavanagh and Mary Hand, as well as better known residents such as Brenda Fricker, seen polishing her Oscar at home.

And of course many other films were shot there, including a drama starring Richard Burton called, *The Spy Who Came in From the Cold* that featured Cork Street.[12]

Celebrated in Literature

Besides being gifted with many local writers, The Liberties have long been celebrated in literature. James Joyce's *Finnegan's Wake* features Adam & Eve's church amongst other places. Playing games with language he reversed the nickname of the church and called it 'Eve and Adam's'.[13] *Ulysses* features Watling Street, opposite the brewery, and 'Mr Kernan turned and walked down the slope of Watling Street by the corner of Guinness visitors' waiting room.' Leopold Bloom doubted that it was possible to cross Dublin without passing a pub on every corner and in The Liberties that was certainly the case for very many years, with Francis Street alone having nine pubs at one time. 'Be interesting some day get a pass through Hancock to see the brewery', Bloom mused. In Crane Street, the Guinness Hop Store visitors' centre facilitates tasting of 'the wine of the country' as Joyce called Guinness stout. He also referred to it in *Finnegan's Wake* as the 'frothy freshener'. Joyce even tackled Dean Swift of St Patrick's Cathedral with Stephen Dedalus saying he was 'a hater of his kind'. Fumbally Lane and its 'tanyard smells' also features in *Ulysses*.[14]

The James Stephens' book *The Charwoman's Daughter* (1912), was set in The Liberties, and is based on his experiences of living there in the late nineteenth and early twentieth centuries. He lived at Thomas Court, just off Thomas Street.[15]

The Liberties area has many literary associations that are sometimes overlooked, including an impressive list of authors with local links. James Clarence Mangan was born on Fishamble Street and lived beside Bride Street; he died prematurely of cholera in the Meath Hospital. He is celebrated at Clarence Mangan Square and Clarence Mangan Road. The whole Liberties district was Jonathan Swift's domain when he was dean of St Patrick's Cathedral in the 1700s and some of his best writings are based on his experiences and observations of The Liberties, including *A Modest Proposal*, *Gulliver's Travels*, and the *Drapier Letters*. And one of the city's great jewels, Marsh's Library, had as writers in residence, as it were, Thomas Moore, who wrote his *Odes of Anacreon* there, and Charles Maturin, author of the influential *Melmoth the Wanderer*.

Sean O'Connor was born on Francis Street and is the father of award-winning author Joseph O'Connor and singer Sinead O'Connor. Speaking at the Ark Children's Centre in Temple Bar, Joseph O'Connor noted that Francis Street and The Liberties had a big influence on his father. This influence has been passed on to the son and several of the stories and songs he wrote were inspired by The Liberties, and have appeared in Joseph O'Connor's fiction and other writings.[16]

The Liberties are still producing much talent. Liz Gillis, author of *The Fall of Dublin*, is from The Liberties. Lar Redmond grew up in Emerald Square (off Cork Street) and wrote a book of the same name. Mairin Johnston is well remembered for her great read, *Around the Banks of Pimlico*. Poet Christine Broe also grew up in The Liberties; her father had a sweet shop in Dean Street and her mother had a second-hand furniture shop 'Moylans', also in Dean Street. Educated at the Holy Faith, the Coombe, she said she used to 'haunt' the Kevin Street Library as a child.[17]

Thomas Phelan grew up in Hanbury Lane in the heart of The Liberties. His book, *Hanbury Lane from Whence I Came*, is about his memories of growing up in The Liberties. Liam O'Meara hails from Ushers Quay and his most famous book *The Bayno* recounts the story of the play centre in the Iveagh Trust building overlooking St Patrick's Park. He has also written a book on Zozimus, the infamous nineteenth-century irreverent poet, balladeer and beggar who loved to lambast politicians and those in authority in his rhymes. *Down Cobbled Streets – A Liberties Childhood*, recounts the early life of Phil O'Keefe who hailed from the Thomas Court/Thomas Court Bawn area. She vividly re-creates Liberties life in the 1930s and beyond.

Former resident Jim Smyth wrote a book, *The Pipes, The Pipes Are Calling*, the story of twentieth-century Dublin and a little boy who was born, raised and grew up in The Liberties, next to the Forty Steps. He says:

I loved The Liberties, from my first remembrances of the streets and alleyways. As a young lad I was early on amused that an alleyway could be called Dirty Lane, and right behind it was a street called Mullinahack (now Oliver Bond Street), and Cherry Steps were nearby. I remember The Liberties was an 'up-and-down' area, we were always walking steep up and low down the streets, up and down.[18]

Another former resident, Joan Duffy, wrote a memorable story, *Growing Up in the Bond* about life in the Oliver Bond Street residential development.

Who Gives a Damn Anyway was the title used for a book published in 1993 about the plight of the old School Street and Thomas Court Bawn Flats. What comes out of this book is that the communities of The Liberties believe in spirit, community effort and tireless work to improve their lot. Despite the challenges the area faced, the locals worked hard to turn their area around and transformed it into a functioning, supportive and proud community. Now they have the School Street Family Centre and The Liberties Counselling Service among other facilities. And this spirit is very much in evidence right across the different communities of The Liberties. A spirit that has been forged over generations, in the smithy of tenements, poverty, hardship and friendship.[19] Another community also put its experiences on paper: The SICCDA Heritage Centre (now based at Meath Street) had its fascinating account *Talking Liberties* published in 1995.

A little booklet called *Little Saints of The Liberties* by Malachy Cullen also did much to celebrate this indomitable spirit of the mothers of The Liberties who reared their families in extremely hard times. The booklet contains personal recollections by Fr Cullen who was based in the Augustinian Priory in John's Lane in the 1940s and 1950s. He remembers some of the wonderful characters of bygone times, and unfolds for us a hidden treasure of those he calls 'God's aristocrats'.[20]

Writer Siobhán Parkinson set her book, *Kate*, in 1930s Liberties. Her story concerns a local girl who goes to her very first Irish dancing lesson and is smitten: it's like flying, she decides. It's the best thing she's ever done. But, coming from a poor family in The Liberties in the 1930s, how can Kate continue with her dancing? How could she ever manage to buy a fancy dancing costume? Still, Kate has her dreams – and sometimes dreams come true, even if not in the way we imagine![21]

And there are many other locals who have written on The Liberties, including Vicky Cremin, Grace O'Keefe, and Phil O'Keefe. The artist and writer Chris Reid also has done much to capture, in art and in print, the essence of the area.

Poet and playwright Fintan O'Higgins is also from The Liberties and, tongue-in-cheek, noted, 'it is said of the city of Dublin that you cannot lob a brick in the place without braining some class of a poet'![22] Well, this is certainly the case with The Liberties.

Pádraig J. Daly's poetry immortalised daily life in The Liberties. His poems of place offer a celebration of the beauty of the landscape, the people and the area. Likewise with renowned Liberties poet Christine Broe who grew up in The Liberties and continues to be inspired and influenced by the area of her upbringing.

And still another poet, Gerard Smyth, was born and grew up in The Liberties (Francis Street), an area that has influenced, and features in, much of the poetry he has written. 'Marbles' is a poem about playing marbles as a boy:

> I loved their colours rolling on the path,
> the spherical motion, the smack
> when glass hit glass. We had fistfuls of them,
> collections stashed in cloth bags
> that we clutched like a treasure chest.

'Shop of Cures', is about the Mushatt brothers who had a chemist's shop in Francis Street, next door to the Hazlehatch Dairy:

> They came with their afflictions to the shop of cures:
> those in need of small mercies, or small miracles.
> Some with fire in their throats, an ache in their bones,
> with ailments, agonies, a rasp in their chests.
>
> Like sorcerer and apprentice, the apothecaries
> in mint white coats, kept to their side of the counter
> among the remedies, spooning powders into the mix,
> deciphering the medicine scripts.

'Sam's Junkshop', another poem, features another landmark that was between the pharmacy and the dairy/bakery and the Draper's Shop (O'Hora's was on the other side). Gerard Smyth noted that Patrick Kavanagh once said that after a poet learns to speak for himself he must speak on behalf of others – 'that is really what I am doing in these poems – especially in "Survivors", about men in the area who had fought in the first World War, but could not speak about that back in the 60s' when he was growing up there. Other memorable poems on The Liberties include: 'The Forty Steps' ('running down the Forty Steps of the medieval passage-way'); 'Return'; 'All That is Left'; 'In the Brazen Head'.[23]

Visit to The Liberties by the Royals (King George and Queen Mary) in 1911. A stop at St Patrick's Cathedral also featured in their stay in Dublin. (Courtesy of RTÉ)

Celebrated in Art – The Boundary Kings

Such is the uniqueness of The Liberties that it has captured the attention and imagination of many artists over time. Chris Reid, mentioned above, has his plaques with anecdotes and memories of local residents of the Iveagh Trust Buildings adorning the walls of the area.[24]

Hugely prolific Irish sculptor Patrick O'Reilly's street sculpture of multi-coloured heads, 'The Boundary Kings', was erected in 1998 outside the Vicar Street music venue. He chose the colours from Celtic illuminated manuscripts. These totem-like structures with disgruntled or startled faces are a particularly eye-catching feature of Thomas Street.[25] These, combined with the glass façade of the Vicar Street music venue and the yellow stalwart arch of Chadwick's Builders adjacent, certainly create a concoction to catch the eye of the passer-by.

One of the most renowned eighteenth-century Irish landscape painters, George Barrett (Senior) (1732–1784) hailed from The Liberties. The son of a clothier, he was initially apprenticed to a corset-maker before studying drawing and painting under Robert West at the Royal Dublin Society School in George's Lane. While at art school, he earned money by colouring prints for a print-seller in Nicholas Street and after graduating he worked for a time as an art teacher in a Dublin school.[26]

It is not surprising that the National College of Art and Design (NCAD) should be located in Thomas Street given the artistic and architectural riches of the area. The famous stained-glass window artist and illustrator of books, Harry Clarke, has some examples of his finest works in John's Lane church on

Thomas Street and St Nicholas of Myra church in Francis Street. The NCAD building that was once the old Thomas Street Fire Station is now called Harry Clarke House.

James Malton's Prints of Dublin illustrate many locations in The Liberties ranging from streets to churches. Malton's prints include: 'The West front of St Patrick's in 1793', 'St Patrick's from the old street market about 1890' and 'St Catherine's Church, Thomas Street'.[27]

The great Irish painter Walter Osborne also captured poignant scenes, including a painting, now in the National Gallery of Ireland, of Patrick Street. The gallery also contains an 1818 watercolour painting depicting St Luke's church with a graveyard in front.

Alexander Williams RHA (1864 – 1930) had a series of Liberties paintings from around 1885:

1. 'St Audoen's Arch, a bit of the old city wall, Dublin.' This watercolour shows the only surviving medieval gate in Dublin, St Audoen's Arch, The Old City Wall, prior to its restoration in the 1880s. At that time battlements were added to the top of the gate and later all the tenement houses shown by Williams were cleared away, leaving Cook Street with an uninterrupted view of the medieval city wall. The horizontal timber support across the alley shows just how decrepit the houses were. Beyond the arch two figures stand beneath the shadow of St Audoen's church. The puddle in the cobbled street and the broken-down cart complete the picture of urban decay.

2. 'Spitalfields, Francis Street, Dublin'. This view of St Nicholas of Myra church seen from Spitalfields gives us an interesting glimpse of city life. A butcher's stall, complete with chopping block takes up the path and gutter, and a variety of figures stand in conversation.

3. 'Old Clothes Shop, Patrick Street, Dublin', also *c.* 1885. This view, taken from Patrick Street looking up to the back of St Nicholas of Myra shows old clothes shops, located in lean-to buildings. In the foreground, a group of women rummage through a pile of old clothes, while stalls provide the means for displaying other wares.

4. 'Watercolour of Slums of Wormwood Gate, *c.* 1890'. This image captures the sense of poverty, decay and loss of these originally fine buildings at the junction of Cook Street and Mullinahack.

This historic centre of Dublin city changed very little until quite recently and many older people still remember the dilapidated and run-down streets of The Liberties. These four paintings by Alexander Williams, 'in a charmingly naïve way', according to historian and artist Peter Pearson, depict the life and architecture of The Liberties at that time.[28]

Other paintings include an oil painting 'John Dillon Street, Liberties' by Fergal Flanagan, and John Cruise's 'The Interior of St Patrick's Before Restoration', (n.d. but probably 1870s).

Jerry Marjoram is one of the great enthusiasts in Irish art. He was born in The Liberties area in 1936. He began to paint for pleasure, but the hobby soon became a passion. He entered the College of Art under the tutorship of Maurice McGonigal, and while there was also taught by Sean Keating. His first major break came when Combridge's in Grafton Street took him on. There was soon a fast-growing demand for his paintings, so he gave up his job in 1970 to paint full-time. Since then he has had many solo exhibitions in Dublin and Galway. He is thought to be the first visual artist from The Liberties to have had a one-man show in Dublin.

Celebrated in Sport

The Liberties has many celebrated sporting heroes. Anne O'Connor of St Thomas's Road in the Tenters swam in the 1968 and 1972 Olympics for Ireland.

Brian Kerr, educated at 'Jambo', St James's Street CBS, managed the Irish soccer team from 2003. He had been the most successful manager of the Republic of Ireland at underage level and craved the opportunity to manage the senior team. His appointment was therefore the fulfilment of a cherished dream. One of his achievements was to persuade Roy Keane to play for Ireland again. He has one of the best win ratios of any Irish manager.

Dan Donnelly, the legendary boxer who died in 1820, owned Fallon's Capstan Bar on Dean Street for a number of years. He also lived in Francis Street. Formerly a carpenter, he fought celebrated bouts against English challengers in 1814 and 1815, in both cases at the Curragh, where 'Donnelly's Hollow' is still marked. He was buried near The Liberties in Bully's Acre cemetery, Kilmainham.

Tony Byrne, a successful Liberties businessman, was born on Winetavern Street. He had two serious passions in life, the cinema and football. As a child, the Tivoli on Francis Street was one of his local cinemas and he and his close friend Johnny Giles never missed a programme there. He also pursed his love for football and played for Shamrock Rovers and Shelbourne. He later owned the latter club for a number of years.

Another famous footballer and talented hurler to boot, was Meath Street's Kevin Moran, of Dublin Gaelic football team fame, who then went on to even more stardom with Manchester United. The family had a grocery and newsagents shop in Meath Street, called The Coconut, where his mother (a very talented business-woman) supplied all the traders going to the football matches with their supplies. (The family later moved out to Driminagh and opened up another Coconut shop!)

There, he played football with Good Counsel GAA Club. He was regarded as the best attacking half-back in Gaelic football for many years and was on the team when Dublin became All-Ireland Football Champions in 1976.[29]

Dublin had not beaten Kerry in a championship match since the All-Ireland semi-final of 1934. In the meantime, Kerry had beaten Dublin in two finals (1955 and 1975) and four semis. The country was entranced by the prospect of the final. Unlike the previous year, tickets sold out in record time and 73,588 attended the final. The opening moments of the match are remembered today for the greatest near-miss in the history of All-Ireland Finals when, after forty-five seconds, Kevin Moran burst through the Kerry defence only to blaze the ball inches wide.

For Dublin manager Kevin Heffernan, the dream of beating the Kingdom had been realised. 'I've waited 21 years for this victory' he remarked after the game. The Liberties and Dublin went suitably 'bananas'. *The Irish Times* reported on 27 September 1976: 'Old men and their wives, their sons and daughters and grandchildren were all proudly wearing their tribal emblems. 'The Jacks are Back', the little chisellers were shouting.'[30] Kevin Moran was part of those memorable days in the 1970s and he went on to win many more epic battles with 'the Dubs'.

Kevin had a high profile through his GAA exploits. However, it was while playing for UCD's Pegasus FC that his soccer skills came to the attention of the famous Manchester United football scout, Billy Behan. The then Manchester United manager, Dave Sexton, signed him to Manchester United in 1978. He made his debut on 30 April 1979 against Southampton. Moran went on to make 289 appearances for United, scored a total of twenty-four goals and won two FA Cup winners medals with the club.

He also played for the Republic of Ireland and was an integral part of the Jack Charlton squad that made the historic breakthrough when Ireland qualified for a first major football championship finals in the 1980s. He was a major part of an unforgettable 1–0 victory over a strong English team in the opening match of the Euro '88 finals. He played for Ireland seventy-one times and scored six goals for his country. There must have been something in those 'liquorice allsorts' in his mother's shop on Meath Street!

It is still possible to see the faded words 'Meath Mart' on the brickwork of his former home.

Street Characters

As one of the oldest areas in Dublin, The Liberties gave the city plenty of characters, not least 'Bang Bang'. Thomas Dudley (or 'Lord Dudley' as he called himself) became known around Dublin in the 1950s and 1960s for the mock shoot-outs he staged, inspired by his love of cowboy films, but with a large church key in place of a gun. While standing on the back platform of the old-style buses he would pretend to shoot all and sundry with his mock gun. He would point his huge key at his intended victim and shout, 'Bang, Bang ...' He lived at Mill Lane and later at 50b Bridgefoot Street for many years. Locals sang the following at the time:

> And we all went up to the Mero, hey there, who's your man
> It's only Johnny Forty Coats, sure he's desperate man
> Bang Bang shoots the buses with his golden key
> Hey hi diddley I and out goes she.

According to writer and former Pimlico (South Summer Street, Marrowbone Lane) resident, Isobel Smyth:

> We reached most places on foot and often encountered 'Bang Bang' on our travels. He was an auld Dublin character who staged mock shoot-outs with the passing public. His '45' was a long church key worn thin and shiny which he aimed at people who, in general, participated in his good natured antics by returning fire with their finger, taking cover in doorways, even clutching their chest and falling down 'dead' on the city streets.[31]

In February 2011, The Lord Mayor of Dublin, Gerry Breen presented Dublin City Archivist, Dr Mary Clark with that famous key. According to the Lord Mayor:

> Bang Bang was a great and entertaining character from Dublin. Many people remember his energy and his love of fun and humour. 2011 marked the 30th anniversary of his death and I think that it is very fitting that his key will now remain in safe keeping in the city he gave so much joy to.

A great friend of Thomas Dudley had held the key for many years and presented it to the Lord Mayor.[32]

Other famous characters include Damn the Weather, Hairy Lemon and the blind beggar Zozimus from Faddle Alley. Then we had Endimion, and not forgetting Oney the funeral-goer who loved following hearses. Also, Peg-the-man and the irrepressible Cantering Jack – a busking fiddler and dancer in odd boots who followed carriages for miles until paid by the passengers to go away! Who remembers The Bird Flanagan? President Keeley? Tie Me Up? Lino? All Parcels? Siki 'Cyclon e' Warren? Lillian Mc Evoy? Shell Shock Joe? The Toucher Doyle? Bugler Dunne? Jumbo No Toes? Mad Mary and Jack the Tumbler? And Hairy Yank?

'Bang Bang' was a great Liberties character. He was born in a house in Bridgefoot St not far from that of the famous actor Jimmy O'Dea. (Courtesy of Dublin.ie Forums/Damntheweather)

Billy-in-the-bowl? Dandyorum? Stoney Pockets? The Dear Man? And of course Fat Mary, the prima donna of Dublin streets. Dusty Lawlor is remembered with a painting in Tom Kennedy's pub on Thomas Street. Each of these characters has a story to tell.[33]

The most famous legendary character of Dublin was probably Molly Malone. Walton Music's Victorian-style image of Molly for their sheet music of 'Cockles and Mussels' became the image for her sculpture on Dublin's Grafton Street. According to folklore Molly's parents were in the fish-selling business, and resided near Fishamble Street. According to the City Fathers who erected the monument in her memory, every day Molly wheeled her wheelbarrow from The Liberties to the more fashionable Grafton Street, crying 'Cockles and Mussels' as she went. The legend has gathered apace over the years and as well as being known and sung internationally, the popular song 'Cockles and Mussels' has become a sort of unofficial anthem of Dublin city. The song's tragic heroine Molly Malone and her barrow have come to stand as one of the most familiar symbols of the capital.

Today, the call to indulge in fish has been taken up in The Liberties by Leo Burdock's (Dublin's oldest chipper!) of No. 2 Werburgh Street. Burdock's, famous for its cod and chips, has been a household name for generations of Liberties residents. They have been trading in fish and chips since 1913. There were other relations of Burdock's in the same business in the 1930s at No. 11 Dolphin Barn Street. In 1958 Burdocks were also at No. 6 Marrowbone Lane. There is an interesting 'Wall of Fame' plaque on the outside No. 2 Werburgh Street that shows it has been frequented by Cabinet Ministers, rock stars, actors, poets, foreign visitors and many famous people who have popped in for the unique fish and chips. You might meet Billy Connolly, Kate Moss, Rod Stewart, Naomi Campbell or Bruce Springsteen in the queue; they have all eaten there!

This poem is also included on the Wall of Fame:

<blockquote>
In the year nine hundred and eighty eight,
As everyone must know,
The Vikings came to Dublin,
</blockquote>

'Cos they had no where else to go,
They landed on Wood Quay, where they all jumped off their ships,
And legged it to Burdocks,
For a little bag of chips.'

(From Tommy Flanagan's Millennium Song, 'A Little Bag of Chips')[34]

The Liberties Today

In their book, *Re-Drawing Dublin*, Kearns and Ruimy suggest that the many inner-city areas (including The Liberties) are often seen through rose-tinted spectacles, particularly by those who don't live there. They say, 'Disadvantaged areas in need of urban regeneration are very often seen through the prism of a form of 'urban nostalgia'. This is perhaps natural but nevertheless quite unhealthy. The past is somehow imagined as a better place when confronted with what seem like the overwhelming challenges of the area today.'[35]

In October 2007, Dublin City Council revealed plans for a multi-million euro redevelopment of The Liberties. They argued that lack of investment and the rationalisation of traditional industry throughout the twentieth century combined to cause both physical and social decay and this was therefore an area crying out for a major urban renewal project. Yet these plans met with strong opposition from residents of the area, claiming that the character of one of the city's oldest surviving areas would be destroyed by such redevelopment.

According to one commentator, despite its clear weaknesses, there is much to celebrate about The Liberties and a great deal of potential lies within its streets. And this is a view echoed by others. For many it is the authenticity of the area, which makes it attractive to live in. The centrality of the location is one of its greatest assets. The area is also home to Ireland's number one tourist attraction – the Guinness Storehouse – an institution, which is hugely important, both historically and culturally for the city and the wider country.

Businesses also thrive in the area. The Digital Hub and Digital Exchange next to the Guinness brewery continue to grow and foster some of the most innovative digital enterprises in the country, as does the Digital Depot, on the other side of Thomas Street. The Liberties Enterprise Centre at Newmarket Square, and Fumbally Lane business centres at Fumbally Court and Fumbally Square, are all hives of entrepreneurial activity. And across The Liberties we have countless small businesses, homes and communities, that all add up to make this The Liberties.

The Liberties also continues to boast architectural importance and gems within The Liberties include the terraced townhouses around John Dillon Street, Reginald Street, Gray Street and others, NCAD's Red Square, the stunning

Victorian Iveagh Trust buildings, the church steeples and the dominating storehouses of Guinness.

The Liberties is not over-rated, it's under-realised, noted a visitor. Investment is certainly needed but the potential of the area is huge, everybody knows this; all that is required to begin to deliver on that potential is a bit of hard work, in-depth research, planning, skill, vision and leadership from the City Council. Yes, there is indeed hope, particularly when we see the work of An Taisce, the Dublin Civic Trust and the Dublin City Council's reports/integrated plans for the area. Moreover when one

Lennon's Dairy and Grocery, Chamber Street, 1964. (Courtesy of Dublin City Public Libraries)

sees the vibrant community spirit at work everywhere, one cannot fail to be moved. The Carman's Hall Community centre, St Nicholas of Myra Heritage Centre, The Liberties Heritage Project, SICCDA and the numerous groups working in the area stand out. These, and the various parish councils and community groups point to local spirit at its very best.

Some say the heart of The Liberties is the area bounded by Francis Street, Pimlico, the Coombe, Meath Street and Thomas Street. For years, prior to the explosion of the Celtic Tiger, these streets were thronged with shoppers looking for bargains. The suburban retail developments temporarily brought to an end the halcyon days of the Liberty Bazaar, the Bull Ring, The Iveagh Markets and Liberty Market, as well as the vast multitude of on-street traders selling clothing, fruit & veg and various 'odds and ends'. But, in true Liberties spirit, the heart is pumping again.

Pride of the Coombe: From Biddy to Bottler

Let's give the last word to Brendan Grace, the renowned Irish comedian and singer, who also hails from the Liberties. Amongst his numerous successes, it is for his inimitable portrayal of the antics of the mischievous schoolboy, Bottler, that he will forever be celebrated. 'Apart from being an Irish man, I'm also a Dublin man. And apart from being a Dublin man, I'm a Liberty boy', said Brendan, speaking in October 2012 at the first Liberties Gathering 2013 in Harkin's Pub beside the Guinness Storehouse, where he was re-united with former showband members of The Gingermen, after more than forty years.

NOTES

Introduction

1. James Malton *A Picturesque and Descriptive View of the City of Dublin* (1799)
2. South Inner City Community Development Association Heritage Centre *Talking Liberties* (1995); Dublin Civic Trust *Thomas Street: Improving the Public Face of an Historic City Centre Street* (2012); Bernadette Flanagan *The Spirit of the City: Voices from Dublin's Liberties* (1999)
3. Dublin City Council 'The Liberties Local Area Plan, September 2008'

1. The Gaelic, Viking and Norman Origins of Dublin

1. John Gilbert *A History of the City of Dublin* (1854)
2. Christine Casey *Dublin: The city within the Grand and Royal Canals and the Circular Road with the Phoenix Park* (2005)
3. J.C. Beckett *The Making of Modern Ireland 1603–1923* (1966)
4. James Collin *Life in Old Dublin* (1913)

2. Henry II: Liberties or Franchises?

1. Kenneth Milne (ed.) *Christ Church Cathedral, Dublin: A History* (2000)
2. Kenneth Milne *The Four Liberties 1660–1850* (2009) 'Introduction', pp.46–7
3. Elgy Gillespie (ed.) *The Liberties of Dublin* (1973)
4. Herbert Wood (ed.) *Court Book of the Liberty of St Sepulchre Within the Jurisdiction of the Archbishop of Dublin* 'Introduction' (1930)
5. Milne *The Four Liberties*, 'introduction', pp. 37–45 and 'conclusion'
6. *ibid.*, pp. 18–20, pp. 21–30 and pp. 37–45
7. Charles Brooking *Map of the City and Suburbs of Dublin* (1728)
8. National Library of Ireland *Survey of The Liberties and franchises of Dublin City as ridden and perambulated every third year* (1815)
9. 'Riding the Franchises', leaflet in Dublin City Council Archives

3. The Middle Ages

1. Friends of Medieval Dublin
2. Howard B. Clarke (Dublin City Council) *The Four Parts of Dublin: High Life and Low Life in Medieval Dublin* (2002)
3. Howard B. Clarke *Dublin c. 840 to c. 1540: The Medieval Town in the Modern City* 2nd ed. (2002)

4. Silken Thomas and William Brabazon

1. R.D. Edwards (ed.) *Reformation to Restoration: Ireland 1534–1660* (1987)
2. R.D. Edwards *Church and State in Tudor Ireland* (1935); Gillian Nells/*Sunday Business Post* 'The *Business Post* Interview: Anthony and Fionnuala Ardee', 1 July 2012
3. Turtle Bunbury *The Landed Gentry & Aristocracy of Co. Wicklow* (2005)
4. Henry Boylan *Dictionary of National Biography* (1998)
5. S.J. Connolly (ed.) *The Oxford Companion to Irish History* (1998); Brabazons information according to UCC History Lecturer Hiram Morgan/HM
6. Colm Lennon 'The Great Explosion in Dublin, 1597' *Dublin Historical Record*, pp. 7–20 (1988)
7. Mary Daly *The Deposed Capital: A Social and Economic History, 1860–1914* (1984)

5. The Huguenots

1. Raymond Hylton *Ireland's Huguenots and their Refuge, 1662–1745: An Unlikely Haven* (2005)
2. Robin D. Gwynn *Huguenot Heritage: The History and Contribution of the Huguenots in Britain* (1985)
3. Danny Parkinson *Huguenot Cemetery 1693* (1988)
4. Samuel Smiles *The Huguenots: Their Settlements, Churches, and Industries in England and Ireland* (1881)
5. Samuel James Knox *Ireland's Debt to the Huguenots* (1959)
6. *ibid.*
7. Grace Lee *Lawless: The Huguenot Settlements in Ireland* (1936)
8. C.E.J. Caldicott, H. Gough, J-P Pittion. (eds) *The Huguenots and Ireland: Anatomy of an Emigration* (1985)
9. 'Huguenot Society of Great Britain and Ireland' *Proceedings of the Huguenot Society of Great Britain and Ireland* (1987)
10. Report of the Joint Committee on the Huguenot Cemetery Dublin (Peter Street) Bill, 1965, together with the proceedings of the Joint Committee, 1966; The Huguenot Cemetery Dublin (Peter Street) Act, 1966
11. National Library of Ireland 'Reports of the Wide Streets Commissioners'
12. Niall McCullough (ed.) *A Vision of the City: Dublin and the Wide Streets Commissioners* (1991)
13. Niall McCullough *Dublin: An Urban History* (1989)

6. The United Irishmen

1. Robert Madden *The United Irishmen – Their Lives and Times*, 4 vols (1842–1846)
2. John T. Gilbert *A History of the City of Dublin* (1854)
3. John T. Gilbert *Dublin, History of the City*, 3 vols (1854–9)
4. *A Compendium of Irish Biography* (1878)
5. Madden *The United Irishmen*

6. Patrick Geoghegan *Robert Emmet: A Life* (2002)

7. Ruan O'Donnell *Robert Emmet and the Rebellion of 1798* (2003)

8. Elgy Gillespie (ed.) 'Emmett's Dublin and the Irish Insurrections' in *The Liberties of Dublin* (1973)

9. T.D., A.M., and D.B. Sullivan, re-Edited by Seán Ua Cellaigh, *Speeches from the Dock* (1953)

10. Gilbert *A History of the City of Dublin*

7. From Daniel O'Connell to the Irish Tricolour

1. National Library of Ireland *Irish History, Genealogy and Culture: The Penal Laws*; O Eamonn Ciardha *Ireland and the Jacobite Cause, 1685–1766* (2004); Donegal Genealogy Resources *The Penal Code 1695–C.1793* (1998/2008)

2. Nicholas Donnelly *A History of Francis Street Parish* (1908)

3. Peter and Fiona Somerset Fry *A History of Ireland* (1991)

4. *Catholic Encyclopaedia* (1911)

5. Edgar Sanderson *The British Empire in the Nineteenth Century* (1898), chapter v

6. Donnelly, p. 5

7. Desmond Bowen *Souperism: Myth and Reality* (1970); Cormac Ó Gráda *Studies in Economic and Social history: The Great Irish Famine* (1989)

8. Nicholas Donnelly *History of the Parish of Francis Street* (1903/1908); see Millie Lawler *St Nicholas of Myra and its two Architects: An Historical and Architectural Survey; St Nicholas of Myra Francis Street Parish* for a historical overview

9. Emmet Larkin 'Devotional Revolution in Ireland 1850–1875', in *The American Historical Review*, 77 (1972); Emmet Larkin *The Roman Catholic Church and the Emergence of the Modern Irish Political System* (1975); Emmet Larkin *The Making of the Roman Catholic Church in Ireland, 1850–1860* (1980)

10. Patrick Corish *The Irish Historical Experience*, (1985), pp. 123–4; Desmond Keenan *The Catholic Church in the Nineteenth Century* (1983)

11. Reports of Commissioners Appointed to Enquire into the Municipal Corporations of Ireland 1835 and 1836, conclusion

12. Municipal Corporations (Ireland) Act, 1841; Manor Court of Saint Sepulchre Abolition Act 1856

13. Kenneth Milne *The Four Liberties*, p. 47

14. *The Irish Times*, 9 April 2012; *Irish Independent*, 9 April 2012

8. Forged in the Smithy: Poverty and Tenements

1. James Whitelaw *Essay on the Population of Dublin in 1798* (1805)

2. James Stephens *The Charwoman's Daughter* (1912)

3. Dublin Corporation 'Inspectors' Report of Housing Conditions' (1909)

4. Chris Reid *Heirlooms & Hand-me-downs: Stories from Nicholas Street, Bride Street, Bride Road and the Rosser, Dublin* (2011)

5. Seamus Hughes *Poverty in Dublin* (1914)

6. Maurice Curtis *The Splendid Cause* (2008)

7. Maurice Curtis *Challenge to Democracy: Militant Catholicism in Ireland in Modern Ireland* (2010)

8. Society of St Vincent de Paul 'Annual Reports 1910–1920'

9. Little Flower Penny Dinners 'Annual Reports 1913–1916'; Sick and Indigent Roomkeepers Society 'Annual Reports, 1900–1920'

10. *The Irish Times*, 15 July 1911; Vicky Cremin *The Liberty Crèche 1893–1993: A Hundred Years of Childcare in Inner City Dublin* (1993); Tessa Fleming's reminiscences on the Royal visit
11. *The Irish Times*, 23 August 1911
12. Irish Transport and General Workers' Union (ITGWU) 'Annual Report 1913–1914'
13. *ibid.*
14. Robert Collis *Marrowbone Lane* (1938)
15. Hilda Tweedy *A Link in the Chain: The Irish Housewives Association 1942–1992* (1992)
16. Bill Cullen *It's a Long Way From Penny Apples* (2008)
17. Kevin C. Kearns *Dublin Tenement Life: An Oral History* (2000)
18. Bernard Neary *Lugs: The Life and Times of Jim Branigan* (1985)
19. Maurice Curtis, personal reminiscences of Lugs Branigan

9. The 1916 Rising and The Liberties

1. Brian Hughes *Michael Mallin* (2012)
2. Éirígí website, 'Republican History – Michael Mallin' 8 May 2012
3. Department of An Taoiseach 'The Easter Rising'
4. Francis X. Martin *Leaders and Men of the Easter Rising: Dublin 1916* (1967)
5. Oliver MacDonagh *Ireland: The Union and its Aftermath* (1977)
6. National Library of Ireland *Those Who Set the Stage: The 1916 Rising – Personalities and Perspectives* (2009)
7. John A. Murphy *Ireland in the Twentieth Century* (1986)
8. National Library of Ireland *Con Colbert: The 1916 Rising – Personalities and Perspectives* (2011)
9. The National Archives *Con Colbert*
10. Joe Lee *Ireland 1912–1985* (1990)
11. F.S.L. Lyons *Ireland Since the Famine* (1985)
12. Dermot Keogh *Twentieth Century Ireland* (2005)

10. The Wood Quay Campaign and the Knight

1. Friends of Medieval Dublin
2. Patrick F. Wallace (ed.), *Medieval Dublin Excavations Series B. Miscellanea* (1990); John Bradley (ed.) *Viking Dublin Exposed, The Wood Quay Saga*
3. Anonymous *Viking and Medieval Dublin: National Museum Excavations, 1962–1973: catalogue of exhibition* (1973)
4. Paul Clerkin *Architecture Discussion Forums/Archiseek: Wood Quay – Viking Remains*, 30 December 2008
5. *ibid.*
6. H.B. Clarke (ed.). *Medieval Dublin: The Making of a Metropolis* (1990); H.B. Clarke (ed.) *Medieval Dublin: The Living City* (1990)
7. John Bradley (ed.) *Viking Dublin Exposed, The Wood Quay* Saga (1984); Thomas Farel Heffernan *Wood Quay - The Clash Over Dublin's Viking Past* (2011)
8. Christine Broe (and Michael O'Flanagan/Terence Kearns) biographical information on John Gallagher
    Isabel Bennett (ed.) *Excavations 1989: Summary Accounts of Archaeological Excavations in Ireland* (1990); Isabel Bennett (ed.) *Excavations 1997: Summary Accounts of Archaeological Excavations in Ireland* (1998)
9. Reproduced by kind permission of Liberties poet Christine Broe

11. Boots, Brews, Biscuits and the Golden Triangle

1. John Gallagher interview in *Dublin Tenement Life: An Oral History* by Terence Kearns (1995)
2. Dublin City Council 'The Liberties Local Area Plan, September 2008' (2008); Liberties Heritage Association and Maintenance Projects, under the supervision of John Gallagher, Bernard Warfield and John Brogan; photographic exhibition (2011/12)
3. Dublin City Council /Heritage Office *East West Cultural Alignment Dublin* (2012)
4. The Roe Family for a history of Roe's Distillery; Eugene Coyne of Guinness's Brewery for information on Roe's Distillery
5. Eamon MacThomais *Thom's Street Directory and Almanac*
6. Diageo/Guinness Brewery/Visitor's Centre and the marketing department for a history of Guinness's Brewery
7. P. Lynch and J. Vaizey *Guinness's Brewery in the Irish Economy 1759–1876* (1960)
8. Diageo/Guinness Brewery/Visitor's Centre
9. Flann O'Brien 'The Workman's Friend' poem, *c.* 1950
10. Anto Howard *Slow Dublin* (2010)
11. Dublin.ie Forums for reminiscences of Guinness Brewery smells
12. June O'Reilly of the Tenters for memories of the Guinness Brewery aroma
13. A. Barnard *The Noted Breweries and Distilleries of Great Britain and Ireland* (*c.* 1890, reprint 1969)
14. Little Books of Ireland *Irish Whiskies: Past and Present* (1993)
15. The Roe Family for a history of Roe's Distillery; Eugene Coyne of Guinness's Brewery for information on Roe's Distillery; M. Magee *1000 Years of Irish Whiskey* (1980); A. Barnard *The Noted Breweries and Distilleries of Great Britain and Ireland* (*c.* 1890; reprint 1969)
16. *ibid.*
17. E.B. McGuire *Irish Whiskey: A History of Distilling, the Spirit Trade and Excise Controls in Ireland* (1973); Midleton Distilleries, Cork
18. B. Townsend *The Lost Distilleries of Ireland* (1997); Powers Whiskey *Jameson Whiskey/Midleton Distilleries, Cork* for additional material on the history of Powers and Jameson whiskies
19. NCAD, Thomas Street
20. Powers Whiskey, *Jameson Whiskey/Midleton Distilleries, Cork* for additional material on the history of Powers and Jameson whiskies.
21. Séamus Ó Maitiú *W. & R. Jacob - Celebrating 150 Years of Irish Biscuit Making* (2008)
22. Jacob/Fruitfield for additional information on the history of Jacob's.
23. *ibid.*
24. *ibid.*; RTÉ Archives Library for information on sponsored programmes including 'Dear Frankie' lunchtime programme, sponsored by Jacob's

12. Stairways to Heaven: Landscape of Spires

1. Dublin.ie Forums/Liberty thread; Liberties resident, 'Christy', speaking to author
2. Central Catholic Library, Leaflets of parishes/churches of Dublin in the Irish Room; *New Catholic Encyclopaedia* (1967)
3. James Malton *A Picturesque and Descriptive View of the City of Dublin* (1799); *St Patrick's Cathedral* booklet (2005); Dean, staff and guides of St Patrick's Cathedral; Charles Read and Sinead Hernon of St Patrick's Cathedral
4. *ibid.*; Eamon MacThomais; For additional information on the clock – Joe Curtis *Times, Chimes and Charms of Dublin: A Unique Guide to Dublin and its Clocks* (1992)
5. Clive Probyn, 'Swift, Jonathan (1667–1745)', *Oxford Dictionary of National Biography* (2004)

6. *Gulliver's Travels*, complete, authoritative text with biographical and historical contexts (1995)

7. Clive Probyn, 'Swift, Jonathan (1667–1745)', *Oxford Dictionary of National Biography* (2004); Eamon MacThomais

8. *A Modest Proposal for Preventing the Children of Poor People in Ireland Being a Burden on Their Parents or Country, and for Making Them Beneficial to the Publick* (1729)

9. Sabine Baltes *Jonathan Swift's Allies: The Wood's Halfpence Controversy in Ireland, 1724–1725* Ph.D Thesis (2004); Libraryireland.com also for Wood's Halfpence Controversy and other writings of Dean Swift; *ibid.*, St Patrick's Cathedral

10. *ibid.*; St Patrick's Cathedral booklet; Eamon MacThomais

11. *Irish Independent*, 27 December 1997; *Irish Independent* 19 February 2001

12. Kenneth Milne (ed.) *Christ Church Cathedral, Dublin: A History* (2000); Stuart Kinsella *Christ Church Cathedral Dublin: A Visitor's Guide* (2012)

13. Dublin.ie Forums/Liberties thread; Peter Costello *Dublin Churches* (1989)

14. *ibid.*; Milne; Kinsella; Eamon MacThomais

15. Dublin.ie Forums/Liberties thread

16. Leaflet on Christ Church Cathedral in the Central Catholic Library

17. *ibid.*; Milne; Kinsella; Peter Costello *Dublin Churches* (1989); Maurice Craig *James Malton's Dublin Views* (1981)

18. Kinsella; Milne; Peter Costello *Dublin Churches* (1989)

19. Philip Dixon Hardy 'The Four Courts', *Dublin Penny Journal* Vol. 1. No. 18, 27 October 1832

20. St Audoen's Catholic church, High Street

21. Maurice Craig *Dublin 1660 – 1860: The Shaping of the City* (2009)

22. St Audoen's Catholic church, High Street

23. St Audoen's (C of I) church Visitor Centre

24. *ibid.* Office of Public Works *St Audoen's Church Visitor's Guide*; Additional information thanks to Tony Dolan and Darina McCarthy of the OPW

25. Brother Giles O'Halloran of the Augustinians for information on John's Lane church

26. *ibid.*

27. *ibid.*

28. *ibid.*

29. *ibid.*

30. Malachy Cullen *Little Saints of The Liberties* (1991)

31. Padraig J. Daly *The Last Dreamers: New and Selected Poems* (1999/2010)

32. Church of the Immaculate Conception/Adam & Eve's, Merchant Quay

33. St James's Catholic church, James's Street. Leaflet on the history of the church

34. Maurice Craig *Dublin 1660 – 1860: The Shaping of the City* (2009)

35. St Catherine's church, Thomas Street. CORE leaflet on history of the church.

36. St Catherine's church, Meath Street for a history of the church.

37. *The Irish Examiner* 4 January 2012; CiNews

38. St Nicholas of Myra church; Millie Lawlor on the history of the church

39. Nicholas Donnelly *History of Dublin Parishes* (1903–1908)

40. *ibid.*; St Nicholas of Myra church; Millie Lawlor on the history of the church

41. Liam O'Meara *Within and Without, Dublin Churches of St. Nicholas, and Exploring the Manx Connection* (2008)

42. The Moravian Community leaflet

43. The parish church of St Werburgh, Dublin leaflet

44. John Gilbert *History of the City of Dublin* (1854)

45. St Werburgh's church, Werburgh Street leaflet

46. Peter Costello *St Werburgh's Church: Dublin Churches* (1989); Central Catholic Library (CCL). The best repository in Dublin for the history of the city's churches. Also contains

Donnelly's *History of Dublin Parishes* pamphlets, histories of St Patrick's Cathedral and Christ Church Cathedral, both St Audoen's, both St James's and both St Catherine's. See: CCL, the Irish Room.

13. A Tour of The Liberties

1. Douglas Bennett *Encyclopaedia of Dublin* (1991)
2. Christopher T. McCready *Dublin Street Names: Dated and Explained* (1892)
3. *Thom's Irish Almanac and Official Directory*
4. Maurice Curtis *Portobello* (2012)
5. Dublin City Council/Kevin Street Library
6. Excavations.ie
7. Kevin Street Garda station. Helpful Gardaí at the station advised me on history and archaeology of the old palace of St Sepulchre
8. Moravian Religious Community
9. Dublin Institute of Technology, Kevin Street
10. For Charles Dickens Irish Tours of 1858 and 1867 see: the *Irish Examiner*, 7 February 2012; *The Irish Times* 4/8 February 2012. Karl Whitney also of *The Irish Times* has written on the visit – see karlwhitney.com
11. Jim Cooke 'Charles Dickens: A Dublin Chronicler', paper read at the Old Dublin Society 1 March 1989, also published in *Dublin Historical Record*, Vol. 42. No. 3 June 1989; The Old Dublin Society
12. F.H.A. Aalen *The Iveagh Trust: The First Hundred Years 1890–1990* (1990); John Power *Thesis on Architecture of Public Bathing Facilities in Dublin City* (2008)
13. Liam O'Meara *The Bayno, a History of the Iveagh Trust Play-Centre marking the Centenary of its Founding* (2009)
14. Henry Boylan *A Dictionary of Irish Biography*, 3rd edition (1998)
15. Chris Reid *Heirlooms & Hand-me-downs: Stories from Nicholas Street, Bride Street, Bride Road and the Rosser, Dublin* (2011)
16. *ibid.*
17. John Gilbert *A History of the City of Dublin* (1854); *Gulliver's Travels*, complete, authoritative text with biographical and historical contexts (1995)
18. Clive Probyn, 'Swift, Jonathan (1667–1745)', *Oxford Dictionary of National Biography* (2004)
19. W.H. Grattan Flood *John Field of Dublin* (1920); Patrick Piggott *The Life and Music of John Field, 1782–1837, Creator of the Nocturne* (1973)
20. Franz Liszt's preface to his edition of Field's nocturnes (1859) (English translation by Julius Schuberth, 1859)
21. The National Gallery *The Bird Market by John Butler Yeats*
22. Noel Haughton; he has been actively involved with the market for over fifty years
23. The National Archives, Bishop Street
24. Henry Boylan *A Dictionary of Irish Biography* (1978)
25. 'James Clarence Mangan' *Catholic Encyclopaedia* (1913)
26. *Irish Press*, 3 April 1949; *The Irish Times*, 2 May 1954
27. Marsh's Library, courtesy of Muriel McCarthy
28. Muriel McCarthy *All Graduates and Gentlemen: Marsh's Library* (2003)
29. Dublin City Council Parks Department: St Patrick's Park
30. The Liberties College, Bull Alley Street
31. Nicholas Donnelly *A Short History of Dublin Parishes* (1903–1908)
32. Maurice Craig *James Malton's Views of Dublin* (1981)

33. Henry Boylan *A Dictionary of Irish Biography* (1978)
34. Puesoccurences.com, the Irish history blog
35. Jonathan Hynes of the Harding Hotel, Fishamble Street/Copper Alley
36. *Evening Herald*, 8 January 2011
37. *Irish Central*, 12 January 2011
38. The Eamon McLoughlin/Phil O'Grady of 93FM.
39. Dublin.ie Forums: The Liberties thread; Kenneth Milne *Christ Church Cathedral: A History* (2010)
40. Dublinia Exhibition; Central Catholic Library for articles/pamphlets on Christ Church Cathedral
41. Courtesy of Dublinia
42. Douglas Bennett *Encyclopaedia of Dublin* (1991); Dublin City Council. Research/brochures on old city walls of Dublin.
43. Christopher T. McCready *Dublin Street Names: Dated and Explained* (1892)
44. John Gilbert *A History of the City of Dublin* (1854); Dublin.ie Forums: The Liberties thread
45. *Thom's Irish Almanac and Official Directory*; St Audoen's (C of I) Visitors' Centre
46. The Carmelites, Whitefriar Street church; Central Catholic Library for history of the Carmelites
47. Joan Duffy *Growing up in the Bond* (2006)
48. Scoilnet *A Walk Around Medieval Dublin*; Joe Curtis *Times, Chimes and Charms of Dublin: A Unique Guide to Dublin and its Clocks* (1992)
49. Eamon MacThomáis *The Liberties* DVD (1978)
50. *ibid.*
51. John Gilbert *A History of the City of Dublin* (1854)
52. O'Shea's the Merchant Pub; the Brazen Head Pub
53. Henry Boylan *A Dictionary of Irish Biography* (1998), p. 314
54. *ibid.*
55. *The Irish Times* 'Jimmy O'Dea dies after 40 years on the Irish stage', 8 January 1965
56. John Gilbert *A History of the City of Dublin*, p.191
57. Howard B. Clarke, *Medieval Dublin* (1990)
58. Dublin City Council, 'Map of City Defences'
59. John Gilbert *A History of the City of Dublin* (1854); Dublin.ie Forums: The Liberties thread; Tony O'Rourke of O'Rourkes, Bridgefoot Street; The Mendicity Institution, Island Street; Audrey Woods *Dublin Outsiders: A History of the Mendicity Institution 1818–1998* (1999)
60. James Joyce *Finnegan's Wake* (1938)
61. Liberties Heritage Group *The Guinness Years* (2002)
62. John Gilbert *A History of the City of Dublin* (1854)
63. Howard B. Clarke *Medieval Dublin* (1990)
64. Eamon MacThomáis *The Liberties* DVD (1978)
65. *The Irish Times*, 6 July 2011
66. MRCB Paints, Cornmarket - The Coughlan Family
67. Excavations.ie
68. Archiseek, the forum for the discussion of matters architecture/archaeology
69. Dublin City Council; Dublin Civic Trust, reports on the excavations of the High Street/Lamb Alley area
70. *Dublin Penny Journal*, Vol. 1, No. 22, 24 November 1832: 'The Dolocher (a legend of the Black Dog Prison, Dublin)'
71. *ibid.*
72. *ibid.*
73. *ibid.*
74. Dublin.ie Forums/South Inner City thread
75. *ibid.*; Dublin Civic Trust; Mother Redcaps Tavern

76. An Taisce/Tailors' Hall, Back Lane

77. Murial McCarthy, librarian at Marsh's Library – leaflet on The Liberties

78. Emmeline Henderson Thomas Street, Dublin Civic Trust, 2001. P.5. Christine Casey
    Thomas Street. Dublin (2005); Christine Casey *Dublin: The City Within the Grand and Royal
    Canals and the Circular Road with the Phoenix Park* (2005); Dublin Civic Trust; *The Irish
    Times* 17 April 2012; *The Irish Times* 9 September 2011, expressions of concern about
    neglected Thomas Street heritage area

79. Dublin City/Planning and Conservation Department *Newmarket and Weavers' Sqaure* (2009)

80. Dublin City Council 'The Liberties Local Area Plan, September 2008'

81. Dublin City Council /Heritage Office *East West Cultural Alignment Dublin* (2012)

82. Dublin City Council/An Taisce *Thomas Street Proposed Architectural Conservation Area* (*c*. 2005)

83. Dublin City Council /Heritage Office *East West Cultural Alignment Dublin* (2012); Thomas
    Phelan *Hanbury Lane from Whence I Came: Memories of Growing Up in Dublin's Liberties*
    (1998)

84. Dublin City Council *The Liberties Local Area Plan*, September 2008

85. Emmeline Henderson *Thomas Street* Dublin Civic Trust, 2001

86. Liberties Heritage Association and Maintenance Projects, under the supervision of John
    Gallagher, Bernard Warfield and John Brogan; Photographic Exhibition (2011/12)

87. Eamon MacThomais *The Liberties* DVD (1978); 25th Anniversary Liberties Festival
    Programme, 1993; 'The Liberties' by Eamon MacThomais

88. Patrick O'Reilly *The Boundary Kings pieces of sculpture*

89. Eugene Coyne of Guinness's Brewery for information on Roe's Distillery

90. The Roe Family

91. Dublin.ie Forums/South Inner City thread/Liberties thread

92. Dublin.ie Forums; Archiseek; 25th Anniversary Liberties Festival Programme, 1993

93. The IAWS, Thomas Street

94. Lawrence Weiner, *c*. 1969

95. Diageo/The Guinness Brewery Visitor's Centre

96. The National College of Art and Design

97. Thanks to Archiseek for information on Joseph Fade

98. Chadwicks Builders Supplies, Thomas Street

99. Dublin.ie Forums/The Liberties

100. Thanks to Tayto Crisps

101. St Patrick's Hospital; Old Kilmainham Village entrance

102. William T. Cosgrave; Oireachtas Members Database, retrieved 1 June 2009; William
     Thomas Cosgrave ElectionsIreland.org, retrieved 1 June 2009; Anthony Jordan *W.T.
     Cosgrave 18880–1965 Founder of Modern Ireland* (2006), p. 48

103. St James's CBS Past Pupils' Union

104. *St James's Hospital: History of the South Dublin Union*

105. Eamon MacThomais *The Liberties* DVD (1978); John Gilbert, *ibid.*

106. Thoms Directories and Almanancs for the streets of Dublin

107. Dublin.ie Forums/The Liberties: thread on Pimlico

108. Pete St John 'Dublin in the Rare Old Times'

109. Eamon MacThomais *The Liberties* DVD (1978)

110. Mairín Johnston *Around the Banks of Pimlico* (1985)

111. *Irish Independent* 9 May 2008

112. James Stephens *The Charwoman's Daughter* (1912)

113. Graham Hickey *Francis and Meath Streets: Dublin Civic Trust* (2009)

114. *ibid.*; Liberties Heritage Association and Maintenance Projects, under the supervision of
     John Gallagher, Bernard Warfield and John Brogan; Photographic exhibition (2011/12)

115. Thanks to the many shop-owners and businesses in Meath Street for helping with the

history of Meath Street, and in particular Declan Larkin of Larkins's Butchers; *The Liberty*, August 2012; Miriam Lord in the *Irish Independent* 10 January 2002; Jack Roche speaking to the author 31 August 2012

116. Vicky Cremin *The Liberty Crèche 1893–1993: A Hundred Years of Childcare in Inner City Dublin* (1993); An interview with staff of the Liberty Crèche, Meath Street

117. *ibid.*

118. *Irish Independent*, 22 April 2004

119. John Boylan *Dictionary of Irish Biography* 3rd edition (1998), p.153

120. G.B. Smith 'Gray, Edmund Dwyer (1845–1888)' *Oxford Dictionary of National Biography* (2004); online edn, January 2006, accessed 7 May 2008

121. Graham Hickey *Francis and Meath Streets: Dublin Civic Trust* (2009); F.H.A. Aalen *The Iveagh Trust: The First Hundred Years 1890–1990* (1990)

122. *ibid.*

123. Boniface Hanley *Frank Duff One of the Best* (1982); Maurice Curtis *The Splendid Cause* (2008), p.91–6

124. George P. Kearns *Old Dublin Cinemas* (2008)

125. For the story of Mushatt's: Sean Foley of Foley's Chemists on Thomas and Meath Streets. They have a museum in the Thomas Street branch dedicated to Mushatt's; Dublin.ie Forums; Terence Kearns *Dublin's Tenements: An Oral History* (1995)

126. Gerard Smyth *The Fullness of Time: New and Selected Poems* (2010)

127. Emmet Scanlon of Tom De Paor Architects

128. John Gallagher of Carman's Hall Community Centre

129. For information on Fallon's The Capstan Bar: Information and leaflet courtesy of Calum McPartland of Fallon's

130. 'Dan Donnelly', International Boxing Hall of Fame, retrieved 31 July 2010

131. Igoe, Vivien *Dublin Burial Grounds & Graveyards* (2001); OPW/Royal Hospital Kilmainham – Bully's Acre Cemetery

132. William Frazer/Dublin City Council *Newmarket and Weavers' Square* (2009), p.2; The Environment Group of the South West Inner City Network, Carman's Court, 14 Carman's Hall, D.8. A mandate for the community representative's to The Liberties/ Coombe integrated area plan, executive summary (2001)

133. *Faulkners Journal*, November 1750; National Library of Ireland 'John Van Nost' *Dictionary of Irish Artists* (1913)

134. *Hibernian Magazine*, June 1775; 'John Van Nost' *Dictionary of Irish Artists* (1913)

135. For Charles Dickens, Irish Tour of 1858 and 1867 see: *Irish Examiner*, 7 February 2012; *Irish Times*, 4/8 February 2012. Karl Whitney also of *The Irish Times* has written on the visit – see karlwhitney.com

136. Jim Cooke 'Charles Dickens: A Dublin Chronicler', paper read at the Old Dublin Society 1 March 1989, also published in *Dublin Historical Record*, Vol. 42. No. 3, June 1989

137. Thanks to Sisters of Charity of the Holy Faith Convent, the Coombe

138. Dublin Corporation memorial plaque on old entrance/portico to Coombe Hospital

139. *The Irish Times*, 'Jimmy O'Dea dies after 40 years on the Irish stage', 8 January 1965

140. Henry Boylan *A Dictionary of Irish Biography*, 3rd Edition (1998), p.314

141. *The Irish Times*, 5 January 1950; *The Irish Times*, 6 November 1931; 'Jimmy O'Dea', *The Irish Times*, 25 September 1959

142. Isobel Smyth, writer and former Pimlico resident. She also wrote a book, *A Southside Childhood* (2008), recounting her memories of growing up in Pimlico and The Liberties

143. Dublin.ie Forums/South West Inner City – Liberties thread

144. Excavations.ie

145. Former Watkins Brewery, 10 Ardee Street

146. *Thom's Directory and Almanac*; John Gilbert *A History of Dublin* (1854); Eamon MacThomais, *The Liberties* DVD

147. Excavations.ie; Dublin City Council 'The Liberties Local Area Plan, September 2008'

148. Eugene J. Foley 'Donnelly's of Cork Street.' Paper Read to the Old Dublin Society, 25 March 1998 also published in *Dublin Historical Record* Vol. 51, No. 1, Spring 1998

149. Lar Redmond *Emerald Square* (1990); Lar Redmond *Show us the Moon* (1988)

150. The Quakers HQ, Fade Street, Dublin, for the history of old Cork Street Fever Hospital; Sharon Fitzpatrick, former manager of Brú Caoimhín, for information on the hospital; *Report of House of Recovery and Fever Hospital* (1817)

151. Brú Caoimhín/HSE Cork Street for information on history of the building

152. The Carmelite Fathers at Whitefriar Street church for information on Fr Spratt

153. The Mercy Sisters, Sophia House, Ormond Street/Cork Street/Weavers' Square

154. Dublin.ie Forums/The Liberties and Cork Street

155. Robert Collis *Marrowbone Lane* (1938)

156. Dublin City Council Waterworks Department, Marrowbone Lane; Dublin.ie Forums/ The Liberties – 'Back of the Pipes'

157. William O. Frazer /Dublin City Council *Newmarket and Weavers' Square* (2009), p.8

158. *ibid.* pp. 10–14

159. Liberties Heritage Association and Maintenance Projects, under the supervision of John Gallagher, Bernard Warfield and John Brogan; photographic exhibition (2011/12)

160. For stories on O'Keefe's: the reminiscences of many locals (in particular former resident 'Paddy' and past pupils of Donore Avenue school. Also Dublin.ie Forums/The Liberties thread

161. Dublin City Council plaque in The Tenters

162. Dublin.ie Forums/The Liberties thread; William O. Frazer/Dublin City Council Planning and Conservation Department *Newmarket and Weavers' Square* (2009)

163. Thanks to Karl Whitney of *The Irish Times*

164. Presentation Sisters, Warrenmount Covent; Adult Learning Centre, Warrenmount

165. Rachel Mc Rory 'History of 12 Fumbally Lane' (Unpublished thesis N.D.)

166. *ibid.*; Éamon MacThomáis *The Liberties* DVD (1978)

167. Department of Taoiseach – Taoiseach's Speeches Archive 6 April 2006; Fumbally Exchange/Fumbally Square/Fumbally Court

168. McCready, Christopher T. *Dublin Street Names: Dated and Explained* (1892)

169. Christine Casey *Dublin: The City Within the Grand and Royal Canals and the Circular Road with the Phoenix Park* (2005); Peter Pearson *The Heart of Dublin: Resurgence of an Historic City* (2000)

170. Liam O'Meara *Zozimus* (2012)

171. *The Dublin People*, 5 March 2012

172. Eamon MacThomais *The Liberties* DVD (1978)

173. *The Dublin People*, 5 March 2012

174. Eamon MacThomais *The Liberties* DVD (1978)

175. Prospect Cemetery Glasnevin, Dublin

176. Dublin City Council Parks Department *The Cabbage Garden Park*

177. Maurice Curtis *Rathmines* (2011)

178. Dublin City Council Parks Department *The Cabbage Garden Park*

179. *ibid.*; Preserved Huguenot section of the Cabbage Garden Park

180. Atkinson's House, 21 New Street; Dublin Civic Trust

181. Atkinsonsties.com., for a history of Atkinson's Royal Irish Poplin

182. Maurice Curtis *Portobello* (2012)

14. Celebrating The Liberties

1. U2 'Wake Up Dead Man'
2. Pete St John 'Dublin in the Rare Old Times', 'The Fields of Athenry'
3. The Dubliners 'Tim Finnegan's Wake'
4. The Dubliners 'The Ragman's Ball'
5. *The Liberty January* 2010
6. The Wolfe Tones website
7. The Dubliners website
8. The Dublin City Ramblers website
9. The Chieftains, The Pipers and Rambling House websites
10. Mick O'Connor *History of the Pipers' Club* (2007)
11. *The Irish Times* 6/9 April 2012
12. Tom Burke and Shane Hogan *The Liberties*
13. James Joyce *Finnegan's Wake* (1939)
14. James Joyce *Ulysses* (1922)
15. James Stephens *The Charwoman's Daughter* (1912)
16. Joseph O'Connor 'The Ark Blog': joseph-oconnor-launches-storyspark
17. Christine Broe *Selected Poems* (2004)
18. Jim Smyth *The Pipes, The Pipes Are Calling* (2010)
19. School Street/Thomas Court Bawn *Who Gives a Damn Anyway* (1993)
20. Malachy Cullen *Little Saints of The Liberties* (1991)
21. Siobhán Parkinson *Kate* (2006)
22. Seven Towers Agency (2009)
23. Gerard Smyth *The Fullness of Time: New and Selected Poems* (2010)
24. Chris Reid *Heirlooms & Hand-me-downs: Stories from Nicholas Street, Bride Street, Bride Road and the Rosser, Dublin* (2011)
25. Patrick O'Reilly website
26. Walter Strickland *Dictionary of Irish Artists* (1913)
27. James Malton *Prints of Dublin* (1792 – 1799)
28. Alexander Williams *Paintings late Nineteenth Century*. Commentary on first three paintings courtesy of Peter Pearson and the Gorry Gallery
29. Declan Larkin of Larkin's Butcher's, Meath Street; Gaelic Athletic Association; Football Association of Ireland; Soccer Ireland - biographical information on Kevin Moran
30. *The Irish Times* 27 September 1976
31. Isobel Smyth *A Southside Childhood* (2011)
32. Dublin City Council press release, 3 February 2011
33. Dublin.ie Forums 'Local History Area Dublin South West'
34. Tommy Flanagan *Millennium Song: A Little Bag of Chips*, courtesy of Burdock's
35. Paul Kearns and Motti Ruimy *Re-Drawing Dublin* 'Introduction' (2010)

BIBLIOGRAPHY

Bardon, Carol and Jonathan *If Ever You Go to Dublin Town* (1988)

Barnard, A *The Noted Breweries and Distilleries of Great Britain and Ireland* (*c.* 1890; Reprint 1969)

Bennett, Douglas *Encyclopaedia of Dublin* (1991)

Boland, Patrick *Tales from a City Farmyard* (1995)

Bradley, John (ed.) *Viking Dublin Exposed: The Wood Quay Saga* (1984)

Casey, Christine *Thomas Street, Dublin* (2005)

Casey, Christine *Dublin: The City Within the Grand and Royal Canals and the Circular Road with the Phoenix Park* (2005)

Cullen O.S.A., Malachy (illustrated by Niamh Foran) *Little Saints of The Liberties* (1991)

Costello, Peter *Dublin Churches* (1989)

Craig, Maurice *James Malton's Dublin Views* (1981)

Craig, Maurice *Dublin 1660 – 1860 The Shaping of the City* (2009)

Cremin, Vicky *The Liberty Crèche 1893–1993. A Hundred Years of Childcare in Inner City Dublin* (1993)

Cullen, Malachy *Little Saints of The Liberties* (1991)

Curtis, Maurice *The Challenge to Democracy: Militant Catholicism in Modern Ireland* (2010)

Curtis, Maurice *Rathmines* (2011)

Curtis, Maurice *Portobello* (2012)

Daly, Mary *The Deposed Capital: A Social and Economic History, 1860 – 1914* (1984)

Daly, Padraig J. *The Last Dreamers: New and Selected Poems* (1999/2010)

Dublin City/Planning and Conservation Department *Newmarket and Weavers Sqaure* (2009)

Dublin City Council 'The Liberties Local Area Plan, September 2008' (2008)

Dublin City Council/An Taisce (Dublin Civic Trust) 'Thomas Street: Proposed Architectural Conservation Area' (*c.* 2005)

Dublin City Council /Heritage Office 'East West Cultural Alignment Dublin' (2012)

Dublin Civic Trust 'Thomas Street: Improving the Public Face of an Historic City Centre Street' (2012)

Dublin Penny Journal, Vol. 1, Number 22, November 24, 1832: 'The Dolocher (a legend of the Black Dog Prison, Dublin)'.

Duffy, Joan *Growing up in the Bond* (2006)

The Environment Group of the South West Inner City Network, Carman's Court, 14 Carman's Hall, D.8 'A mandate for the community representative's to The Liberties/ Coombe integrated area plan, executive summary' (2001)

Flanagan, Bernadette *The Spirit of the City: Voices from Dublin's Liberties* (1999)

Foley, Eugene J. 'Donnelly's of Cork Street', paper read to the Old Dublin Society, 25 March 1998. *Dublin Historical Record* Vol. 51, No. 1, Spring (1998)

Frazer, William O. /Dublin City Council 'Newmarket and Weavers' Square' (2009)

Gilbert, John *A History of the City of Dublin* (1854)

Gillespie, Elgy (ed.) *The Liberties of Dublin* (1973)

Gillis, Liz. *The Fall of Dublin: Military History of the Irish Civil War* (2011)

Grattan Flood, W.H. *John Field of Dublin* (1920)

Hardy, Philip Dixon 'The Four Courts', *Dublin Penny Journal*, Vol. 1. No. 18, 27 October 1832

Heffernan, Thomas Farel *Wood Quay – The Clash Over Dublin's Viking Past* (2011)

Henderson, Emmeline *Thomas Street: Dublin Civic Trust* (2001)

Hickey, Graham *Francis and Meath Streets: Dublin Civic Trust* (2009)

Hopkins, Frank *Rare Old Dublin* (2002)

Howard, Anto *Slow Dublin* (2010)

Hughes, Brian *Michael Mallin* (2012)

Igoe, Vivien *Dublin Burial Grounds & Graveyards* (2001)

Johnston, Mairín *Around the Banks of Pimlico* (1985)

Kearns, Kevin C. *Dublin Tenement Life: An Oral History* (1995)

Kearns, Paul and Ruimy, Motti *Re-Drawing Dublin* (2010)

Kinsella, Stuart *Christ Church Cathedral Dublin* (2012)

Lawler, Millie *St Nicholas of Myra Church: An Historical and Architectural Survey* (N.D.)

Liberties Festival Committee *The Liberties Festival 1980* (1980)

Liberties Heritage Association and Maintenance Projects, under the supervision of John Gallagher, Bernard Warfield and John Brogan 'Photographic Exhibition' (2011/12)

The Liberty, a local online publication

Liberties Association *The Liberties Magazine* (1976)

Little Books of Ireland *Irish Whiskies: Past and Present* (1993)

Lynch, P., and Vaizey, J. *Guinness's Brewery in the Irish Economy 1759–1876* (1960)

Magee, M. *1000 Years of Irish Whiskey* (1980)

MacThomáis, Eamon *The Liberties DVD* (1978)

McCready, Christopher T. *Dublin Street Names: Dated and Explained* (1892)

McCullough, Niall *Dublin: An Urban History* (2008)

McGuire, E. B. *Irish Whiskey: A History of Distilling, the Spirit Trade and Excise Controls in Ireland* (1973)

Mc Rory, Rachel *History of 12 Fumbally Lane* (Unpublished thesis N.D.)

James Malton *A Picturesque and Descriptive View of the City of Dublin* (1799)

Milne, Kenneth (ed.) *Christ Church Cathedral, Dublin: A History* (2000)

Milne, Kenneth *The Four Liberties 1660–1850* (2009)

Neary, Bernard *Lugs: The Life and Times of Jim Branigan* (1985)

Nisi, Valentine, Davenport, Glorianna and Haahr, Mads MediaLabEurope/TCD, Dublin. *A Mediated Portrait of the Dublin Liberties* (c. 2008)

O'Connor, Mick *History of the Pipers' Club* (c. 2007)

O'Keefe, Grace *The Liberties of Dublin* (N.D.)

O'Keefe, Phil *Down Cobbled Streets: A Liberties Childhood* (1995)

Ó Maitiú, Séamus *W & R Jacob – Celebrating 150 Years of Irish Biscuit Making* (2008)

O'Meara, Liam *Zozimus* (2012)

O'Meara, Liam *The Bayno, a history of the Iveagh Trust Play-Centre marking the centenary of its founding* (2009)

O'Meara, Liam *Within and Without, Dublin Churches of St. Nicholas, and Exploring the Manx Connection* (2008)

Parkinson, Siobhán *Kate* (2011)

Pearson, Peter *The Heart of Dublin: Resurgence of an Historic City* (2000)

Phelan, Thomas *Hanbury Lane from Whence I Came. Memories of Growing Up in Dublin's Liberties* (1998)

Reid, Chris *Heirlooms & Hand-me-downs: Stories from Nicholas Street, Bride Street, Bride Road*

and the Rosser, Dublin (2011)
Redmond, Lar *Emerald Square* (1990)
Redmond, Lar *Show us the Moon* (1988)
Smyth, Gerard *The Fullness of Time: New and Selected Poems* (2010)
Smyth, Jim *The Pipes, the Pipes, They are Calling (Growing up in The Liberties)* (2010)
South Inner City Community Development Association Heritage Centre *Talking Liberties* (1995)
Stephens, James *The Charwoman's Daughter* (1912)
Thom's Irish Almanac and Official Directory
Townsend, B. *The Lost Distilleries of Ireland* (1997)
Whitelaw, James *Essay on the Population of Dublin in 1798* (1805)

ALSO:

The Liberties: Portrayal of Famous Dublin Area (2008): A series of twelve short films, each focused on a different character within Dublin's Liberties community. Directed and produced by Tom Burke and Shane Hogan of Areaman Productions, this fifty-two minute documentary was produced in association with RTÉ Factual. It celebrates ordinary people living in The Liberties – such as tailor Eugene Fagan, Meath Street butcher Declan Larkin, and flower ladies Phyllis Kavanagh and Mary Hand, as well as better-known residents such as Brenda Fricker.

Memoirs of Guinness: A series of twelve video podcasts that recount local people's memories of the Guinness Company. The idea for this project came from a local history group, D8CEC, who along with elevate Learning @ The Digital Hub approached Diageo with a proposal to contribute to the Guinness 250 celebrations. The idea was to capture local stories and broadcast them as a series of podcasts. Four local history groups, D8CEC, Nicholas of Myra, Dolphins Barn and Bluebell participated in the creation of the podcasts. Over thirty people received training and the podcasts are the culmination of their work. Their stories capture the influence of the Guinness Company on life in Dublin during the last century, particularly for those living in the shadows of the brewery.

If you enjoyed this book, you may also be interested in…

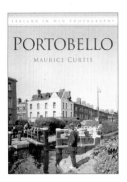

Portobello In Old Photographs
MAURICE CURTIS

In this book, Maurice Curtis, takes the reader on a visual tour of Portobello through the decades, recounting both the familiar and the events and places that have faded over time, revealing many fascinating details, including the fact that Dublin's Portobello was named after an area on the East Coast of Panama! This, and much more, is captured in a timeless volume, which pays fitting tribute to this well-loved part of the city.

978 1 84588 737 7

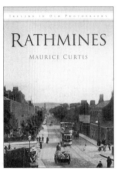

Rathmines In Old Photographs
MAURICE CURTIS

Rathmines is one of the country's most well-known suburbs, home to heads of government, vast swathes of students and local families alike. In his latest book, writer and historian Maurice Curtis takes the reader on a visual tour of Rathmine through the decades, recounting both the familiar and the forgotten, those feature and events that may have faded over time. Illustrated with over 150 archive photographs, this fascinating book pays fitting tribute to the place Rathmines has carved in the history of all who have passed through it.

978 1 84588 704 9

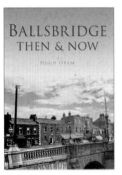

Ballsbridge Then & Now
HUGH ORAM

Ballsbridge, the 'embassy belt' at the leafy heart of South Dublin, is home to the Royal Dublin Society (RDS), the British and American embassies, the Aviva Stadium, and an array of the great houses of Ireland. Aside from the area's conspicuous grandeur, it is also steeped in history. Herbert Park was the site of th visit of King George V and throughout its wide streets are statues and mementos the great moments of the Irish state. This book captures the changing face of one of the most striking parts of all Ireland.

978 1 84588 726 1

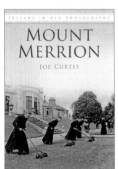

Mount Merrion In Old Photographs
JOE CURTIS

Mount Merrion lies on the south side of Dublin, 'between the mountains and th sea'. In 1711, the Fitzwilliam family walled the area to serve as their private coun estate, and the 300th anniversary of this has sparked a new and enthusiastic intere in the history of the area. The early days of rustic open fields and tree-lined lanes are still in evidence, and this book by local historian and long-time Mount Merr resident Joe Curtis continues that celebration.

978 1 84588 747 6

Visit our website and discover thousands of other History Press books.

www.thehistorypress.ie